Contents

New Institutions for Participatory Democracy in Latin America

New Institutions for Participatory Democracy in Latin America

Voice and Consequence

Edited by Maxwell A. Cameron, Eric Hershberg,
and Kenneth E. Sharpe

First published in hardcover in 2012 by
PALGRAVE MACMILLAN®
in the United States—a division of St. Martin's Press LLC,
175 Fifth Avenue, New York, NY 10010.

Where this book is distributed in the UK, Europe and the rest of the World,
this is by Palgrave Macmillan, a division of Macmillan Publishers Limited,
registered in England, company number 785998, of Houndmills,
Basingstoke, Hampshire RG21 6XS.

Palgrave Macmillan is the global academic imprint of the above
companies and has companies and representatives throughout the world.

Palgrave® and Macmillan® are registered trademarks in the United
States, the United Kingdom, Europe and other countries.

ISBN: 978–1–137–48546–5

Translations of Chapters 2, 3, 7, and 9 copyright © Judy Rein, 2012.

Library of Congress Cataloging-in-Publication Data is available from the
Library of Congress.

A catalogue record of the book is available from the British Library.

Design by Integra Software Services

First PALGRAVE MACMILLAN paperback edition: November 2014

10 9 8 7 6 5 4 3 2 1

Figures, Graphs, and Tables

Foreword

Mark E. Warren

Over the last three decades, the world has entered into a new phase in the development of democracy. The fact that so many countries have transitioned to choosing political elites through competitive elections is hugely important to the cause of democracy. But there has been another huge shift as well: we are entering a new phase of experimentation with participatory governance, involving a variety of ways of directly engaging citizens with government. The trend affects almost every country, across many kinds of political systems, from Canada to China, Germany to Japan, and from India to Brazil. If there is a broad explanation for this shift, it is that the more familiar ways in which governments generate legitimacy—elections, ideology, personal charisma, or economic performance—are increasingly inadequate to governing complex societies. Governments have broad platforms, purposes, and agendas. But governing is specific, policy focused, and particular in its effects, so that the people affected by any particular act of governing are likely to be different from those who support a government more generally, and much more intensely interested in results. Moreover their capacities to force the attentiveness of governments are increasing. In an era in which governments are less likely to have a monopoly over citizens' livelihoods, information flows ever more freely and nongovernmental organizations are increasingly ubiquitous. Citizens have more capacities to frustrate governance as usual. Increasingly, governments respond with new forms of citizen participation.

But the variety of purposes, locations, institutional designs, norms, and effectiveness of participatory responses is almost endless. Political scientists face an enormous challenge in simply describing this new landscape, let alone assessing whether democracy is helped or hindered. Nowhere is this truer than in Latin America, the focus of this book. While virtually all of Latin America's governments have functioning electoral systems, their democratic performance ranges from the exceptionally poor (as in several of the

Central American countries) to pretty good (Chile, followed by Uruguay). So we would expect participatory innovations to have quite different kinds of political functions and niches. Some new kinds of participation, such as the national conferences in Brazil, integrate broadly representative citizen input directly into national legislative and administrative processes, probably increasing the inclusiveness, representativeness, and responsiveness of policy-making processes. Other forms of participation, such as Bolivia's autonomous self-governing indigenous communities, most certainly compete with electoral representation, and probably exist (in part) because electoral institutions produce very little democratic responsiveness to these communities. Still other new forms of participation may actually strengthen autocracy. For example, Venezuela's community councils, may serve to strengthen Chávez's autocratic powers relative to constitutionally established institutions. That said, they may also generate citizenship capabilities that may, at some point, exceed Chávez's ability to control them.

This book represents an important and sophisticated step forward in this mapping and assessing of participatory innovations in Latin America. The editors and authors have chosen a theoretically driven, empirically attentive approach to this enormous variety of new forms. The approach involves three important moves. The first is to view each participatory innovation within its context, as part of a system of institutions. Thus, it makes little sense to view a similar institutional form—say, community councils of various kinds—outside of its function within a broader ecology of institutions. Mechanisms of direct participation may serve one kind of function in Venezuela (providing a basis of support for Chávez), and quite another in Brazil (extending universal health care). The second move is to abstract democratic norms from any particular institutional form. The contributors to this book understand that "democracy" is, normatively speaking, a composite concept. It involves, at the very least, norms of inclusion, representation, responsiveness, accountability, and citizen education. It may involve institutions and practices that disrupt clientelism, enable indigenous norms of justice, or provide more legitimacy for existing institutions. These norms may be enhanced in one or more dimensions—say, by improving responsiveness and accountability. But they may sometimes trade off, as when increased opportunities for participation strengthen clientelistic relationships. Nor is there any necessity that new forms of participation will strengthen any norm of democracy at all: new forms of participation may, sometimes, be used primarily by those who are already well organized and well resourced; they may enable new forms of clientelism; they may strengthen autocracy. The third move, then, is to ask how each particular innovation functions within its context, measuring its functions against the several norms of democracy, in such a way that it is possible to both decompose "participation" into its many varieties and ask what each particular variety contributes to democracy.

We should notice that although this method is attentive to democratic theory, it is not captive of received conceptual polarities between "representative" and "direct" democracy, or between "liberal" and "participatory" democracy. As the practices evolve, these received categories turn out to be insufficiently complex—and, indeed, inattentive to the wide variety of political functions and norms an innovation may serve. The finer-grained form of analysis and normative parsing is increasingly used within the fields of democratic theory and comparative democratization to map these new domains. This book is a sophisticated contribution to the exciting new field of research democratic innovation.

Acknowledgments

The preparation of this book involved a substantial collective effort. It began with a proposal to the Ford Foundation. We are grateful for the constant support and encouragement of Felipe Agüero in the Foundation's Santiago office. The Ford Foundation provided the funding necessary both to support project field research and to hold two workshops, one in Washington DC, in June 2010, and another in Buenos Aires in December of that year. Our deliberations benefited immensely from the participation at those meetings by Robert Albro, Santiago Anria, Cynthia Arnson, Eddie Condor, Tulia Falleti, Manuel Antonio Garretón, Anne Gillman, Karina Gregori, Sam Handlin, Carlos Meléndez, Andrew Selee, and Mark Warren. We also benefited from the written feedback of Abe Lowenthal.

Rebecca Monnerat provided efficient project management support at the University of British Columbia. Jason Tockman, Jorge Madrazo, Nick Harper, Julia Malmo-Laycock, Yayoi Sekine, and Amielle del Rosario provided able research assistance. Funding for including research assistants came primarily from a Social Sciences and Humanities Research Council grant, supplemented by a UBC Arts Undergraduate Research Award grant, which allowed us to enable the research assistants join the meeting in Washington DC. At the American University, Andrea Mesa and Sebastian Bitar of the staff of the Center for Latin American and Latino Studies helped with the Washington DC and Buenos Aires workshops, respectively. Alicia Lissidini was a gracious host throughout our meeting at the Universidad San Martin in Buenos Aires. We are grateful to Marcelo Cavarozzi for supporting that event and to Vanina Lago for handling administrative arrangements in Buenos Aires.

We appreciate the thorough work of Judy Rein, who translated chapters 2, 4, 7, and 9 from the original Spanish. It has been a pleasure to work with Farideh Koohi-Kamali, Sara Doskow, and their colleagues at Palgrave Macmillan, which has provided efficient and timely assistance throughout the manuscript preparation process. Four anonymous reviewers provided extremely helpful and constructive advice on earlier drafts of the chapters, and the final product has been strengthened considerably as a result. We are grateful for Sebastian Bitar's capable assistance in compiling the index.

Finally, we wish to thank the contributors to the book. Our intellectual exchanges over the past two years have challenged us as editors to sharpen our articulation of the particular dynamics that we aim to illuminate in the book, and to better situate our work in the literature on comparative politics and democratic theory. This has been a truly collaborative endeavor, and we have learned a great deal from our colleagues.

CHAPTER 1

Voice and Consequence: Direct Participation and Democracy in Latin America

Maxwell A. Cameron, Eric Hershberg, and Kenneth E. Sharpe

Democracy in Contention

A remarkable transformation has swept Latin America. During the last three decades, in country after country, authoritarian governments have given way to democratically elected ones. Moreover, there are signs, especially in the last decade, that some democratic institutions are themselves being refashioned; institutions of direct, popular participation are emerging that are quite different from the elected, representative institutions normally associated with democracy in Western Europe and North America.[1] These new forms of popular political participation are giving voice to groups that are often not heard in the elections, or through the parties that are at the heart of representative democracy. They are far more institutionalized than many of the traditional ways through which the excluded project their concerns and demands, such as public hearings, petitions, sit-ins, demonstrations, strikes, and land seizures. These new forms of voice allow for the inclusion of not only legitimate but also *frequently* marginalized perspectives. They also encourage more deliberation among the citizenry and between the citizenry and elected officials.

In some countries, like Brazil and Venezuela, new institutional spaces for participation are changing the political landscape. Institutions for popular participation in setting municipal budgets have taken root in many cities in Brazil and have begun to spread elsewhere (Abers, 2000; Baiocchi, 2003,

2005; Wampler, 2007; Wampler and Avritzer, 2005). In Venezuela, tens of thousands of community councils have mobilized citizens, with government support, to design and implement local development projects. Advisory councils in Brazil and Mexico have, with varying degrees of success, enabled local citizens and policy experts to gain the ear of government officials and influence policy planning and legislation. In Uruguay, Venezuela, and Bolivia, referenda, recall elections to remove public officials and citizen initiatives have been encouraged (Lissidini, 2011; Altman, 2010). Governments in Ecuador, Peru, and Bolivia have incorporated such mechanisms of direct citizen participation outside the channels of representative democracy and into new constitutions (Cameron and Sharpe, 2010).

These new forms of participation do not rely solely or primarily on traditional institutions of representative democracy, neither do they take place through legislative votes or party bargaining or in the corridors of power. And the groups that participate are often ones that have been historically excluded not only by traditional patron–client and authoritarian institutions but by electoral, representative democracy as well. In fact, the rise of these participatory institutions, and of new forms of popular intervention in politics, may be related to crises in representation resulting from policy failures of governments that emerged from the wave of electoral transitions that began nearly three decades ago (Mainwaring et al., 2006).

This new wave of participation raises important questions for understanding and assessing the nature of democratization in Latin America and for rethinking the very meaning of democracy. These are the central themes of this book, in which the contributors first describe these new forms of participation, analyze their relationship to the broader political system and their aims and purposes, and consider whether and in what ways they give voice to those previously excluded. The latter highlights our interest in the consequences of these new forms of voice. In particular, we aim to understand whether these new forms of participation challenge or complement traditional institutions of representation based on electoral participation (Selee and Peruzzotti, 2009: 3–6). Do they hold governments and elected officials more accountable than elections? To what extent is the participation they elicit "real" or "manipulated," and does it sustain or challenge traditional forms of clientelism? Do these institutions make the political system more responsive in terms of policy (for example, on the allocation of goods, the "who gets what, when, where, and how" aspect of politics) and decision making? How do these institutions affect the *quality* of citizens' voices: do they educate citizens to have the virtues and skills to exercise their voices effectively—to gather information, deliberate, reason publicly, imagine alternatives, and influence policy makers and regulators?

Beyond the "Crisis of Representation"

The important recent work by Andrew Selee and Enrique Peruzzotti (2009) and their collaborators in *Participatory Innovation and Representative Democracy in Latin America* suggests that the new forms of institutionalized direct democracy in the region respond to "the emergence of a growing gap between citizens and the political system" (2009: 2). There are deficits in representation caused, among other things, by severe weaknesses in mechanisms of accountability and the "defective functioning" of electoral and party systems as well as the courts (2009: 3). Recent scholarship on democracy in Latin America underlines the kinds of problems that have created the need, and sometimes the demand, for more direct citizen participation (Cameron and Luna, 2010).

We build on this literature, but we do not necessarily take representative democracy as our main point of reference. We recognize that Latin American democracies have emerged from distinctive historical trajectories, and that they need not necessarily converge on the model of representative democracy. Indeed, it is important to recognize the complexity and the contested meaning of the core concepts of democracy as it emerges in the region.

The transition from authoritarian regimes to elected democratic governments has been a surprisingly stable achievement, all the more remarkable when considered in light of the frequent coups and democratic breakdowns that have characterized Latin America's history. Effective and legitimate governance has nonetheless proven elusive, and by the waning years of the twentieth century pessimism about the quality of democracy had become ubiquitous. Although democracy was working as a mechanism for selecting leaders, democratically elected leaders exhibited a remarkable penchant for governing undemocratically. Unresponsiveness to the wishes of the public, a long tradition in most Latin American states, proved hard to change. The elected governments often failed to provide physical or social security or economic well-being, and were plagued by levels of corruption, clientelism, and unaccountability that undermined legitimacy (Hagopian and Mainwaring, 2005; Drake and Hershberg, 2006). Fundamental flaws persisted with regard to electoral procedures, adherence to constitutional provisions, and the separation, coordination, and balance of powers between the executive and competing branches of government, as well as the availability of opportunities for citizen participation in public affairs. In the most dramatic cases, this led to ruptures in democratic regimes, as in the Peruvian *autogolpe*[2] of 1992. In other countries of Latin America, leaders like Carlos Menem (Argentina), Alan García (Peru), Fernando Collor de Mello (Brazil), Ernesto Samper (Colombia), Abdalá Bucaram (Ecuador), and Gonzalo Sánchez de Lozada (Bolivia) seemed determined to govern erratically or autocratically.

The failure of democratization to catalyze meaningful improvements in public responsiveness, accountability, and effective representation, not to mention participation, led to considerable malaise. Observers lamented anemic public support for democracy as a preferred system of government, the inclination of charismatic leaders to bypass democratic procedures and impose their will instead through plebiscitary means, and the endemic weakness of state institutions (UNDP, 2006).

It was not simply the lack of political accountability, representation, and responsiveness in these new democracies, but also their unresponsiveness to the negative impact neoliberal economic strategies had on the lower and middle classes that fanned discontent and created pressures for greater voice for citizens. In fact, governments were encouraged to weaken certain state institutions—those involved in regulating the economy, enforcing environmental and regulatory laws, and providing social and public services. This formed part of their drive to impose unpopular austerity and structural adjustment strategies, to dismantle and privatize state industries, to weaken trade unions and popular organizations, and to undermine the economic position of agricultural producers, small manufacturers, and business sectors that depended on the protections of import substitution strategies being eroded by government-backed free trade policies. As these elected governments institutionalized the neoliberal model—indeed sometimes "constitutionalized" it through enabling legislation accompanying trade agreements—lack of responsiveness, accountability, and representation became integral to the economic strategy.

Anemic public support for democracy as a preferred system of government was noted by a number of researchers who pointed out the endemic weakness of Latin American states (Mainwaring and Scully, 2010: 374–77) and the tendency of charismatic leaders to bypass democratic institutions. The failure to extend democratic citizenship to what Guillermo O'Donnell labeled the "brown spaces" that marked vast swaths of cities and countryside alike, and the pervasive and seemingly intractable poverty that diminished the life chances of nearly half of the region's inhabitants, called into question the capacity of democratic institutions to enhance the public good (O'Donnell, 1993). Among the consequences, in the early twenty-first century, there were signs of increasing backlash by a wide range of movements and groups. At times these forces fought for ethnic inclusion (Yashar, 2005) and at others they demanded repeal of neoliberal economic policies that were associated with socioeconomic polarization (Silva, 2009).

But the emergence of popular organizations and protests is not the central concern in the book. Rather, our focus is on the creation of new institutions that may provide avenues for citizens to exercise their voice. Throughout the region there have arisen new institutions of direct, participatory democracy, frequently aimed at bringing new forms of accountability, responsiveness, and, indeed, representation, to supplement the traditional institutions of electoral democracy. These new institutions for participation are changing the character of representative democracy—with its reliance on elections, parties, and exclusive policy making by legislatures and executives—even while, as Panizza (2009: 255) has pointed out, they need not be seen as undermining it.

The Framework: Institutionalized Voice and Its Consequences

There has been a long-standing and extensive tradition of participatory politics in many Latin American nations, from Christian base communities in Brazil after Vatican II, Argentina's Madres in the Plaza de Mayo, to insurrectionary movements in Central America in the 1970s and 1980s. Thus, Latin America has long been seen as a region of powerful social movements, contentious politics, and grassroots political struggles (Lehmann, 1990: 148–214). Many of these movements operated outside the confines of the state. Indeed, they deliberately fought to preserve their autonomy from the perceived risks of encroachments by the state, and they bemoaned the demobilization of civil society that followed processes of democratization. As new political spaces for participation opened up following military rule, social movement leaders often became candidates for office and took up posts in governments at every level. While the move to electoral democracy was welcomed, many advocates of popular participation lamented the decline in civic engagement that resulted.

The kind of popular participation that we are analyzing is unlike earlier waves of participatory politics in that it does not eschew links with the state. Indeed, it is sometimes spurred by the growing awareness of the state's incapacity to deliver public goods on its own, which leads to the recognition of the need to work with the state to provide these goods. Sometimes institutions for direct citizen participation are even promoted by the state. Participatory budgeting institutions in Brazil, for example, had the support of elected representatives—local mayors from the Workers Party (*Partido dos Travalhadores* PT), a national party—as well as a social base among middle-class voters, business groups, organized labor, and the church (Abers, 2000; Fung, 2011). Further, many of the changes we are witnessing are not only institutionalized but are also "constitutionalized," often in direct response to neoliberalism. Popular organizations and populist leaders have sometimes (in Venezuela, Bolivia, and Ecuador, for example) enshrined these new forms of direct participation in constitutions in an attempt to make them permanent features of new political orders. In some settings, the very processes of constitutional change are, as in the case of Bolivia, designed to be participatory in one way or another.

Such new forms of participation risk several major antidemocratic pitfalls. One danger is the state devolution of power and responsibility for the provision of critical social goods onto civil society groups without the transfer of corresponding resources. It is sometimes convenient for elites to embrace the value of "civil society autonomy" as a way to shrink the state and its expenditures, and encourage a "do it yourself," "pick yourself up by your own bootstraps" ethic of turning over responsibility of everything from public education, road building, health care, and social services to citizens groups or local (often unfunded) municipal governments or market actors (Pateman, 2012: 15). Blessing "civil society" and local participatory institutions can be consistent with a neoliberal politics where state institutions shirk core responsibilities and offload the slack to the "third sector." This pitfall is not inevitable and in some countries (Brazil and Bolivia, for example) the emerging project around participation stresses both an expansion of state responsibilities over the economy and social welfare and efforts to increase the voice of citizens through institutionalized direct participation. Borrowing a term from the United Nations Development Program (UNDP), such efforts might be seen as aiming at "a citizens' democracy" (UNDP, 2006; OAS and UNDP, 2010).

A second potential antidemocratic pitfall in the expansion of institutions of direct participation is that autocratic leaders may deploy those institutions not to buttress citizen autonomy but to maximize their own power at the expense of their opponents. Contemporary analysts of Latin America echo historians of democratic Athens in noting the risks that demagogues can mobilize and manipulate the participation of the masses—the demos—for their own purposes. When powerful executives or dominant parties draw on clientelist mechanisms to mobilize constituents against competing institutions that might check their authority, and to deprive oppositions of opportunities to influence allocation of critical resources, participation takes on a profoundly antidemocratic character. The case of Venezuela under Chávez offers an example of a process of political change that has witnessed an explosion of participation of various forms, often at the expense of representatives, especially of the opposition, such as mayors, governors, and legislators. Institutionalizing popular participation can thus risk eroding the accountability and checks and balances of political institutions that depend on the periodic election of representatives. From this perspective, more "participation" implies less "representation," and vice versa.

Finally, absent appropriate institutional safeguards, popular participation in decision making may also come into conflict with the protection of rights and interests of minorities, including those of economic elites. Latin American politics have historically been susceptible to plebiscitarian tendencies, and that is very much evident today. It is arguably in this vein that some leading political scientists see increasing evidence of the eclipse of democracy, particularly in the Andes, and the emergence of "competitive authoritarianism" (Levitsky and Way, 2010).

Yet an undue focus on the antidemocratic potential of participation runs the risk of distracting us from the myriad ways in which the expansion of institutionalized spaces in which voice can be expressed might deepen the democratizing aspects of the important yet frequently unsatisfying regime transitions that swept the region during the last two decades of the twentieth century. We argue that there are diverse models of democracy in contention in Latin America today (and hence the proliferation of adjectives—"participatory," "liberal," "polyarchic," "representative"), and that the erosion of one form might strengthen or weaken another. It is entirely possible that a highly participatory system can hold regular elections that are genuinely competitive, and promote grassroots participation in ways that are meaningful for citizens, even as the representative features of the constitutional order are eroded. This possibility is all the more worth considering to the extent that the crisis of representation in Latin American democracies, and the failure of electoral democracies in the region to guarantee rights and justice to all of the citizenry, has often been so severe that vast segments of the population have never acquired much of a stake in representative institutions per se.

Several chapters in this book demonstrate that the various pitfalls we have identified are not inevitable. Huntingtonian fears notwithstanding, inclusion may strengthen stability; participation may teach judiciousness; through new institutional mechanisms excluded minority interests—or majorities, in the case of indigenous peoples in some settings—may be given voice for the first time; elected representatives may be made more accountable. Unless we appreciate the ways in which new patterns of participation and representation are reconfiguring politics in Latin America, we risk overstating the dangers to democracy and underestimating the potential benefits of political change. In short, the analysis of the dynamics of the democratic gains and pitfalls needs to be carefully nuanced. Moreover, processes of change in participation can rarely be plotted in a linear and predictable manner: in one institutional space after another, unanticipated consequences and transformations abound.

To navigate these waters analytically, we asked contributors to this book to think about a set of normative and empirical issues. We started by recognizing the crucial importance of electoral participation, and then asked in what ways it was insufficient. One of the classical objections to the notion that voting should be the central or only form of political participation is the idea that active citizenship is required to sustain and give vitality to democratic institutions. The Schumpeterian model of democracy—which puts primary emphasis on the competitive electoral struggle of party elites for votes—invites us to be citizens for the one day when we vote, and then asks us to go back to our private affairs. Our choice, and voice, is limited to the ballot.

This widely accepted model of democracy—elected representatives chosen from competing elites in free and fair elections—is often taken as the norm. But theorists of "deliberative democracy," from J. S. Mill to more contemporary theorists like Mark Warren, Archon Fung, Amy Gutmann, and Dennis Thomson, have challenged this vision, arguing that the kind of citizenship that is required to generate the public goods we want as citizens, including the preservation of democracy itself, may demand more than periodic choices at the ballot box (Pateman, 2012). More robust mechanisms for exercising citizenship may be necessary to ensure effective representation, expand inclusion, bolster responsiveness, disrupt clientelism, raise accountability, educate citizens, guarantee political stability, and enable local judicial practices to function well. The upsurge of institutionalized direct participation in Latin America indicates that this is not simply a theoretical issue: it is precisely because democracy without institutionalized voice is insufficient and the emergence of new forms of popular and citizen participation have the potential to strengthen democracy considerably. Free and fair elections, party systems, and constitutional institutions (the rule of law, a separate executive, legislature, and judiciary, a system of checks and balances), even when backed by a free press and civil liberties, seem not to have ensured opportunities for people to participate in the decisions that directly affect them. Having emerged from the intense privatization of their lives imposed by the terror of dictatorships and the disruptive effects of economic crises that beset the region for two decades beginning during the 1980s, Latin American citizens today seem to want more say in public affairs.

Albert O. Hirschman had an important insight about the limits of the Schumpeterian model of competitive electoral democracy. In *Exit, Voice, and Loyalty* he argued that the model conceived of democracy as a kind of market competition among elites, with the voter assuming the role of captive consumer faced with two choices: accept the offer of one's party, exit the party and choose another, or exit the system altogether by abstaining from voting. The power in such a system, said Hirschman, lies with elites; the voter as captive consumer, forced into loyalty or exit, is the "epitome of powerlessness" (Hirschman, 1970: 70). But Hirschman insisted that voters can do more than vote or abstain: they can exercise voice. Such voice embodies an underlying normative principle of democracy, the idea that people should have a say in the collective decisions that affect their lives. And it is not just a theoretical principal: it is embodied in many of the new forms of participation that are sweeping Latin America today.

In a retrospective essay on his earlier writing, Hirschman (1981: 213–223) outlined a number of criteria to identify situations in which voice is likely to be preferred to exit. The first was situations in which striving for an aim or goal cannot be neatly separated from its possession. He used the "public good" or "public happiness" as examples. We may not ever achieve the public good, but we take pleasure from participation in a movement that strives to bring it about. Second, voice may be a mechanism through which we overcome uncertainty or ignorance about the goods we want. Parents who want to know whether their kids are getting a good education, for example, may seek involvement in schools or daycares. Finally, there may be situations in which exit is costly, because preserving a relationship is important. Hirschman draws an analogy between marriages and vertically integrated firms. Both involve complex relationships in which exit entails a heavy cost (the need to start over with a new partner). In such cases, voice becomes a relatively more attractive way of managing friction. This is what Hirschman called "institutionalized voice" (1981: 222). The explosion of participation in Latin America, and its institutionalization through various mechanisms, may well reflect such voice-prone situations.

Along these lines there are two central questions that are addressed by our authors. A first core question is what do these new forms of participation look like? There are different mechanisms or innovations for direct participation. The first type consists of those we designate as electoral or vote dependent: mechanisms that break out of the normal bounds of periodic election of elites and elite agenda setting. Recalls allow voters to throw elites out before the next election; referenda allow citizens to decide on legislation or constitution change, taking the decision out of the hands of the elected elites working in legislatures; citizen initiatives allow interest groups to set the legislative agenda and bypass the legislature. All of these mechanisms involve bypassing the traditional institutions or periodic elections and decisions taken by legislatures; they also bypass traditional checks and balances. They may be held between elections, but they involve voting.

The second set of institutions operates between elections; they are participatory but not necessarily electoral. One form this may take is as consultative institutions such as consultative councils in Mexico. Here it is essential to determine the extent to which they have a real impact on agenda setting or policy outcomes. Other institutions may aim at policy making through both agenda setting and implementation, as is the case with communal councils in Venezuela. Direct participation between elections may be part of the legislative process (national conferences in Brazil) or the judiciary (communal indigenous justice). Finally, direct participation may revolve around budgeting and spending, as occurs in the participatory budgeting processes in Brazil and elsewhere.

Also of particular interest are the ways that some of these new forms of direct participation have been crucial in creating fundamental constitutional changes. Direct participation through constituent assemblies has been important in shaping the new constitutions of a number of Andean countries, and the book includes a study of Bolivia to examine whether the process of constitution making empowers or weakens representative bodies like legislatures and political parties.

A second core objective of the book is to assess the consequences of these new forms of institutionalized voice through direct participation on some of the fundamental aims and purposes of democracy. The following are among the main criteria we use to evaluate this aspect of the emerging institutional landscape.

Inclusion. Inclusion can be achieved in many ways, from suffrage to street protests. The conquest of the universal mass franchise was clearly a momentous event from the point of view of social inclusion—and a relatively recent one in some countries in the Latin American region where until recently, for example, illiterates could not vote—that opened the door to other struggles for the opportunity to participate as citizens. But not all decisions can be made on the basis of the principle of one-person, one-vote; sometimes other forms of participation that reward active citizenship and community involvement are desirable, especially when they hold the potential to include historically marginalized populations. In such cases, formal equality may have to be balanced against other forms of sociability that have the potential to reinforce democratic practices and institutions. The case of elections for indigenous authorities in Mexico, analyzed in the chapter by Todd Eisenstadt and Jennifer Yelle, provides a valuable example of hybrid logics of participation involving voting and customary practices, as does the current efforts of the Bolivian government to combine communal with participatory and representative democracy, discussed in the chapter by Jose Luis Exeni.

Representation. Pressure for participation may intensify where established representative institutions, such as party systems, have collapsed or where legislatures have fallen into disrepute. But mechanisms of direct participation may also proliferate alongside strong parties, legislatures, and interest associations, sometimes even strengthening them. Uruguay is an example of a case in which parties and legislatures have used referenda to reinforce representation. In Brazil, the policy conferences analyzed in this book by Thamy Pogrebinschi are often initiated by the executive but nested within legislatures (at both state and national levels) and they generate proposals that may be submitted to the legislature and passed into law. Here, again, the issue is not participation versus representation but how to balance the two. In particular, if there is active deliberation outside the legislature, lawmakers may feel pressure from below to act as agents of society. They may have more scope for deliberation and autonomy when social attentions are diverted elsewhere. As a general rule, Latin American legislatures have not done a good job of capturing public opinion and translating it into law, so a major hope for participatory democrats is that a more active citizenry will lead to less passive and reactive legislatures. In the case of Venezuela, however, although implementation of the new community council system has enlivened the local arena, it has also made the task of repairing the already weak representative institutions more complicated.

Responsiveness. By responsiveness we mean whether political decisions or other outcomes reflect what policymakers hear from citizens who are participating through these new institutions. The impact of voice may occur at different levels: (1) legislation, (2) policy decision-making, and (3) policy implementation. When does such responsiveness lead to a more equitable distribution of public goods, and when does it simply reward those with the most voice? Michael McCarthy's analysis of community councils suggests that to understand the rationale and appeal of these entities we must think more about how they enable civil society to "co-produce" public goods. The community council system also has a partisan logic, as it seeks to galvanize support for President Chávez and his party, and there are tensions between the councils and traditional forms of representation (the power of locally elected mayors and other officials is curtailed). But despite such threats to traditional electoral institutions already weakened by previous governments, Chávez's supporters often fervently embrace these participatory innovations as examples of a more meaningful or "protagonistic" democracy in action.

Disrupting Clientelism. There is a lively debate in the region over whether new mechanisms of popular participation are undermining clientelism or reinforcing it. New mechanisms of participation could help to break up clientelistic networks or provide new guises for the reassertion of older patterns of partisanship, brokerage politics, and even corruption. Clientelism is a powerful informal institution that may persist, whether because it provides benefits—though highly unequal—to both patrons and clients or because longstanding cultures of "doing politics" may be very difficult to overcome. The ideas of exit, voice, and loyalty are fruitful in this context because clientelism is, almost by definition, a system in which loyalty and exit are the only options. Yet these options rarely operate in isolation, as illustrated by the ways in which the ruling party in Mexico (the Institutional

Revolutionary Party, PRI) used indigenous governance to create barriers to entry for competitors. The PRI may have promoted *usos y costumbres*, indigenous customary law, leading to political logics beyond their immediate control, in order to ensure that the areas in which their influence was in decline were not captured by the opposition (Eisenstadt and Yelle, this volume).

Accountability. Some of the institutionalized mechanisms of direct participation that we are interested in—recall, referenda, citizens initiatives—offer instruments to check legislators and hold them accountable by removing them from office, by rejecting laws they have passed, or by passing laws they may have refused to enact. Guillermo O'Donnell has dubbed this "vertical accountability." Vertical accountability can trigger "horizontal accountability," in which one set of public agencies monitors and oversees the operation of another. But there are also alternative forms of accountability involving citizen control over public officials, sometimes called "social accountability" or, in Spanish, *control social.* Some of these mechanisms have been institutionalized or even incorporated into new constitutions. Citizen control refers to the watchdog role of civil society actors who are empowered to monitor wrongdoing and instigate existing accountability mechanisms to enforce existing rules and procedures (Peruzzotti and Smulovitz, 2002).

Before writing about vertical and horizontal *accountability*, O'Donnell, inspired by Hirschman, coined the terms "vertical voice" and "horizontal voice" (O'Donnell, 1986). He argued that horizontal voice—people (customers, citizens, clients) talking to others like themselves—was a necessary precondition to vertical voice, which results when people talk to those in power, such as managers, governors, or bosses. If people are not able to exercise horizontal voice they cannot hold rulers to account. That is one of the reasons that participatory development is hindered in settings characterized by the absence of a strong civil society, a phenomenon that is illustrated in this book by the analyses of Nicaragua (Gisela Zaremberg), and Recife, Brazil (Françoise Montambeault). A weak civil society allows parties and bosses to capture the spaces for direct participation and use them for their own purposes.

Educating Citizens. How do these new participatory institutions affect the *quality* of citizens' voices? For many of the new forms of institutionalized participation in Latin America to work, citizens have to learn how to exercise their voice in ways that strive to some level of agreement on agendas, decisions, and coherent policies. Democratic theorists from Mill onward have posited that democracy is enriched to the extent that citizens are informed, trust one another, are able to deliberate about policy issues, respect the law, are open to compromise, and are tolerant of differences. The proliferation of spaces in which participation takes place in Latin America in this respect marks a watershed in what some analysts have labeled "schooling" for democracy.

Institutional design is important if institutionalized voice is to be effective. For participatory institutions to work, it is not sufficient for citizens to "come together" in these forums to exercise their voice, or that policy elites and representatives happen to listen to them. Rather, these institutions need to structure participation and encourage discussions that enable citizens to accomplish a certain purpose (e.g., to decide on a portion of the local budget, to recommend policies to legislatures or government ministries on a particular issue). That often means that the new institutions need to be organized in a way so they can encourage and educate citizens to have the virtues and skills needed to exercise their voices effectively—to gather information, deliberate, reason publicly, imagine alternatives, and influence policy makers and regulators.

Most of the institutions analyzed in this book do not simply elicit and aggregate "preferences." Rather they are getting people to deliberate about, to reflect on, and to develop and refine their preferences in conversations with others. This is true of the advisory councils of experts and stakeholders studied by Hevia and Isunza in Mexico, the policy councils of experts and stakeholders studied by Pogrebinschi in Brazil, the participatory budgeting institutions studied by Montambeault in Brazil, and even the local neighborhood community councils in Venezuela, which must decide which projects to prioritize and how to carry them out.

These institutions are set up to encourage the participants to be *responsible* and to contemplate *more than just their own interests*: to think about what is good for the environment, for public health, for women, for their local neighborhood community, and for the cities of Belo Horizonte or Porto Alegre. Also, in many of these institutionalized structures *experts*, knowledgeable people, are brought into to *work with* citizens and stakeholders: in Venezuela, *tecnicos* (technical experts) from the ministries come into advise *consejos* (councils); in the Mexican and Brazilian councils there are academics and experts as well as local stakeholders. In a region where highly insulated technocrats have frequently exercised overwhelming influence over the allocation of public goods, the creation of spaces in which experts must interact with the citizenry has enormous democratizing potential.

The Structure of the Book

The chapters in this book provide us with a detailed inventory of institutionalized mechanisms of direct participation encompassing much of the Latin

American region. The survey is not exhaustive, but we have sought to identify a wide range of experiences, including both examples of success and failure. As the editors, we asked the contributors to the book to be as vivid and precise as possible in their descriptions of participatory mechanism.

Chapter 2 is an ambitious comparative study of municipal development councils in four countries, in which the Mexican political scientist Gisela Zaremberg identifies sharp differences in the degree to which participatory institutions serve to augment or constrain spaces for the citizenry to exercise control over central authorities. Making sophisticated use of techniques of network analysis borrowed from economic sociologists and geographers, Zaremberg portrays cases where executives deploy these institutions to bypass competing elected officials and reinforce hierarchical control, as well as instances where direct democracy opens avenues for more horizontal accountability and for the bolstering of representative institutions.

In Chapter 3, Thamy Pogrebinschi offers the most comprehensive analysis to date of the national policy conferences on public policies in Brazil, which have proliferated over the past decade and that are resulting in an unprecedented translation of citizen preferences into concrete legislative and regulatory measures. Here we find a remarkable case of participatory processes appearing to strengthen representative institutions—in this instance, both the legislature and the executive—and encouraging the latter to focus policy on the interests and demands of disadvantaged groups, ranging from racial and sexual minorities to senior citizens and people with disabilities. Whereas much of the social scientific literature to date has considered participatory institutions that operate strictly at the local level, Pogrebinschi's analysis provides an invaluable contribution to democratic theory by illuminating processes of direct democracy that take place nationally.

Whereas Zaremberg focuses on heterogeneity across countries, anthropologists Felipe Hevia J. and Ernesto Isunza Vera shed light in Chapter 4 on the factors that generate variation within a single national context, that of Mexico, where advisory councils to the federal government have exhibited strikingly different degrees of success. They look at the system of "consultative councils" (*consejos consultativos*) that began to be set up in Mexico in the early 1980s. They first consider the history and relative success of the Sustainable Development Councils that draw on a fairly wide range of civil society and government participants. In explaining how and why they have exerted some influence on the policies and regulations of the Ministry of the Environment, they are then able to account for why direct participation has been much less successful in other consultative councils (there are about 160 in total) in sectors like education, culture, health, and economic development. They analyze the character of these other participatory mechanisms but put particular emphasis on the continued closed and corporatist character of the Mexican state even after the defeat of the ruling party in 2000.

The degree to which a single institutional innovation can play out differently across contexts within a single nation is the central theme of Chapter 5, by the Canadian political scientist Francoise Montembeault. This chapter focuses on the widely analyzed experience of participatory budgeting in Brazil, but it does so by moving beyond the case of Porto Alegre, which has occupied most of the literature published to date. Whereas Montembeault's research largely confirms the optimistic accounts of Porto Alegre, which find an impressive degree of openness and transparency giving rise to greater degrees of accountability, her examination of participatory budgeting in Belo Horizonte and Recife shows how the same institutional mechanism can be captured by elites ruling through clientelist practices. The interaction between direct democracy and representative democracy emerges clearly in this chapter, as the nature of political parties turns out to be a critical determinant of the impact of participatory budgeting.

The role of political parties and of clientelism is also clear in Michael M. McCarthy's nuanced study of community councils in Venezuela. Deftly avoiding the temptation that plagues much of the literature to either celebrate or condemn the mechanisms through which *chavismo* has sought to bypass representative institutions, McCarthy chronicles in Chapter 6 the ways in which the Chávez government encouraged local "community councils" (over 35,000 of them) that were enabled to plan and execute local projects, such as electrification, road building, and the provision of potable water. McCarthy's subtle analysis of this politicized popular participation explores the ways in which the participatory strategy of the Chávez government simultaneously enhances top–down control by the executive at the same time that it empowers previously excluded citizens to make the government more responsive to their needs, hold public officials accountable, educate citizens, and encourage citizens to share responsibility with the government for the provision and allocation of public goods and services.

In Chapter 7, Alicia Lissidini examines direct democracy in Uruguay and Venezuela. Her focus is on electoral mechanisms of direct participation, especially referenda, plebiscites, and citizen initiatives. Both Uruguay and Venezuela have emerged as exemplars of Latin America's left turns, but they use direct democracy in different ways. In Uruguay, which has a long tradition of progressive constitutionalism, referenda are instruments wielded by political parties in the legislature to restrain the power of the executive. In Venezuela, they accomplish the exact opposite, reinforcing the power of the executive and perpetuating clientelism.

Chapter 8, by political scientists Todd A. Eisenstadt and Jennifer Yelle, addresses the central issue of how Latin American democracies are grappling with the challenges of incorporating the voice of indigenous peoples. Their analysis describes both the proliferation of *usos y costumbres* in southern Mexico and its contradictory implications for democratic representation. On the one hand, indigenous communities gain degrees of autonomy that recognize their distinctive histories and their right to self-determination, yet at the same time the authors reveal highly undemocratic practices that prevail in the operation of those institutional spaces. Representation of communities is enhanced through *usos y costumbres*, but representation of individuals living in those communities may not be, and the resulting circumstance highlights the possibility that institutional innovations may undermine important elements of democratic governance.

Chapter 9, by José Luis Exeni, reflects further on the challenges of deepening democracy in plurinational states. He argues that Bolivia's new constitution is an amalgam of three distinct democratic models: representative democracy, direct participatory democracy, and communitarian democracy. The current Bolivian government seeks to enhance indigenous participation at all levels of the state, and this means more indigenous representatives in the legislature, but also in the "plurinational" electoral body, as well as the plurinational constitutional tribunal. Another innovation in terms of participation in and through representation is the election of judges nationwide, as well as participation in new legislative bodies created by the framework law of autonomy and decentralization. But participation does not end with more elections; it also involves the encouragement of direct participation, both electoral (referenda) and nonelectoral (in local self-government). In particular, the communitarian conception of democracy is encouraged through the creation of autonomous self-governing bodies in indigenous communities. Recognizing that reconciliation of these models of democracy is not going to be easy, Exeni's perspective is not uncritical, yet the contribution of his chapter is to show that participation is not simply a set of mechanisms to be practiced at the local level but rather an alternative understanding of democratic politics that can be used to transform and democratize the state as a whole.

In the conclusion, two of the coeditors return to several of the key themes outlined in the introduction and addressed over the course of the book. We emphasize how this book represents a contribution to empirical analysis grounded in democratic theory and practice, and review how it documents and explains not only participatory deepening of democracy but also regressions and failures. We suggest ways in which the book will help move the debate beyond the either/or dichotomy of participation versus representation in Latin America, and also help us to delineate more clearly the diversity of democratic regimes in terms of the ways that they foster, inhibit, or balance mechanisms of participation and representation. Most importantly, the concluding chapter recommends criteria for evaluating the quality of democracy in the region, emphasizing the importance of considering its participatory dimensions.

Taken together, the chapters in this book provide a nuanced overview of direct institutionalized participation, including both electoral and nonelectoral mechanisms. They contribute to our understanding of the diverse models of democratic regimes and the variation in their quality. And we hope they will move the debate on democracy in Latin America away from a perspective that takes one form of democracy as the only relevant normative and empirical standpoint. The normative ground upon which we assess the new institutions of participatory democracy is not necessarily representative democracy. That is not to say that we are hostile to representative democracy, far from it, and for some of our authors it *is* the normative point of departure for analysis. But our book is not designed primarily to ask the question, how can participation improve representative democracy? That is a very important question (addressed by, among others, Selee and Peruzotti). However, in the course of our collective deliberations we came to ask a different one: how can people be given more institutional voice in whatever model of democracy may actually exist?

That focus on institutional voice is, perhaps, the distinctive feature of this book and is what makes it different from most of the other work available in this literature. Like Selee and Peruzotti we see no reason for being suspicious of institutions or institutionalized forms of popular participation. Nor do we genuflect at the altar of social movement autonomy and civil society purity. For that matter, we might challenge the idea that participation is only "good" if it contributes to democracy—let alone representative democracy. We can imagine it as a "good," even in an authoritarian system, or in a marketplace, or in a bureaucracy, although that is beyond the scope of this book. Our purpose here is to examine the multiplicity of ways in which institutionalized voice can be inserted into alternative models of democracy.

Notes

1. The term "direct democracy," as Alicia Lissidini (2008: 13–14) observes, can be used narrowly to refer only to referenda initiated by citizens or more broadly to any form of popular consultation (including plebiscites or recall), as well as a diverse gamut of forms of citizen participation involving firsthand experience (such as

participatory budgeting). We therefore use "direct participation" to refer to all the above, and direct democracy to refer to referenda.
2. Autogolpes, or self-coups, refer to situations in which democratically elected presidents alter or overthrow the constitutional order and rule by decree, typically abolishing legislative and judicial institutions that constrained their powers, at least until a referendum can be held to ratify a new regime with expanded presidential powers.

Bibliography

Abers, Rebecca. (2000). *Inventing Local Democracy: Grassroots Politics in Brazil.* Boulder: Lynne Rienner Publishers.

Altman, David. (2010). "Plebiscitos, referendos e iniciativas populares en América Latina: ¿mecanismos de control político o políticamente controlados?" *Perfiles Latinoamericanos* (No. 35, January–June). FLACSO-México.

Avritzer, Leonardo. (2009). *Participatory Institutions in Democratic Brazil.* Baltimore: Johns Hopkins University Press.

Avrtizer, Leonardo. (2002). *Democracy and the Public Space in Latin America.* Princeton: Princeton University Press.

Baiocchi, Gianpaolo. (2005). *Militants and Citizens: The Politics of Participatory Democracy in Porto Alegre.* Stanford: Stanford University Press.

Baiocchi, Gianpaolo. (2003). "Participation, Activism and Politics: The Porto Alegre Experiment," in A. Fung and E. O. Wright, eds. *Deepening Democracy: Institutional Innovations in Empowered Participatory Governance.* London: Verso.

Cameron, Maxwell A. and Kenneth Sharpe. (2010). "Andean Left Turns: Constituent Power and Constitution Making," in Cameron and Hershberg, eds. *Latin America's Left Turns: Politics, Policies and Trajectories of Change.* Boulder, CO: Lynne Rienner Publishers.

Cameron, Maxwell A. and Juan Pablo Luna, eds. (2010). *Democracia en la region andina: Diversidad y desafíos.* Lima: Instituto de Estudios Peruanos.

Dagnino, Evelina, Alberto J. Olvera, and Aldo Panfichi, eds. (2006). *La disputa por la construcción democrática en América Latina.* México: FCE, CIESAS, Universidad Veracruzana.

Drake, Paul and Eric Hershberg, eds. (2006). *State and Society in Conflict: Comparative Perspectives on Andean Crises.* Pittsburgh, PA: University of Pittsburgh Press.

Fung, Archon. (2011). "Reinventing Democracy in Latin America," *Perspectives on Politics,* Vol. 9 (December): 857–871.

Hagopian, Frances and Scott P. Mainwaring, eds. (2005). *The Third Wave of Democratization in Latin America: Advances and Setbacks.* New York: Cambridge University Press.

Hirschman, Albert O. (1981). *Essays in Trespassing: Economics to Politics and Beyond.* Cambridge: Cambridge University Press.

Hirschman, Albert O. (1970). *Exit, Voice, and Loyalty: Responses to Decline in Firms, Organizations and States.* Cambridge: Harvard University Press.

Lehmann, David. (1990). *Democracy and Development in Latin America: Economics, Politics and Religion in the Post-War Period.* Philadelphia, PA: Temple University Press.

Levitsky, Steven and Lucan Way. (2010). *Competitive Authoritarianism: Hybrid Regimes After the Cold War.* New York: Cambridge University Press.

Lissidini, Alicia. (2011). *Democracia directa en América Latina: entre la delegación y la participación.* Buenos Aires: Consejo Latinoamericano de Ciencias Sociales.

Lissidini, Alicia. (2008). "Democracia directa Latinoamericana: riesgos y oportunidades," in Lissidini et al. eds. *Democracia directa en América Latina.* Buenos Aires: Prometeo Libros.

Mainwaring, Scott, Ana María Bejarano and Eduardo Pizarro Leongómez, eds. (2006). *The Crisis of Democratic Representation in the Andes.* Stanford: Stanford University Press.

Mainwaring, Scott and Timothy R. Scully (2010). "Democratic Governance in Latin America: Eleven Lessons from Recent Experience," in Mainwaring and Scully, eds. *Democratic Governance in Latin America.* Stanford: Stanford University Press.

Munck, Gerardo L. (2010). "Repensando la cuestión democrática: la región andina en el nuevo siglo," en *Revista de Ciencia Política* (Volumen 20, No. 1), pp. 149–161. Santiago: Universidad Católica de Chile.

O'Donnell, Guillermo (1993). "Privatization Is Not Democratization: The Browning of Latin America," *New Perspectives Quarterly,* Vol. 10, No 4 (Fall): 50–53.

O'Donnell, Guillermo (1986). "On the Fruitful Convergences of Hirschman's *Exit, Voice, and Loyalty* and *Shifting Involvements*: Reflections from the Recent Argentine Experience," in Foxley et al. eds. *Development, Democracy, and the Art of Trespassing: Essays in Honor of Albert O. Hirschman.* Notre Dame, IN: University of Notre Dame Press.

OAS and UNDP (2010). *Nuestra Democracia.* Mexico: Fondo de Cultura Económica.

Panizza, Francisco. (2009). *Contemporary Latin America: Development and Democracy Beyond the Washington Consensus.* London: Zed Books.

Pateman, Carole. (2012). "Participatory Politics Revisited," *Perspectives on Politics,* Vol. 10, No. 1 (March): 7–19.

Peruzzotti, E., and C. Smulovitz. (2002). *Controlando la política. Ciudadanos y medios en las nuevas democracias latinoamericanas.* Buenos Aires: Temas.

Santos, Boaventura de Sousa and Leonardo Avritzer. (2004). "Para ampliar el canon democrático," en Santos (coordinador): *Democratizar la democracia. Los caminos de la democracia participativa.* México D.F.: Fondo de Cultura Económica.

Schumpeter, Joseph A. (1942). *Capitalism, Socialism, and Democracy.* New York: Harper & Row.

Selee, Andrew and Enrique Peruzzott, eds. (2009). *Participatory Innovation and Representative Democracy in Latin America.* Washington, D.C. and Baltimore: Woodrow Wilson Center Press and the Johns Hopkins University Press.

Silva, Eduardo. (2009). *Challenging Neoliberalism in Latin America.* Cambridge UK: Cambridge University Press.

UNDP (2006). *Democracy in Latin America: Toward a Citizens' Democracy*. New York: United Nations Development Programme.

Van Cott, Donna Lee. (2008). *Radical Democracy in the Andes*. Cambridge: Cambridge University Press.

Wampler, Brian. (2007). *Participatory Budgeting in Brazil: Contestation, Cooperation, Accountability*. University Park: Penn State Press.

Wampler, Brian and Leonardo Avritzer. (2005). "The Spread of Participatory Budgeting in Brazil: From Radical Democracy to Participatory Good Government," *Journal of Latin American Urban Studies*, Vol. 7: 37–51.

Yashar, Deborah J. (2005). *Contesting Citizenship: The Rise of Indigenous Movements*. New York: Cambridge University Press.

CHAPTER 2

"We're Either Burned or Frozen Out": Society and Party Systems in Latin American Municipal Development Councils (Nicaragua, Venezuela, Mexico, and Brazil)

Gisela Zaremberg

Introduction

The demands of democratic opening in Latin America have led to the creation of mechanisms for promoting greater citizen participation, transparency, and accountability (Cunill, 1997; Cheresky and Pousadela, 2001; Dagnino, Olvera, and Panfichi, 2006). Especially noteworthy are efforts to create institutionalized "interfaces" for contact between government and civil society (Isunza and Hevia, 2006; Gurza and Insunza, 2010) in the form of municipal citizens councils.

In the last decade these new spaces have proliferated in Mexico, Nicaragua, Venezuela, and Brazil. There is significant disagreement in the literature on these experiences. Are these new forms of local participation just new ways of hiding old political bad habits? Or to the contrary, are they genuine innovations that open avenues for new processes that are more horizontal and inclusive?[1]

This chapter addresses these questions with the understanding that there is no single representation applicable to all the experiences. Thus, a typology is constructed to capture nuances. We will argue that these experiences constitute new names for old forms of political control when there is a relationship of cooptation or monopoly of intermediation between political parties and the social actors who are involved. At the other extreme, municipal citizens councils become spaces for participation when social actors can dialogue with political actors through various channels to connect with one another. Network analysis is fundamental to this argument, since it provides measures of centrality (especially measures of intermediation) for analyzing the relationships surrounding the councils.

The chapter is divided into four parts. The first is a brief theoretical-methodological overview. In the second part, the municipal development councils are analyzed. Third, we outline a typology of relationships between society and political parties based on an analysis of the networks that operate around the councils. The conclusion summarizes the principal inferences obtained from case comparisons.

Brief Methodological Note

This chapter analyzes the external networks that form around municipal development councils, with a particular focus on the relationships among the councils, social organizations, and political parties. The following councils are studied: Rural Municipal Development Councils (Conselhos Municipais de Desenvolvimento Rural—CMDR) in Brazil (Bahia, sisal-growing region); Rural Municipal Sustainable Development Councils (Consejos Municipales de Desarrollo Rural Sustentable—CMDRS) in México (Oaxaca); Citizen Participation Cabinets (Gabinetes de Participación Ciudadana—GPC) in Nicaragua (Nueva Segovia and León); and Communal Councils (Consejos Comunales—CC) in Venezuela (Zulia). These councils were selected for study because they are highly comparable and all operate in contexts of profound socioeconomic marginalization. We sought to analyze new efforts to exercise "voice," understood in Hirschmanian terms, in contexts where these voices usually face serious difficulties being heard, in order to apprehend what innovative factors can overcome these obstacles.

To select cases, in each country a state with a similar set of socioeconomic conditions was identified. Within each state eight municipalities were chosen based on similar socioeconomic conditions and selection quotas for each country, so that at least one municipality has a significant ethnic minority population, one has female leadership, and two are urban or semi-urban. To assure a selection of socioeconomically similar cases a series of variables were considered.[2] A principal components analysis was conducted with these variables to identify homogeneous groups from which the eight municipalities per country were selected.

Once the qualitative and quantitative information in the field was obtained, one of the analytic strategies concentrated on the internal and external networks that were identified around the councils. Network analysis investigates the relationships among actors, generating a network diagram in which individual or organizational actors are located as points, formally referred to as "nodes." The existence of a relationship is reflected in a line connecting two points or nodes in the network. The lack of relationship is evidenced by the absence of lines between the nodes in question (Harary, 1969).

Each diagram produces a matrix that illustrates different measures. In this instance the focus is on measures of centrality (Freeman, 1977). The measures observed are *degree, betweenness,* and *closeness.* Degree describes the percentage of connections that a node has with respect to the entire network. Degree analysis indicates the most connected person in the group. Betweenness indicates the frequency that a node appears in the shortest line (or geodesic) that connects two others that are not themselves directly connected. This shows when a person or organization is an intermediary between two others in the same group who do not know each other (which can be called a "bridge" person or institution). Finally, the level of closeness indicates the proximity of a node to the rest of the network. This represents the capacity that an actor has to reach the others. A person who is poorly connected to the rest (low centrality, low level of betweenness) by being only connected to an "important" person may have very high closeness.[3] Thus, betweenness indicates monopoly, closeness shows influence, and degree is a measure of popularity.

The third section of this chapter includes an analysis of external relationships constructed around the councils for municipal development, emphasizing the relationships in which benefits are exchanged (e.g., resources, information, etc.). These network relationships are identified by the aforementioned centrality measures in diagrams and tables. A key factor in the analysis is the extent to which betweenness of social organizations and parties (in government and the opposition) is monopolized (or not) by actors in the network.

Finally, data from a total of 400 surveys and 320 in-depth interviews with council members, key informants, and control subjects (100 surveys and 80 interviews in each state) are included in the chapter.

Democratic Innovation? Municipal Development Councils in Brazil and Mexico

Networks in which councils are embedded need to be precisely characterized to validate the bases for comparative analysis. Thus, we begin with a review of the *normative references, objectives, scope of territorial action, thematic areas,* rules for *integration* or membership, and the *functions* and *resources* that the councils manage. This is done without losing sight of the *political project* (Dagnino, 2007) in which the councils are inscribed.

In the Brazilian case, the CMDR were created by presidential decree as part of the National Program for Strengthening Family Farms (Programa Nacional de Fortalecimiento a la Agricultura Familiar—PRONAF) in 1996. The program's purpose is to promote sustainable development in rural areas, and it is based on a strategy of cooperation among municipal, state, and federal authorities; the private sector; and family farmers and their organizations. The partner organizations come together in the National Council for Sustainable Rural Development (Consejo Nacional de Desarrollo Rural Sustentable—CONDRAF). That development policy in Brazil is reflective of a governance framework is not unusual. Indeed, this pattern is observed in several areas of Brazilian public policy (Bresser Pereira and Cunill Grau, 1999; Genro, 2000; Wampler and Avritzer, 2005; Cornwall and Coelho, 2007; Paez de Paula, 2010).

Among the many possible councils to choose from in Bahia, the CMDR were selected for this study because they were highly comparable to the Mexican case, and to a large extent the Nicaraguan and Venezuelan cases as well. The CMDR's formal purpose is to provide the main venues to consider proposals for addressing smallholders' demands and to make public policies for municipal development (Moura, 2007: 245). Their primary function is the creation and implementation of Municipal Plans for Rural Development (Planes Municipales de Desarrollo Rural—PMDR) and the management of resources allocated to carry out the program's objectives. These objectives are formally consistent with those analyzed in the other countries.

Although these geographically focused activities are directed at rural zones, they also affect urban areas where peasants are engaged in agricultural and nonagricultural activities.[4]

The CONDRAF recommends that these CMDRs be comprised of 50 percent of people from civil society and 50 percent of government representatives. This composition differentiates these councils from the rest of the sample. In practice, civil society organizations are represented in excess of the recommended level. In the municipalities we studied, 87 percent of the members surveyed represented social organizations (small farmers' unions, rural organizations, NGOs). In qualitative interviews they reported that the creation of these councils has been a historic demand of the rural movement they belong to.

After 2003, with the PT's Lula da Silva in the presidency, rural development policy was concentrated in two ministries, the Ministry of Agriculture, responsible for agribusiness issues, and the Ministry of

Agricultural Development (MDA), which is responsible for the interests of smallholders. The latter supports intermunicipal councils, called CODES (Conselho de Desenvolvimento Territorial), to address regional development. Within the MDA, the Secretariat for Regional Development (Secretaría de Desarrollo Territorial–SDT) transfers resources from PRONAF (previously under CMDR management) to the CODES (see Moreira and Carneiro, 2012). According to our key informants, this policy was favored by the organizations, because in municipalities run by the opposite parties, municipal leaders *(prefeitos)* had blocked the implementation of resources controlled by the CMDR. It was believed that regional planning could remedy this problem.

In Bahia, which has 417 municipalities, regional policy was made through 26 intermunicipal councils (CODES). This approach was strengthened after 2006, when the PT succeeded in obtaining power after a long hegemony of a group of politicians known as "carlistas."[5] Additionally, in Brazil, especially in the sisal region of Bahia where we carried out our study, there is a diverse network of civil society actors who have roots in an intense history of religious base communities, and who come from modern smallholder unions connected to the grassroots formation of the Bahian PT. This network of endogenous actors is further connected to an accumulation of work done by several international development organizations. The network is stronger and more varied than that found in the rest of our cases. This is true despite the fact that in comparison with other regions of Brazil (especially the south, such as Porto Alegre) the literature suggests that northeastern Brazilian civil society is relatively weak (Avritzer, 2010).

In comparison, at the time of our research, the state of Oaxaca, Mexico, had been governed by the Institutional Revolutionary Party (Partido Revolucionario Institucional—PRI) for 80 years, with a change in power only in July 2010, after the research was concluded. As we will show, this is a significant difference from the Brazilian case, yet it still does not fully explain the degree of variance between the two cases. Lack of alternation in power coexists with the formal democratic game of competitive elections, yet there is informal resistance to the game. Furthermore, the state is very heterogeneous, with 570 municipalities, of which 418 follow a system of *usos y costumbres* (a traditional form of governance based on indigenous practices, addressed by Eisenstadt and Yelle in Chapter 9 of this book).[6] In the social sphere, there are civil society organizations (which are relatively weak)[7] and many corporatist organizations that, as we shall demonstrate, intermediate between parties and government. The latter are rooted in organizations of the past (e.g., the National Peasant Federation and Confederación Nacional Campesina—CNC) but they also come out of new organizations linked to opposition parties, which nonetheless adopt the same political negotiation style of the organizations historically connected to the PRI. Finally, the diverse spectrum of ethnicities, the context of migration, cultural distances, and socioeconomic inequalities all make for a very complex scene.

Mexico began to decentralize beginning in the mid-1980s, which led to the creation of the National System for Democratic Planning (Planning Law) that paved the way for the participation of social sectors in the country's development process. The changes led to the setting up of Planning Councils for State Development (Consejos de Planeación para el Desarrollo de los Estados—COPLADE) and Planning Committees for Municipal Development (Comités de Planeación para el Desarrollo Municipal—COPLADEMUN).[8]

At the time of our research Oaxaca's administrative structure was unusual. It had been decided to merge most of the rural councils with the Municipal Councils for Rural Sustainability (Consejos Municipales de Desarrollo Rural Sustentable—CMDRS), which were created in 2001 by the Law for Sustainable Rural Development. In accordance with this structure, the CMDRS should formally operate within COPLADEMUN. Nevertheless, since municipal governments have the authority to name councils or committees, some have treated the COPLADEMUN or CMDRS bodies in different ways. Our research found that in six of the cases, the body that is officially recognized is the CMDRS, without any corresponding COPLADEMUN body (this is despite the fact that some of the municipalities are more urban). In two other municipalities there is no registered Municipal Development Plan, but in the minutes of hearings for Prioritization of Works and Actions, the CMDRS are the bodies that approve priorities, and there is no information about the COPLADEMUN.[9] Thus, the formal body in our cases is the CMDRS, although interviewees confused the terms "COPLADE" and "CMDRS" constantly, reflecting the low level of awareness of the legal framework.

Formally, the CMDRS are defined as entities through which producers and other rural agents participate in defining regional priorities, and in the planning and distribution of resources that the federal government, states, and municipalities allocate to productive investments and sustainable rural development. These councils would act as consultative bodies to municipal government for the planning and definition of rural development policies and strategies. Basically, CMDRS are the conduits for the Fund for Contributions to Municipal Social Infrastructure Fondo III (Fund III, Mexico) of resources from Branch 33 (Caire, 2009).[10] Nevertheless, in practice, of the 20 functions mandated by law, the CMDRS studied only performed the one for prioritizing work included in Ramo 33 (Branch 33, Mexico).[11]

This complicated series of laws applying to CMDRS and COPLADEMUN seem to contribute to simulation. For one thing, the councilors are not sure of their roles. Additionally, officials cite COPLADEMUN (which in their documents is actually CMDRS) for the requirement of signature approval from councilors for annual resources from Ramo 33 (Branch 33, Mexico). This is the councils' activity that most concerns the municipal leaders who we interviewed. As a result, many of them reduce the councils to one annual meeting exclusively dedicated to this objective.

According to the Law for Sustainable Rural Development, municipal presidents are permanent members of the CMDRS and, unlike in Brazil, they can preside over the councils. The councils are also comprised of the municipal representatives of the agencies in the Inter-Secretarial Commission, officials from state agencies who are appointed by those same agencies, and representatives of social organizations and private economic and social organizations from the municipality's rural sector.

In practice, in the cases studied there is significant manipulation of the selection of members by the municipal president, who has the authority to preside over the councils. One form of this manipulation is promoting election of members from the agencies (or towns) previously selected by the president. In the case of Oaxaca, which is in clear contrast to that of Brazil, the majority of members on the councils from society are essentially "agents," authorities who govern the towns within the municipalities. These authorities are elected via *usos y costumbres,* by the Assembly, and/or by the Council of Elders.

In sum, although the spaces for municipal interface in Oaxaca and Bahia are located in similar socioeconomic contexts (except for the ethnicity variable, which in Bahia involves race), there are important contrasts in the internal composition of the councils, in the centrality of the municipal president, and in the strength and type of civil society.

Democratic Innovation? Municipal Development Councils in Nicaragua and Venezuela

In Nicaragua, the current Citizen Participation Cabinets (GPC) are a reformulated version of the Councils for Citizen Participation (Consejos de Participación Ciudadana—CPC) created by presidential decree in 2007 by the ruling Sandinista National Liberation Front (Frente Sandinista de Liberación Nacional—FSLN). The decree was intended to counteract the old Councils for Municipal Development (Consejos de Desarrollo Municipal—CDM), which the legislature had established in 2003. Until the creation of the CPC/GPC, the highest body for government–civil society dialogue in the municipalities was the CDM. In the municipalities where the FSLN has not won municipal elections (or could not control them through fraud)[12] the CDM continue to function parallel to the GPC. Nevertheless, their relevance is in clear decline. Although several civil society organizations had received international support for capacity building during the 1990s, it does not seem to have been sufficient to have significantly reversed the weakness of the CDM and the ascendancy of the GPC (see Largaespada, 2008).

The formally articulated purpose of the GPC is for the Nicaraguan "people" to organize and participate in comprehensive development, actively and directly supporting the policies of the president of the Republic. This objective is based on a political project that privileges participatory democracy over representative democracy, which has often been assessed in pejorative terms (Prado, 2008).

The GPC are territorially designated in communities, neighborhoods, districts, municipalities, departments, autonomous regions, and at the national level. They are made up of 16 sectors that are responsible for diverse areas of action, with a general coordinator.[13] The 16 officials at the multiple levels (community, *comarca* (a traditional region or local administrative division), neighborhood, etc.) are elected for a period of two years and can be reelected up to two times. The GPC have been part of the National Council for Socio-economic Planning (Consejo Nacional de Planificación Económico Social—CONPES) since 2007.[14] The decree places the National Cabinet of Citizen Authority at the highest level of decision-making within the CONPES, which is constituted by a plenary body.

GPC membership includes an elected representative from each of the sectors in the 15 departments and two autonomous regions of the country, chaired by the president of the Republic and the government's coordinator for the Secretariat of Communication and Citizenship (headed by the first lady), ministers of state, presidents of autonomous and government entities, national police authorities, the board of directors of CONPES, and other government officials appointed by the president. Economic and social sector representatives can become members by requesting approval from the cabinet to join (Stuart Almendárez, 2009).

From the National Cabinet of Citizen Authority down to the *Comarca*, all the bodies are called cabinets. The cabinet for the *Comarca* or the Neighborhood Citizen Authority, which is the lowest level, is made up of two to six representatives. In turn, this cabinet elects a team of 16 coordinators and selects between two and six of them to represent them at the district cabinet. This same process is followed for the municipal and departmental cabinets.

In practice, the membership in the municipal GPC is closely linked to FSLN party militants. Our data reflect this for members of the councils who were interviewed. Notably, all of the interviewees (100 percent) responded that they also considered themselves active members of the FSLN. In comparison, only 22.7 percent of CDM members indicated they had any party affiliation, which was exclusively the opposition party—the Liberal Party (Partido Liberal—PL). This illustrates the level of polarization that affects these spaces.

Additionally, because to date the government has not issued regulations for the decree or the statute to establish the GPC's organization and functions, there are no official data on their specific responsibilities. Nevertheless, our investigation determined that in many councils their role is identified as the implementation of the national executive's programs at the community level. There are very few references to decision-making. Despite this, some GPC members we interviewed had a sense of symbolic "empowerment" as they were able to engage with implementation of policies and/or register complaints at the mayoral level without bureaucratic objections or delays ("now they open the door for me").

Finally, there is no official information on the administration of public resources by the GPC. However, we were able to observe that they do have an important role in the implementation of two of the most important government programs: the food program "Zero Hunger" and the "Zero Usury" program.[15]

In the case of Venezuela, the Venezuelan Communal Councils (CC) are a fundamental piece of a political project that emphasizes participatory democracy in opposition to or of greater priority than representative democracy. Representative democracy is associated with the political period called the "Puntofijo," characterized by the predominance of two parties, Democratic Action and the conservative Christian Democratic coalition COPEI (Comité de Organizaæion Política Electoral Independiente), which were locked into an asphyxiating bipartisan system throughout the four decades prior to President Chávez's election in 1998.

The CC were created by the Communal Councils Law, approved by the National Assembly on April 7, 2006. The CC are consistent with the Bolivarian constitution, which enshrines participation as a central principal of "popular power"—the embodiment of a new basis for sovereignty. The constitutional principal drew on significant participatory experiences that had been a central objective of the left when it joined the Chavista electoral coalition at its beginning. The coalition's military faction has continued to expand on the components originally proposed by the left (see López Maya, 2009).

Currently, the CC are a central part of the "Socialist Revolution for the 21st Century," a political project, which, although vague, was created simultaneously with the Unified Socialist Party of Venezuela (Partido Socialista

Unido de Venezuela—PSUV) to strengthen a second era of Chavista hegemony. Thus, the normative framework for the CC has changed over time. In 2009, the National Assembly passed the Organic Law for Communal Councils, which extended the CC's sphere of action beyond participation, because by definition they are a fundamental vehicle for the construction of the new model of socialist society. This law superseded the Communal Councils Law of 2006.[16]

The development of the CC is oriented, coordinated, and evaluated by the Presidential Commission for Popular Authority, which is appointed by the president of the Republic. This commission is made up of a National Commission for Popular Authority and regional, local, and "special" Popular Authority Commissions.

The CC are formally defined as bodies for participation, coordination, and integration between citizens, community organizations, and social and popular movements that allow the "organized people" to exercise "communitarian government" and to directly manage community-responsive public policies and projects in the construction of the new model of socialist society. To meet their objectives, the CC are required to follow the communal cycle, which is intended to make popular participation and participatory planning that is responsive to community needs effective. It is made up of five phases that need prior approval by the Citizens' Assembly for each council: (1) diagnostics, (2) plan, (3) budget, (4) execution, (5) social audit.

The CC territorial unit is the communities, defined by law as the social group of families and citizens that inhabit a defined geographic area, share a history and common interests, know and relate to one another, use the same public services, and share similar needs and potentials. The communities bring together between 150 and 400 families in urban areas, at least 20 families in rural areas, and at least ten families in indigenous communities.

This is a different delimitation from the municipality, which is the relevant geographic unit for the rest of the councils we consider in our international comparison. We chose the CC in Venezuela because at the time we began our research, the Municipal Planning Councils were extinct and the Communes had not yet appeared on the horizon. Furthermore, the small size of municipalities in Bahia, Oaxaca or Nueva Segovia, and Leon can be closely compared to the communal territories in Zulia, Venezuela. However, as discussed below, the difference in territorial definition is relevant to the consideration of some details that affect the inferences derived from the comparisons.

The CC are formally comprised of (a) the Citizens' Assembly, the Communal Council's highest decision-making body with a minimum of 10 percent participation of community residents over the age of 15; (b) the

Community Coordinating Collective, made up of representatives from the Executive, Administrative and Community Finance, and Social Audit Units; (c) the Executive Unit, comprised of representatives covering various issues (water, education, etc.); (d) the Administrative and Community Finance Unit, which acts as an entity for administration, implementation, investment, credit, savings, and financial intermediation for the resources and funds from the CC (made up of five community residents elected by the Assembly); and (e) the Social Audit Unit that evaluates community management and monitors the activities, resources, and administration of the CC's funds.

The majority of members in the councils we studied in Zulia were housewives, teachers, students, and workers, as illustrated in Table 2.1.

Notably, members of the CC we studied are mostly women, 65.9 percent (34.1 percent men), in contrast to Oaxaca where we found only nine women out of the 92 members interviewed (9.8 percent women and 90.2 percent men). Although 44 percent reported direct affiliation with the PSUV and some belonged to a front that is associated with the party, the rest reported belonging to other organizations, including other popular participation bodies integrated with the Chavista movement (e.g., *Misión Sucre*). However, 30 percent reported not belonging to any organization. This contrasts with the Nicaraguan case, in which membership in the FSLN by GPC members was 100 percent. Thus, the membership landscape of the CC in Venezuela is not as linearly tied to the governing political party as it is in Nicaragua.

CC directly receive financial and nonfinancial resources from various sources. It is formally stipulated that funds approved by state authorities for a specific project cannot be used for purposes other than the initially approved and allocated project without authorization from the state authority that

Table 2.1   Principal employment of members of the CC, Zulia

Occupation	What do you do?	
	Frequency	Percentage
Housewife	24	19.5
Businessperson	5	4.1
Teacher	15	12.2
Municipal employee	3	2.4
Student	25	20.3
Worker	21	17.1
Professional	5	4.1
Other	7	5.7
Unspecified	18	14.6
Total	123	100.0

provided the funds. Resources not earmarked for specific projects must be allocated to internal accounts to be administered by the Administrative and Community Finance Unit following approval from the Citizens' Assembly.

In practice it appears that the CC have insufficient capacity to follow the formal mandates for financial management. Our findings echo those of McCarthy's as outlined in Chapter 6: complaints and comments about the poor use of funds were frequent among interviewees (anti- as well as pro-Chavistas).

This descriptive information provides a basis for weighing the similarities and differences among the cases, leading to a new comparison in analytic terms, as shown in Table 2.2.

This table illustrates the differences and similarities in the councils' internal organization as well as in their political party and social environment. Thus, it is noteworthy that although Mexico and Brazil formally share the same political project with respect to a balance between representative and participatory democracy, the nature of the societies and party systems at the local level are relevant factors that appear to be impacting greater (as in the case of Brazil) or lesser (as in the case of Mexico) effectiveness of the

Table 2.2 Analytical summary of cases

Dimensions	Brazil	Mexico	Nicaragua	Venezuela
Political Project	Representative and participatory democracy	Representative and participatory democracy	Participatory vs. representative democracy	Participatory vs. representative democracy
Role of Municipal President	Not necessarily presiding. Greater manipulation in "carlista" municipalities	Presides and manipulates the selection of members	Non-Sandinista mayoralties are marginalized from the GPC. Sandinista mayoralties are subsumed by the party (recentralization of the national government)	Non-Chavista mayoralties are marginalized from the CC. Chavista mayoralties are subsumed in the CC (recentralization of the national government)
Role of Municipal Legislature (councilors, aldermen, etc.)	Approval required to create a CMDR	Approval required to create a CMDRS (but they tend to be coopted by the municipal president)	No participation. National executive ratifies them	No participation. National executive ratifies them

Membership	Strong and diverse organizations. Manipulation in "carlista" municipalities	Local agents elected by *usos y costumbres*. Significant manipulation by the municipal president in the selection	FSLN militants	Housewives, students, workers. Some are militants in the PSUV or other Chavista groups
Resources	Do not directly control resources. But do make decisions on program implementation	Do not directly control resources. Formally, make programming decisions but in practice only prioritize projects for annual implementation of branch 33	Implement national programs; especially social assistance	Control significant resources and even generate their own. Resource management has gotten out of control
Social Context	Strong civil society organizations. Modern and strong corporatism	Weak civil society. Traditional corporatism	Civil society divorced from "popular" organizations linked to the FSLN	"Popular" society, based on strong and vibrant communitarian organizations
Political Party Context	Alternating political power. Competitive party system	No alternation until 2010. Declining monopoly party system (formally competitive, informally obstructed)	Increasingly monopolistic party system	Increasingly monopolistic party system

Source: Prepared by the author.

formal rules that govern the councils. Despite sharing several norms (especially regarding the role of municipal legislatures and financial management), in Mexico manipulation and simulation of these rules is more evident.

At the same time, while Nicaragua and Venezuela also share the same political project, the vertical composition of the councils and the instrumental use of resources are much more apparent in Nicaragua.

However, this question remains: Why do projects that emphasize participation as a central component arrive at politically different outcomes? In the next section, we will define a typology of relationships among networks connecting local councils and political parties. Through this typology, we will provide an analysis that explains the meaning and nuances of the differences that these experiences impart.

"We're Either Frozen Out or Burned": Cooptation, Mobilization, Participation, and the Vote

Based on the overview above, we will argue here that where there is a party system built on or distorted by a monopoly, and civil society is relatively weak, the relationship among networks around local councils and political parties will be one of cooptation (simulated or instrumental). However, where a party monopoly is built with a strong societal counterpart, the relationship will be based on mobilization. In the context of a relatively consolidated competitive party system combined with an active and strong society, the relationship will be participatory. If the competitive party system is not complemented by this type of society the connection will be one of voting. This means that spaces for participation will be reduced to individual action, through voting, without connection to a collective. (This last type is not addressed in our analysis since none of the cases in our sample corresponds to it.)

For each type of connection there is a corresponding specific type of network, which is constructed based on the network theory (using UCINET data processing). The result is depicted in Table 2.3.

Cooptation reflects very hierarchical networks for participation around the councils. Concretely, this means that there are nodes in these networks (local political secretariats of the Sandinista Front in Nicaragua or cooperative organizations loyal to the PRI in Mexico) that control the intermediation (betweenness) of the circulation of benefits in the network. These monopolistic intermediations are directly linked to the governing party through nodes that the network controls and that guarantee party loyalty. On the society

Table 2.3 Type of connection between society (civil or "popular") and parties at local levels

		PARTIES	
		Monopoly (in creation or distortion)	Competition
S O C I E T Y	Weak	**Cooptation** Simulated (Mexico- Oaxaca) Instrumental (Nicaragua-N Leon)	**Voting** (no case in this study)
	Strong	**Mobilization** (Venezuela-Zulia)	**Participation** (Brazil-Bahía)

Source: Prepared by the author.

side, there are no organizations sufficiently strong to avert this process and dispute the monopoly of intermediation.

Looking at the case of the municipality of Dipilto as paradigmatic for Nicaragua, once we get past the strangeness of a very spidery form, the network reproduced in Figure 2.1 in fact illustrates two distinct schemes. The first is drawn by the solid lines in the network, and the second is pictured by the dotted blue lines. The solid lines represent all forms of exchange of information and services related to decision-making and planning tasks. The dotted lines represent management and operational implementation tasks taken on by the municipal GPC. This superposition of relationships (represented by lines) is distinguishable only in the Nicaraguan case.

The solid lines of the network suggest a mostly hierarchical network that is made up of a vertical line of nodes (actors) and lines (relationships). As the network shows, the president connects with the First Lady; she connects with the political secretary of the FSLN who is linked to the municipal GPC, which in turn is connected to the neighborhood GPC. In other words, with respect to decision-making and planning, the diagram that describes the GPC is hierarchical. The first lady and, in any case, the president directly

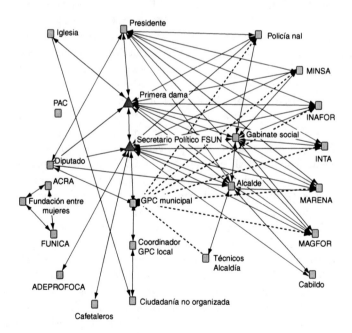

Figure 2.1 Networks for GPC, Dipilto, Nicaragua
Source: Prepared by the author.

approve financing and projects related to national ministry programs that are strongly linked to the GPC (such as "Zero Hunger" and "Zero Usury"). Cooptation is exercised by the intermediation of the first lady through the political secretariat.

If we look at the level of program management (dotted lines), the perspective on the municipal GPC opens up substantially. At the point of implementation, the GPC can go directly to the Ministry of Health without necessarily going through the political secretariat of the FSLN (as shown by the dotted lines). Nevertheless, it cannot do this for making decisions or proposing courses of action.

We are interested in analyzing the dynamics of cooptation constructed by the FSLN as the governing party in order to more deeply understand the dynamics of alternative circuits in the network. The relationships established by the governing party reflect high measures of centrality in the network, since the FSLN's political secretariat and the first lady are in the top positions.

These data show that the FSLN's political secretariat occupies the highest position in all the network's scores for centrality.[17] The secretariat is the node that most often (28,169 times) appears as the shortest path between unknown actors (intermediation). It is also the node that has the most links (degree) and exercises the most influence (closeness). Moreover, the first lady and the president have ample connections in the network (degree) and, after the political secretariat, are the closest to the rest of the network (closeness). Although the president does not occupy a substantial place in intermediation (only the eighth position), the role of intermediation is exercised by the first lady.

Significantly, the mayor occupies the third highest spot for intermediation in the network, yet has little influence or closeness (despite being from the FSLN). This reflects the competition established between the representative structure of mayoralties and the new power that the FSLN and the presidency are exercising at the local level through the GPC as parallel structures for program implementation and management. The mayor still receives demands and must find a way to channel them, but she or he has little influence on how, with how much, and with what to do that.

Finally, civil society organizations not connected to the FSLN or its networks are surviving with foreign support (which is increasingly scarce in Nicaragua), such as the ACRA—Asociación de Cooperación Rural para África y América Latina, the Among Women Foundation, and the FUNICA—Fundación para el Desarrollo Tecnológico, Agropecuario y Forestal de Nicaragua (Nicaraguan Foundation for the Technological, Agrofishery and Forest Development) (they form a triangle, which, like the PAC—Asociación Pueblos en Acción Comunitaria—node, is separated from the network). Women's organizations that address gender and feminist issues

Table 2.4 Scores for centrality, Dipilto, Nicaragua

Actor or Organization	Intermediation (Betweenness)	Actor or organization	Degree	Actor or organization	Closeness
Pol. secretariat FSLN	28.169	Pol. secretariat FSLN	12	Pol. secretariat FSLN	18.699
First lady	13.024	First lady	12	First lady	18.699
Mayor	11.897	President	9	President	17.829
GPC municipal	10.624	Social cabinet	8	Deputy	17.692
Neighborhood coordinator GPC	4.471	Mayor	7	Social cabinet	17.692
Deputy	3.829	MARENA	5	Mayor	17.557
Social cabinet	3.363	MAGFOR	5	MARENA	17.557
President	3.165	Deputy	4	MAGFOR	17.557
Church	2.617	INTA	4	INTA	17.164
MAGFOR	0.732	Police	4	Police	17.164
MARENA	0.732	MINSA	4	MINSA	17.164
Unorganized citizens	0.369	INAFOR	4	GPC municipal	17.164
INTA	0.317	GPC municipal	3	Church	16.788
MINSA	0.317	Among Women Foundation	2	Deputies	16.788
Police	0.317	Church	2	INAFOR	16.547
INAFOR	0.243	Neigh. coord. GPC	2	Coffee growers	16.312
Coffee growers	0.00	ACRA	2	ADEPROFOCA	16.312
Town council	0.00	Town council	2	Technicians	15.436
PAC	0.00	FUNICA	2	Neigh. coord. GPC	15.333
Technical professionals	0.00	Coffee growers	1	Citizens	13.690
FUNICA	0.00	ADEPROFOCA	1	ACRA	4.545
ACRA	0.00	Managers mayoralty	1	FUNICA	4.545
ADEPROFOCA	0.00	Unorganized citizens	1	Among Women Foundation	4.545
Among Women Foundation	0.00	PAC	0	PAC	4.167

Source: Prepared by the author.

are especially likely to have this type of ties. It is no coincidence that the majority of conflicts observed are between these kinds of organizations and those supported by the first lady, which, in alliance with the Church, openly oppose them, even violently.

Mexico also shows signs of cooptation but in a more attenuated and complex way (or as we can say: simulated).

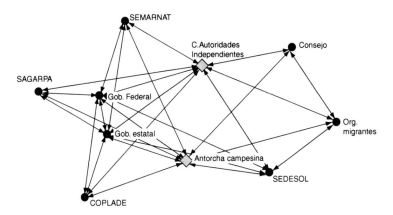

Figure 2.2 Networks for Consejos de Desarrollo Rural Sustentable Municipal (CDRSM), San Juan Ñumí, Oaxaca, Mexico
Source: Prepared by the author.

As illustrated in Figure 2.2 (the municipality of San Juan Ñumí, governed by a municipal president elected by *usos y costumbres*), two organizations, *Antorcha Campesina* and the Council of Independent Authorities (Mexico), share the monopoly of intermediation (*Antorcha Campesina* has a greater measure of concentration in the sense of greater frequency). If we take out these two nodes (rhombuses) we would have two disconnected networks. Thus, the intermediation of these two organizations is crucial. They have the highest scores for measures of centrality (Table 2.5).

The data show that *Antorcha Campesina* and the Council of Independent Authorities, two organizations that engage in corporatist negotiations for benefits from the governing party, appear most frequently (5,417 times) in the shortest paths between two actors who themselves are not directly linked. This provides a sense of the power of cooptation of council (i.e., CDRSM) members' political support by these organizations.

It is also evident that the two organizations are disputing intermediation (the Council of Independent Authorities is the newcomer), reflecting a degree of decomposition of exclusive intermediation by PRI-affiliated organizations. However, this breakdown is not serious, since the two organizations share a mode of mediation similar to that which was typically constructed under PRI hegemony.

There is a noncorporatist organization in the network, the Migrants Organization (Mexico), which a binational group that has the potential for intermediation (it appears in the middle of the list ranking intermediation).

Table 2.5 Scores for centrality, San Juan Ñumí, Oaxaca

Organization	Degree	Organization	Betweenness	Organization	Closeness
Councils of Independent Authorities	8	Councils of Independent Authorities	5.417	Councils of Independent Authorities	90.000
Antorcha Campesina	8	Antorcha Campesina	5.417	Antorcha Campesina	90.000
State gov.	8	State gov.	2.875	Federal gov	81.818
Federal gov.	7	Federal gov.	1.625	State gov.	81.818
SEDESOL	5	Migrants org.	0.792	SEDESOL	69.231
Migrants org.	5	SEDESOL	0.375	SAGARPA	64.286
SAGARPA	4	COPLADE	0.125	COPLADE	64.286
SEMARNAT	4	SAGARPA	0.125	SEMARNAT	64.286
COPLADE	4	SEMARNAT	0.125	Migrants Org.	64.286
Council (CDRSM)	3	Council (CDRSM)	0.125	Council (CDRSM)	60.000

Source: Prepared by the author

Nevertheless, it is far away from the rest of the nodes in the network, which means that its influence is limited.

The network also indicates that there are several federal government agencies that are disconnected from one another and have little closeness power compared to the rest of the actors. They especially enjoy little direct closeness to the council (CDRSM), which in interviews was described as efforts to get close through projects that are always blocked. This underscores the view within the council that the only way to obtain benefits is through the mediation of the two corporatist organizations that negotiate with the PRI in the government (and which have a close personal relationship with the governor, Ulises Ruiz) through a cycle of pressure/negotiation/influence (by deploying sit-ins, marches, etc.).

Finally, significantly, the council itself is at the lowest level of the measures; its powers of connection, intermediation, and closeness are practically null.

These data are useful for identifying the type of connection as simulated cooptation. Thus, as described above, the formal legal frameworks for the councils or committees established in the Law for Sustainable Rural Development and the National System for Democratic Municipal Planning, which regulate the CMDRS and the COPLADEMUN, create bodies that are very inclusive and prominent in local development. However, in reality, in the Oaxacan municipalities studied, although local actors are adept at the formal discourse, they view these councils as bodies that are "empty" of power (which includes the fact that they effectively do not control the political or financial resources necessary to achieve the formally imposed objectives). In this context, the only option is to connect with organizations that monopolize the network of actors for obtaining any benefit.

In contrast, for Nicaragua, we have classified this cooptation as instrumental, especially in comparison with the Venezuelan case. As discussed below, mobilization in the latter country is still loaded with symbolic content that constitutes a more significant level of "voice," whereas in Nicaragua the hierarchical network around the GPC is used for more crudely explicit ends with respect to obtaining benefits from programs centralized by the national executive.

In contrast, mobilization involves centralized networks for participation (in Venezuela, through the presidency) from the base of varied and in many cases vibrant "popular power" organizations. It is a subtle but important difference. In the Venezuelan case the intermediation of benefits takes place as much through loyalty to the PSUV as through federal executive agencies and their local affiliates. Although they all are accountable to the president, who also controls the PSUV, none of these nodes monopolize the intermediation of benefits yet. For example, the "Agrarian Explosion" movement from the Cañada zone in Zulia, although pro-Chavista, opposes the policy of converting individual land titles to a communal land tenure system under the National Fund for Socialist Agrarian Development (Fondo Nacional para el Desarrollo Agrario Socialista—FONDAS). The female leader of the group said, "if FONDAS doesn't give it to us [referring to possible denial of resources from the agency given the group's opposition], we'll go to Misión Robinson, and if that doesn't work, to the Water Technical Roundtable."

This network (seen in Figure 2.3) shows that the Communal Council itself and the presidency have the greatest number of links, together with, and to a lesser extent, FUNDACOMUNAL (Fundación para el Desarrollo y Promoción del Poder Communal, Venezuela). Indeed, these two actors scored at the top of the measure for centrality. The network also shows how the mayor, a position elected through a conventional electoral process, and in this case a member of an opposition party, is excluded from the network (see the node for the mayoralty without any lines linking to the rest of the actors).

The data in Table 2.6 show that the presidency and the Communal Council retain a high degree of centralization of links in the network. Indeed, this network is the most centralized of all the cases in the degree dimension (the centralization of Venezuela's network is 67.78 percent, whereas Nicaragua's is 44.64 percent, Brazil's is 37.5 percent, and Mexico's is 33.33 percent). This means that a large percentage of network connections are linked to only a few actors.

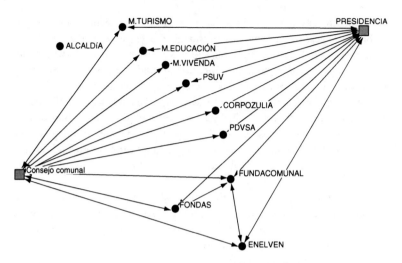

Figure 2.3 Networks for Consejo Comunal, La Cañada, Zulia, Venezuela
Source: Prepared by the author.

Table 2.6 Scores for centrality, La Cañada, Zulia

Organization	Degree	Organization	Betweenness	Organization	Closeness
Presidency	9	Presidency	12.633	Presidency	50.000
Communal Council	9	Communal Council	12.633	Communal Council	50.000
FUNDA-COMUNAL	4	FUNDA-COMUNAL	0.333	FUNDA-COMUNAL	39.286
ENELVEN	3	ENELVEN	0.000	ENELVEN	37.931
FONDAS	3	FONDAS	0.000	FONDAS	37.931
PDVSA	2	PDVSA	0.000	PDVSA	36.667
Housing M.	2	Housing M.	0.000	Housing M.	0.000
CORPOZULIA	2	CORPOZULIA	0.000	CORPOZULIA	0.000
Education M.	2	Education M.	0.000	Education M.	0.000
Tourism M.	2	Tourism M.	0.000	Tourism M.	0.000
Mayoralty	0	Mayoralty	0.000	Mayoralty	0.000

Source: Prepared by the author.
Note: Housing M.: Housing Ministry; Education M.: Education Ministry; Tourism M.: Tourism Ministry.

Nevertheless, centralization is not equivalent to monopoly of inter-mediation. An interesting analysis of this structure allows for understanding what it is that the presidency controls through centralization, what the Communal Council controls, and how intermediation between these two nodes takes place. While the presidency has central control over resources and policy decisions, the council centralizes demands. All federal agencies are required to offer projects to the councils. Although the resources and bureaucratic structures often determine their trajectory, we have found a variety of stories of negotiation, conflict, and appropriation around these projects, especially in places with prior communitarian experiences. Venezuelan society is more vibrant than the Oaxacan society in Mexico or the Segovian in Nicaragua. At the same time, the historically byzantine paths of government bureaucracy have enabled society's base to develop expertise in taking advantage of the lack of coordination among agencies and the duplicative opportunities that they offer in the context of an abundance of resources (at least until the 2008 crisis).

None of this means that over time the model cannot turn into cooptation (toward the end of our fieldwork we observed several attempts to move toward cooptation).[18] To date there is certainly a euphoric attachment to the president, who is seen as the person allowing access to resources that were never before provided by other governments.

Additionally, the network diagram and scores also show that the mayoralty, which is held by the opposition (called A New Time), is completely disconnected from the network. This suggests that the network ties the micro local level directly to the macro national level, skipping over the municipal authorities, which adds to centralization (as opposed to decentralization) in the sense of a new positioning of the national level in control at the local level.

Moreover, with the exception of FUNDACOMUNAL, the rest of the government agencies are not very connected with one another, while the PSUV is explicitly included in the network. In interviews, a large percentage of the councils' membership reported having a clear and explicit political role within the PSUV, which is consistent with the central role that these councils play in the construction of the political project of Socialism of the 21st Century.

Analysis of participation in Brazil offers a comparison with the two types described above, in that it does *not* have nodes with high degrees of centralization (Venezuela) or a hierarchical monopoly of intermediation (Nicaragua, Mexico-Oaxaca). The enormous difference in Brazil-Bahia is a varied, strong, and diverse network of civil society actors related to the Workers Party (PT) grassroots formation in Bahia (the party is on the left of the spectrum).

The network diagram (Figure 2.4) is the only one that has a shape that approaches a hexagon, which indicates greater horizontality (or flatness) in a network. Scores for centrality (displayed in Table 2.7) do not concentrate excessively for any of these actors, which suggests that a range of actors participate in the connection, intermediation, and closeness of the network.

This table is noteworthy, first, for the variety and quantity of actors who filled the interviews in this municipality. There is also some emphasis on

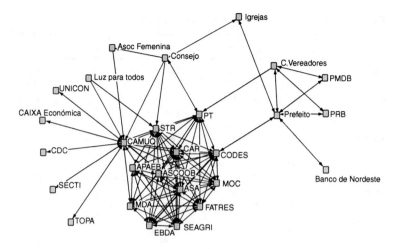

Figure 2.4   Networks for Conselhos do Desenvolvimento Municipal, Queimadas, Bahia, Brazil
Source: Prepared by the author.

the intermediation of the PT (listed second), although the first place for intermediation is held by a cooperative (CAMUQ, Rural Credit Cooperative Central das Associações do Município de Queimadas), and the third place is held by the CMDR itself.

At the time of the interviews, this municipality was governed by the opposition. The PT actors interviewed accused the municipal president of trying to manipulate the selection of members for the CMDR, although the efforts of some organizations (like CAMUQ) succeeded in thwarting the attempt. As discussed above, there is a local conflict between PT supporters and more conservative supporters. The latter view the councils as a PT initiative that undermines their power. Compared with the south, the northeastern states of Brazil exhibit recurring aspects of traditional Bahian politics (Avritzer, 2010; see also Montembeault in Chapter 5 of this book).

Despite these circumstances, the institutional limits of electoral competition in the municipalities have been respected. In fact, the mayor *(prefeito)* and the municipal legislature (town council) are not disconnected from the network. The actors stay within the democratic institutional game and participate (although according to our qualitative information, they do so grudgingly) in the territorial council (CODES). Compared to the other cases, these are significant differences, in that there is greater articulation between mechanisms for participatory and representative democracy.

At the territorial level, the actors interviewed (those in the opposition as well as from local organizations) accused CODES of privileging certain

Table 2.7 Scores for centrality, Queimadas, Bahia, Sisal region

Organization	Degree	Organization	Betweenness	Organization	Closeness
CAMUQ	17	CAMUQ	265.192	CAMUQ	74.286
FATRES	12	PT	188.546	CODES	66.667
CODES	12	Council	159.5	PT	61.905
STR	12	Prefeito	146.333	STR	61.905
APAEB	12	Churches	111	FATRES	59.091
ASCOOB	11	CODES	60.192	ASCOOB	59.091
MDA	11	STR	20.591	CAR	59.091
EBDA	11	C. Councilors	19	ASA	59.091
ASA	11	FATRES	5.359	MOC	56.522
MOC	11	ASCOOB	5.023	APAEB	55.319
PT	10	ASA	4.914	EBDA	55.319
SEAGRI	8	CAR	3.958	SEAGRI	55.319
CAR	8	APAEB	2.908	MDA	54.167
Prefeito	6	MOC	2.683	SECTI	43.333
Council	5	EBDA	1.265	CDC	43.333
C. Councilors	4	MDA	0	TOPA	43.333
PSDB	2	SEAGRI	0	UNICON	43.333
Electricity for all	2	PSDB	0	CAIXA Económica	43.333
PMDB	2	SECTI	0	Council	41.27
Churches	2	PMDB	0	Churches	32.911
SECTI	1	Banco de Nordeste	0	Women's associations	30.233
CDC	1	CDC	0	Prefeito	27.083
TOPA	1	TOPA	0	C. Councilors	21.849
UNICON	1	UNICON	0	PMDB	21.667
Asoc Femenina	1	Women's associations	0	PSDB	21.667
CAIXA Económica	1	CAIXA Económica	0	Banco de Nordeste	21.488
Banco de Nordeste	1	Electricity for all	0	Electricity for all	3.704

Source: Prepared by author.

networks built by social organizations (not necessarily directly linked to the electoral logic) that are more historically deeply rooted in other municipalities (e.g., Valente or Coité). This was a curious finding, which we were able to corroborate. The dynamic of grassroots participation has itself created a type of appropriation of the space for participation at the regional level by social organizations with the most resources and that are most connected to one another, leading to a kind of "participatory aristocracy" within the region's active rural movement.

Finally, voting is the kind of connection typified by a society where the popular base and what we usually call civil society are not deeply entrenched. It is characterized by a lack of ties or of social capital, so that citizens, as individuals, connect with parties specifically for every vote. Scholars who commented on this chapter have suggested that this type of connection also might apply to Chile, among major Latin American countries. This study does not analyze instances of citizen-party linkage limited to the vote, as this was not characteristic of any of the cases in our sample included here, since the research underlying the chapter did not incorporate one.

Conclusion

The analysis indicates that the difference between a case where municipal development council networks are connected in a participatory manner and those where they are linked hierarchically is rooted in the degree of separation/merging (where the key is intermediation) between social organizations and the party system.

Contrary to what most of the literature maintains, strengthening civil society is not sufficient to make participatory processes more democratic. For them to become truly inclusive and plural, reform "from below" is as necessary as reform "from above." The case of Nicaragua provides incontrovertible evidence of this. During the 1990s, the strengthening of autonomous civil society did not coincide with concomitant reforms of the party and electoral system so that it could efficiently connect with a society engaging in new forms of expression.

Moreover, formally promoting a competitive party system is also not sufficient. Without a strong society, formality gives way before thousands of subtle informal strategies and tactics that undermine it. The comparison between Mexico and Brazil makes this clear. Although formally both cases are framed by a democratic game mediated by a competitive party system, in Mexico actual practice is far from this ideal. Party competition is hindered by a series of subtle informal mechanisms of cooptation, simulation, and even violent repression at the same time that the growth of social organizations is asphyxiated by corporatist organizations' monopoly on intermediation. This is the choke point in the network, cutting off paths to alternative means of connection with other worlds of ties that "from below" might open up the competition informally closed from above.

Finally, the comparison between Brazil and Venezuela offers an eloquent perspective on options for the left to advance neglected sectors. When social organizations tied to the left in Venezuela sought electoral power, they did it through a temporary coalition rather than by creating an institutionally consolidated party like the PT. However, when the PT sought to win in the state of Bahia, it did not form a transitory electoral alliance (as Chavismo did with the Movement Toward Socialism (MAS), for example) that easily could be broken or bullied once in power (e.g., as occurred in Venezuela, it could demand allegiance to a single party or threaten expulsion). Instead, the PT's quest for power in Bahia entailed a prolonged and gradual process.

In other words, in the Brazilian case, citizens' "voice" was not merged with the allied party, as may be impending in the Venezuelan case and even more strongly in the Nicaraguan. Nor has voice become frozen, closing up on itself, as occurred in the Oaxacan case in Mexico. The paths to institutional reforms "from above" seem to have crossed with the paths to social transformation "from below," at least initially. Although the Brazilian case is not exempt from difficulties and weaknesses, society and politics do seem to have initiated a dialogue without the aspirations of the former having been completely burned or frozen out.

Notes

*Response from a Nicaraguan interviewee on his organization's relationship with political parties. This work is based on preliminary results from the research titled "When Networks and Hierarchies Meet: State-Civil Society Interfaces in High-Conflict Municipalities (Mexico, Nicaragua, Venezuela and Brazil)," funded by IDRC, Canada, and coordinated by FLACSO, Mexico.

1. For example, see differences in Hawkins and Hansen (2006), Saint-Upéry (2007), García Guadilla (2007), López Maya (2007, 2008), and Arenas (2008) for Venezuela. Fox and Aranda (1996), Fox (2002, 2007), and Gutman (2008) for Oaxaca, Mexico. For Nicaragua see differences between Prado (2008), Borchgrevink (2006), and Largaespada (2008).

2. The variables considered were Population per municipality, Percentage of population that is indigenous, Elections through political parties rather than custom, Electoral violence, Electoral protests, Disappearance of authorities, Female mayors, Marginalization index, Average Municipal Development index, Institutional index, Environmental index, Socioeconomic index, Population density (Rurality). Note that political conflict variables were included. This was done for every country except Brazil, which was used as a counterfactual case so that it could answer the question, why does a case with similar conditions show different levels of political violence? Although political conflict is not the primary issue for this chapter, it is important to consider the role of the Brazilian case (specifically, the sisal-growing region in the state of Bahia) in the methodological design.

3. For example, I can have only three contacts while the rest of the nodes in my network have more than six. Nevertheless, my three contacts are the president of my country of residence, the president of the United States, and the most powerful

businessman in Latin America. Obviously, it is worthwhile to distinguish between degree, in the sense of popularity, and closeness, in the sense of influence.

4. Nonagricultural activities include rural tourism services, artisanal production, family agribusiness, and other services in rural areas that are compatible with rural activities and the best use of family labor (Banco Central de Brasil. Online: http://www.bcb.gov.br/pre/bc_atende/port/pronaf.asp). Accessed: January 25, 2011.

5. The term "carlistas" refers to politicians from a powerful social and economic elite who follow a famous "coronel" from the region called Antonio Carlos Peixoto de Magalhanes. The word "colonel" is analogous to "cacique" in Mexico, used to describe an actor who exercises control over politics in a specific territory.

6. In 1995 the constitution and the State Electoral Law were reformed to legalize municipal elections according to the customs of indigenous peoples. However, several authors note that this law was promoted to facilitate the interests of the PRI, which used it to manipulate informal networks to influence elections. Later, in some cases this system was appropriated by movements fighting for the autonomy of indigenous peoples (Hernández-Díaz and Martínez Juan, 2007; Guerra Pulido, 2010).

7. Oaxacan civil society is characterized here as weak in comparison with other countries, and based on the power they have with respect to the corporatist organizations and the government. This does not mean that these organizations do not do important work in the state.

8. In Oaxaca, under the State Planning Law it is called a State Development Planning Committee and is a decentralized public agency of the state public administration.

9. The Municipal Development Plans for 2008–2010 were consulted for Santiago Niltepec, San Juan Ñumí, Putla Villa de Guerrero, Ayoquezco de Aldama, Eloxochitlán de Flores Magón, and Juchitán de Zaragoza; and Resolutions on Priorities were reviewed for Chalcatongo de Hidalgo and Trinidad Zaachila. These were available on COPLADE's Web page (Coordinación General), Oaxaca, Municipal Information.

10. Branch 33 is a Fund for Federal Contributions to States and Municipalities comprised of seven separate pools of resources, two of which are dedicated directly to municipalities.

11. According to COPLADE's Web page for Oaxaca, the CMDRS have broad and wide-ranging powers; for example, they can promote the Fund for Contributions to Municipal Social Infrastructure (FAISM) and facilitate citizen participation in the programming, execution, and evaluation of projects supported by the fund.

12. In 2008 several national and international electoral observers concluded that approximately 30 municipalities experienced electoral fraud, which led to the exit of international development agencies, such as the Swedish International Development Agency (SIDA), involving the temporary suspension of 37 million dollars.

13. The 16 sectors are as follows: (1) Promotion of citizenship rights (training), (2) Communication and marketing, (3) Citizen security, community exchanges

and solidarity, (4) Women's rights, (5) Child and youth rights, (6) Elder rights, (7) Health, (8) Education, (9) Environment, (10) Transportation and infrastructure, (11) Rural development, (12) Culture, (13) Sports, (14) Proposals to local governments, (15) Promotion of employment, self-employment, and community work, (16) General.

14. Presidential Decree 113/2007, published in the Official Gazette, No. 360, November 29, 2007.
15. See also the Web page of the Nicaraguan presidency.
16. The immediate formal precedent for the CC was the communal councils established by the Local Councils for Public Planning Law (Official Gazette No. 37.463, June 12, 2002). Under the 2006 Communal Councils Law, the network of parish councils was abolished.
17. All of the networks in this study are egocentric; they are constructed from the point of view of interviewees from the municipal GPC as well as control interviews with key informants. Therefore, it is possible that this network illustrates a more local perspective on intermediations.
18. One of the most significant attempts was FUNDACOMUNAL'S arranging for a "single window" for applications for projects (and resources).

Bibliography

Abramovay, Ricardo and Veiga, José Eli da. (1999). *Novas Instituições para o Desenvolvimento Rural: o caso do Programa Nacional de Fortalecimento da Agricultura Familiar (PRONAF)*, IPEA Instituto de Pesquisa Econômica Aplicada, Brasília, Brasil.

Arenas, Nelly. (2008). "El gobierno de Hugo Chávez: de la Asamblea Nacional Constituyente a la propuesta de Reforma Constitucional," paper presented at the international seminar "Populismo en América Latina: más allá de las etiquetas" FLACSO, March.

Avritzer, Leonard. (2010). *Las instituciones participativas en el Brasil democrático*, Universidad Veracruzana, Xalpa. 1st Ed. (2009), Woodrow Wilson Center Press, Washington.

Bartolini, Stefano. (1986). "Partidos y sistemas de partido," in *Manual de Ciencia Política*, Buenos, Aires, Alianza, Universidad, pp. 217–264.

Berríos Ortigoza, Juan Alberto. (2009). *Estudio político-constitucional de los Consejos Comunales: los Consejos Comunales y la Concepción Constitucional de la Democracia Participativa y la Descentralización*. Universidad de Zulia, Venezuela

Bresser Pereira, Luiz Carlos and Cunill Grau, Nuria. (1999). O Público não estatal na Reforma do Estado, Editora da FGV, Río de Janeiro.

Blondel, Jean. (1978). *Political Parties. A Genuine Case for Discontent?* Wilwood House, London.

Borchgrevink, Axel. (2006). "A Study of Civil Society in Nicaragua," paper No. 669, NUPI-NORAD, Oslo.

Caire, Georgina. (2009). "Descentralización participativa en ausencia de recursos: Los Consejos Municipales de Desarrollo Rural Sustentable." Doctoral thesis. FLACSO, Sede México, México DF.

Chamorro F. Carlos. (2008). "El 'poder ciudadano' de Ortega en Nicaragua: ¿participación democrática, o populismo autoritario?" paper presented at the Woodrow Wilson International Center for the conference "Understanding Populism and Popular Participation: A New Look at the 'New Left' in Latin America," Washington D.C., March 10.

Cheresky, Isidoro y Pousadela, Inés (eds.) (2001). *Política e Instituciones en las Nuevas Democracias Latinoamericanas*, Buenos Aires, Piados.

Cohen, Jean and Arato, Andrew. (2001). *Sociedad Civil y Teoría Política*, Fondo de Cultura Económica, Mexico City.

Cornwall, Andrea and Coelho, V.S.R.P. (2007). *Spaces for Change? The Politics of Citizen Participation in New Democratic Arenas*, Zed Books, London.

Cunill Grau Nuria. (1997). *Repensando lo público a través de la sociedad: Nuevas formas de gestión pública y representación social*, CLAD, Editorial Nueva Sociedad, Caracas.

Dagnino, Evelina. (2007). "Citizenship: A Perverse Confluence," *Development in Practice*, Vol. 4, No. 17, pp. 549–556.

Dagnino, Evelina, Olvera, Alberto J. and Panfichi, Aldo (eds) (2006). *La Disputa por la Construcción Democrática en América Latina*, FCE-CIESAS-UV, Mexico City.

Duverger, Maurice. (1981 [1951]). *Los partidos políticos*, Fondo de Cultura Económica, Mexico CITY.

Fox, Jonathan. (2002). "La relación recíproca entre la participación ciudadana y la rendición de cuentas: La experiencia de los Fondos Municipales en el México Rural," *Política y Gobierno*, Vol. IX, No. 1, pp. 95–133.

Fox, Jonathan. (2007). *Accountability Politics: Power and Voice in Rural Mexico*, Oxford Studies in Democratization, Oxford University Press, New York, p. 438.

Fox, J. y Aranda, J. (1996). *Decentralization and Rural Development in Mexico. Community Participation in Oaxaca's Municipal Funds Program*. Monograph Series No. 42. Center of US-Mexico studies, University of California, San Diego. 74 pp.

Freeman, Linton. (1977). "A Set of Measures of Centrality Based on Betweenness," *Sociometry*, Vol. 40, No. 1, pp. 35–41.

Fundação de Apoio aos Trabalhadores Familiares da Região do Sisal e Semi-árido da Bahia. FATRES. (2006). "Diagnóstico dos Conselhos Municipais de Desenvolvimento Rural Sustentable da Região do Sisal Semi-árido da Bahia," Valente, June.

García Guadilla, María Pilar. (2007). "El poder popular y la democracia participative en Venezuela. Los consejos comunales," paper presented at the XXVII International Congress of the Latina American Studies Association (LASA), Montreal, Canada, September 5–8.

Genro, Tarso. (2000). "Co-gestão: reforma democrática do Estado," in Nilton B Fischer and Jacqueline Moll (organizadores), *Por uma nova esfera pública. A experiência do ornamento participativo*, Vozez, Petrópolis.

Guerra Pulido, Maira Melissa. (2010). "Eficiencia electoral en Oaxaca: partidos políticos versus usos y costumbres," paper presented at the II Latin American and Caribbean Congress for Social Sciences, May 26, 27 and 28.

Gurza Lavalle, Adrián and Insunza Vera, Ernesto. (2010). (coordinators) *La innovación democrática en América Latina. Tramas y nudos de la representación, la participación y el control social*, Centro de Investigaciones y Estudios Superiores en Antropología Social, Universidad Veracruzana (Publicaciones de la Casa Chata), México.

Gutman, Matthew. (2008). "Academic Freedom under Assault in Oaxaca: The LASA Delegation Report," *LASA FORUM*, Vol. XXXIX, No. I, Winter, pp. 6–8.

Hawkins, Kirk and Hansen, David. (2006). "Dependant Civil Society. The Círculos Bolivarianos in Venezuela," *Latin American Research Review*, Vol. 41, No. 1, February, pp. 103–132.

Harary, Frank. (1969). *Graph Theory*, Addison-Wesley Publishing Company, Massachusetts.

Hernández Díaz, Jorge and Martínez Juan, Victor Leonel. (2007). *Dilemas de la institución municipal y los dilemas en los municipios: una incursión en la experiencia oaxaqueña*, Miguel Angel Porrúa, México DF.

Isunza Vera, Ernesto y Hevia de la Jara, Felipe (2006). "Relaciones Sociedad Civil- Estado en México. Un ensayo de interpretación", en Cuadernos para la Democratización, nro 4, CIESAS, Universidad Veracruzana, México DF.

La Palombara, Joseph and Weiner, Myron. (1966). *Political Parties and Political Development*,. Princeton, NJ: Princeton University Press.

Largaespada, Angie. (2008). Las Organizaciones civiles como instancias de intermediación entre el Estado y la ciudadanía, Tesis para obtener el grado de Maestra en Gobierno y Asuntos Públicos, FLACSO, Sede México.

León Álvarez, María Elena. (2009). "Los consejos comunales y la corresponsabilidad en la educación en Venezuela: Análisis Crítico," Trabajo presentado en las II Jornadas de Investigación y Postgrado de la División de Estudios para Graduados de la Facultad de Ciencias Jurídicas y Políticas de la Universidad del Zulia, October 26, 27, and 28.

López Maya, Margarita. (2009). La participación en la Constitución, leyes y normas (versión preliminar), Capítulo II, mimeo presented at the Seminario Internacional sobre Participación y Políticas Públicas, FLACSO, México DF, 31 octubre.

—— (2008). "Venezuela: ascenso y gobierno de Hugo Chávez y sus fuerzas bolivarianas", ponencia presentada en el Seminario Internacional"Populismo en América Latina: más allá de las etiquetas" FLACSO, 14 marzo.

—— (2007). "¿Socialismo democrático en 2007?" January 8, 2007, available at http://www.aporrea.org. Accessed: November 4, 2010.

Mainwaring, Scott. (1999). *Rethinking Party System in the Third Wave of Democratization. The Case of Brazil*, Stanford University Press, California.

Moura, Joana Teresa Vaz de. (2007). "Os Conselhos Municipais De Desenvolvimento Rural (CMDRs) e a construção democrática: esfera pública de debate entre agricultores familiares e o Estado?" *Organizações Rurais & Agroindustriais*, Universidade Federal de Lavras, Brasil, Año/Vol. 9, No. 002, pp. 241–255.

Moreira Gislene and Carneiro Eliana. (2012). "La dinámica participativa en el semiárido brasilero: el caso del Territorio del Sisal en la Era Lula," in Redes y Jerarquías: participación, representación y gobernanza local en América Latina, FLACSO, México DF.

Paez de Paula, Ana Paula. (2010). "Entre el gerencialismo y la gestión social: en busca de un nuevo modelo para la administración pública brasilera", in Isunza Vera, Ernesto and Stuart Almendárez, Roberto (2009) (Coordinator), *Consejos del poder ciudadano y gestión pública en Nicaragua*, Centro de Estudios y Análisis Político (CEAP), Nicaragua, July.

Prado Ortiz, Silvio. (2008). *Modelos de participación ciudadana y presupuestos municipales. Entre los CDM y los CPC*, Centro de Estudios y Análisis Político (CEAP), Nicaragua, March.

—— (2007). "Las relaciones Estado-Sociedad Civil en Nicaragua," paper presented at the Foro de la Sociedad Civil, Managua, March.

Rae, Douglas. (1971). *The Political Consequences of Electoral Laws*, Yale University Press, New Haven.

Sartori, Giovanni. (1980 [1976]). *Partidos y Sistemas de Partidos*, Universidad Madrid, Editorial Alianza.

Saint-Upéry, Marc. (2007). "Ocho preguntas y ocho respuestas sobre la Venezuela de Hugo Chávez. El enigma bolivariano," *La Insignia*, November 6, 2007, available at http://www.lainsignia.org.

Stuart Almendárez, Roberto. (2009). *Consejos del Poder Ciudadano y Gestión Pública en Nicaragua, Centro de Estudios y Análisis Político (CEAP)*, Managua, July.

Wampler, Brian and Leonardo Avritzer. (2005). "The Spread of Participatory Budgeting in Brazil: From Radical Democracy to Participatory Good Government," *Journal of Latin American Urban Studies*, Vol. 7, pp. 37–51.

CHAPTER 3

Participation as Representation: Democratic Policymaking in Brazil

Thamy Pogrebinschi

That political representation faces a crisis has become an old and worn-out claim. It is a claim as old as political representation itself, the essential principles of which have been translated into a set of institutional devices that have remained in place almost intact since the eighteenth century (Manin, 1996; Urbinati, 2006). If the structure of representative government has not been significantly modified since its inception, one can perhaps assume that some of the symptoms of crisis (low electoral turnout, rising political apathy, distrust in political institutions and actors, decrease of party membership and mobilization, proportionality deficits of electoral systems, etc.) may simply be indications of a transformation in how political representation expresses itself.

We are certainly witnessing one such transformation in contemporary politics. In recent years, one can increasingly observe the emergence of concurrent models of governance. Participatory and deliberative models of democracy have frequently been proposed as alternatives supposedly capable of correcting the purported flaws of representative government and its institutions. Strong engagement with participatory and deliberative designs of democracy has become an observable trend within academia, as suggested by an extensive scholarly work (Pateman, 1970; Mansbridge, 1983; Barber, 1984; Cohen, 1989; Fishkin, 1991; Habermas, 1998; Gutmann, 1996; Bohman, 1996; Dryzek, 2000; Fung, 2003; Avritzer, 2009; Sintomer, 2007; Geissel, 2009), which has extended itself beyond the university to other spheres. Governments have increasingly institutionalized new participatory practices and deliberative experiences around the world.

Brazil has always followed in step with this trend, especially since 1989, when the participatory budget was first implemented in Porto Alegre; it became a standard case study on this topic and was replicated by other cities in Brazil and abroad. Since then, several participatory experiments propelled by the 1988 constitution and by the democratic governments that followed it—notably the presidency of Luiz Inácio Lula da Silva—have been increasingly institutionalized. Such experiments range from the more traditional (referendums and plebiscites) to the less well-known, such as the public policy conferences. They encompass the restructuring and expansion of previously existing initiatives, such as national policy councils, public hearings, and local administration councils as well as the rehabilitation of less notorious practices, such as audit offices and discussion and negotiation roundtables.

In observing these new democratic practices in Brazil and abroad, one quickly notes a consistent attempt to expand citizen participation beyond the right to vote. The main underlying assumption of these initiatives is to allow citizens to become more directly involved in the administration of all things public, particularly the design, implementation, and control over public policy. The expected outcome of these practices is to enable citizens to express their preferences in a way that is not directly mediated by political parties and professional politicians.

This much is clear, yet there are other truths to be uncovered. If the new democratic practices expand direct citizen participation, this does not mean that traditional political institutions have become less apt to represent them. Participative practices strengthen democracy by broadening the role of citizens. However, evidence indicates that this does not occur at the cost of diminishing the role of political representation and its institutions.

The relationship between representative and participatory practices of democracy is not trivial. Its clarification is necessary in order to avoid academic opportunism, prejudicial as it is to ideas, or political opportunism, harmful as it is to institutions. Those who suppose that political representation faces a crisis typically become engaged in the defense of participatory and deliberative models of democracy as a means of delegitimizing the legislative branch, jeopardizing its capacity to express popular sovereignty. However, the emergence of new democratic spaces, as well as of new actors involved in the administration of public goods, can be perceived as a means of strengthening political representation rather than a sign of its weakening.

The aim of this chapter is to support the above arguments through a study of arguably the major participatory experiment currently being held in Brazil: the national public policy conferences (*conferências nacionais de políticas públicas*). The national policy conferences consist of participatory spaces designed to deliberate on guidelines for the formulation of public policy at the federal level. They are summoned to convene by the executive branch through its ministries and secretariats, are organized according to policy areas and issues, and involve the equal participation of representatives from the government and civil society. The NPC consist of meetings at the municipal, state, or regional levels, and the aggregate results of the deliberations occurring during those stages are the object of deliberation in the national conference itself, attended by the delegates from the previous rounds. This culminates in the production of a final document containing the guidelines for the design of public policy—the result of a long process of deliberation and consensus formation between government and civil society.

Observing some features and impacts of the national policy conferences in Brazil, I argue first that there is no necessary competition between participation and representation. Democratic innovations enlarge citizens' direct participation, but that does not imply that traditional political institutions have become less apt to represent them. Second, there might be cooperation between participation and representation. Participatory practices do not undermine political representation and representative institutions; they may in fact strengthen them. Third, the alleged crisis of representative government is but a transformation that involves greater participation and deliberation. There may be no empirical correlation between the strengthening of participatory and deliberative practices of democracy and a supposed weakness of representative institutions. Fourth, the more participatory and deliberative practices are institutionalized, the more stable representative government might become. Institutionalized participation increases both legitimacy and accountability of representative institutions and actors, as well as the enforcement of policies and legislation. Fifth, the institutionalization of participatory innovations within representative institutions changes the relation between the state and civil society, and thus impacts the liberal principles of democracy. Once civil society is enabled to act within the state and take part in national-level policy-making and law-making processes, institutional redesign might follow a pragmatic model of democracy.

The National Public Policy Conferences

Although Brazil's practice of holding national public policy conferences dates back to 1941, these conferences have only very recently acquired a clear deliberative and participatory character. In the years following the enactment of the 1988 constitution, several participatory experiments were designed and implemented in Brazil, but the national policy conferences gained expression and visibility only after 2003, when the Workers' Party (PT, *Partido dos Trabalhadores*) reached the federal government, and Lula took office as president. Only since 2003 have national policy conferences become recurrent, wide-ranging, inclusive, and broad.

Mostly in response to demands from civil society, national public policy conferences have been replicated and sustained by ministries, secretariats, national councils, and, in few cases, legislation that has established that conferences be held as part of the decision-making process of certain policy areas. As Graph 3.1 indicates, they have become closely associated with the PT government, with 73 percent of the national conferences held between 1988 and 2010 taking place during Lula's presidency (2003–2010). An average of 9.2 national conferences was held each year during his eight years of government (amounting to 74).[1] Before the PT took hold of the federal government the national policy conferences were scarcely held. In Fernando Henrique Cardoso's eight years of mandate, his government was in charge of 19 national policy conferences. Such an average of 2.3 conferences per year indicates the low disposition of the Brazilian Social Democracy Party (Partido da Social Democracia Brasileira—PSDB) to endorse participatory mechanisms of governance, in particular the national public policy conferences. The fact that the latter only became effective and turned out to be an important democratic mechanism starting with Lula's government indicates the participatory approach to governance endorsed by the Workers' Party (Pogrebinschi, 2012a).

The national policy conferences have become wider-ranging in that they encompass an increasingly greater number of policy issues under public

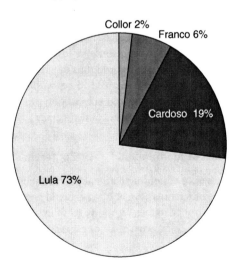

Graph 3.1 Distribution by governments (1988–2010)

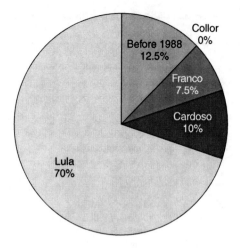

Graph 3.2 Introduction of policy issues by government (Before 1988–2010)

deliberation, no longer being restricted to health-related issues, as was the case in the 1940s. National policy conferences first arose out of Brazil's health reform movement, which has traditionally been a very strong and organized form within civil society since long before re-democratization in 1985. Only after the enactment of the new constitution in 1988 did other policy areas began to be deliberated in national conferences, although these were still very limited until Lula took office in 2003. Human rights and social assistance issues have become increasingly institutionalized since the latter half of the 1990s. Graph 3.2 shows how the PT government was responsible for introducing 70 percent of policy issues deliberated in the national conferences from 1988 to 2010.

From 2003 forward, the conferences have covered a vast array of new areas of public policy, the discussion of which has been divided into around 40 issues (see Table 3.1). From education and culture to fishing and rural development, the national conferences have been deliberating on a wide range of policy issues, especially those related to minority groups' interests and rights. 28 of the 40 policy issue areas addressed were introduced during Lula administrations. Luiz Dulci, Lula's minister of the General-Secretary in 2010, defended the policy conferences, asserting that since the PT took office, "social participation has been adopted as a democratic method of public administration."[2]

National policy conferences have also become more inclusive as a result of the increase in their range and breadth, since they gradually assemble more diverse and heterogeneous social groups, especially representatives of

Table 3.1 Policy areas and issues deliberated in the national conferences between 1988 and 2010

Policy Area	Policy Issues
Health	Health Oral health Workers' health Health of indigenous peoples Mental health Environmental health Science, technology, and innovation in health Management of labor and education in health Medication and pharmaceutical care
Minorities and human rights	Human rights Rights of children and adolescents Rights of the elderly Rights of people with disabilities Gays, lesbians, bisexuals, transvestites, and transsexuals Indigenous people Public policies for women Youth Promotion of racial equality Brazilian communities abroad
State, economy, and development	Food and nutritional safety Science, technology, and innovation Solidary economy Local productive arrangements Aquaculture and fishing Sustainable and solidary rural development Cities Public security Communication Environment Environment and children and adolescents Civil defense and humanitarian assistance Human resources of federal public administration
Education, culture, social assistance, and sports	Social assistance Basic education Professional and technological education Indigenous education Culture Sports

civil society originating from nongovernmental organizations (NGOs), social movements, labor unions, business associations, and other entities, professional or otherwise. Since 2003, several conferences concentrating on the deliberation of policies related to minority groups have taken place, and participation has grown among women, Afro-Brazilians, indigenous people, the lesbian, gay, bisexual, and transgender (LGBT) community, people with disabilities, and youth, among others. In this way, national policy conferences can be seen as a political process inclusive of minority groups. Of the national conferences held from 1988 to 2010, 35.6 percent focused on policy issues related to minority groups and human rights. Considering only the national conferences held during Lula governments, those dedicated specifically to minority group issues account for 31 percent of the total—a substantial number.

Finally, national public policy conferences became *broader* due to the fact that they have involved a progressively larger number of people, participating either directly as delegates in the national stage of deliberation; indirectly in the preceding state, municipal, or regional levels or in the so-called free conferences; or electronically in the so-called virtual conferences. On average, the national conference itself brings together about 3,000 delegates, but the number of participants increases significantly if one takes into consideration all those involved in the entire process.

Official data from the federal government estimate that about 5 million people have participated in the 74 national policy conferences that took place in Brazil between 2003 and 2010.[3] This number may not be high if one keeps in mind that Brazil has a population of about 190 million people, but compared to other participatory practices worldwide it is very impressive. Some national conferences may involve hundreds of thousands of participants. In the First National Conference on Public Security held in 2009, for example, 524,461 people were involved in the process. Of these, 225,395 persons participated directly, in face-to-face deliberation, while 256,598 took part online. In the entire country, 514 municipalities were involved in 266 municipal conferences, reaching 44,651 participants. Every one of Brazil's 27 states held conferences, during which 17,439 representatives deliberated over the policy guidelines that were then taken up to the national level. In addition, 1,140 free conferences were organized by different sectors of civil society, bringing together 66,847 people that did not participate at other stages. Finally, the national conference was held comprising 3,060 representatives.

These numbers suggest that the national policy conferences are designed to allow for more democratic policymaking in Brazil. Rather than formulating policies from the top–down through a formal process that might at best involve the aid of technical expertise, the government encourages civil society to join the task of designing new policies, and while doing so, to revise old ones. It is Brazil's federal government that convenes a national conference, with the president's decree to initiate the process following either a governmental perception that a certain area is in need of new policies or an external demand from civil society. In general, both actors in the national conferences process—government and civil society—join from the start as partners in the task of organizing these new venues for democracy.

Notwithstanding its nonbinding character, from 2003 forward, the participatory conference process can be said to have undergone a deliberative, normative, and representative turn (Pogrebinschi, 2010a). It is deliberative in the sense that national conferences have been oriented toward consensus formation based on public deliberation processes aimed at opinion and will formation, involving representatives from civil society and the government in equal number. Most conferences are composed of 60 percent of participants from civil society and 40 percent from the government. Some also include a proportion of representatives from the workers concerned with the policy area or issue under deliberation. The deliberative process comprises several levels. As can be seen in Figure 3.1, the deliberation starts in the local (municipal) or regional (aggregation of municipalities) levels, continues in all the 27 states,

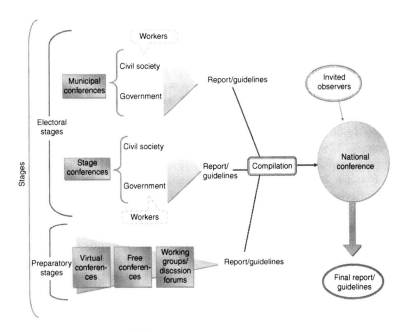

Figure 3.1 The process of deliberation

and is concluded at the national conference that is usually held in Brasilia, the country's capital. Some national conferences also review the discussions that had taken place during "free conferences" that were organized by civil society groups or "virtual conferences" that aggregate contributions submitted over the Internet. The results of the free and virtual conferences are included in materials distributed to participants in the national conference, which are deliberated along with the results from the local and state conferences.

Although the national stage of the conferences usually last three or four days, the entire process usually takes over a year. Every national conference begins to be prepared from the moment the executive decree that summons it to convene is enacted, and the commission that will coordinate it is installed. This commission is composed of members of the government and of civil society, and the same occurs at most of the conferences themselves at all levels (some include a third caucus, made up of representatives of the workers and professional associations involved on the policy area under discussion). Once the rules for the conference are approved, a schedule is drafted, and the methodology that will be used to aggregate deliberations is issued.

No single methodology is applied to all conferences, and some of them involve very complex systems of preference prioritization (instead of simple preference aggregation), which are applied both at the various stages of a single conference (from working groups' deliberations to the final plenary) and at the stages that precede the national one. No guidelines approved at the local, regional, or state levels are excluded from the deliberation that takes place in the national conference, and even conflicting guidelines approved at the different levels may be resubmitted to deliberation at the national stage. Even when deliberation ends in a vote, as is the case in the final plenary that concludes the national conferences, majority is not always the rule: an equal proportion of votes among state and civil society delegates may have to be achieved in certain cases in order to form a consensus and have a policy guideline included in the final report.

It is precisely because final results fulfill the inclusive procedures described above that national policy conferences have a high degree of public legitimacy, and can be said to have undertaken a normative turn. Since 2003, the deliberations of almost all national conferences have culminated in the drafting of a final document, which has been submitted to debate, voting, and approval based on the distinct strategies and methods of preference aggregation at different levels and moments. As a result, the policy conferences have been gaining credibility and have generated expectations that are not only cognitive but also normative for those involved in the process, as well as by those who, despite nonparticipation and the nonbinding aspect of national conferences, are indirectly affected by their eventual consequences.

The strictly representative dimension inherent to the national conferences, as instances of participation and deliberation, is reinforced by (1) the participatory composition and organization of national conferences; (2) the deliberative dimension of its working groups, panels, and final assembly sessions; and (3) the normative character of the final reports, which condense the resolutions, guidelines, and motions debated and approved by majorities in compliance with a set of rules that seeks to ensure the legitimacy of the outcome, regardless of its content. Perhaps due to the implied delegation of the executive that summons them, the national conferences are an addition to the ensemble of practices that constitute a so-called "new ecology of representation," embodying a mode of "informal representation" (Castiglione and Warren, 2006).

The process through which national conferences are organized and evolve leads to an interesting distinction between "participants" and "representatives," which is helpful to understand in relation to the new and informal ecology of representation. The municipal and regional conferences are entirely open to participation, and there has been over the past few years extensive advertisement calling on people to come and engage. At the local stage, one of the main purposes is to elect the delegates that will take part into the following levels. Because anyone can show up to a municipal conference, anyone can therefore be elected to go to the subsequent stage, and it is the participants themselves that are responsible for the election. The government may nominate representatives, but it has no influence over who is chosen among civil society participants. Usually civil society groups indicate one or more of their members to represent them at local conferences, and they must be elected at the local level in order to advance to the next levels. Among the delegates, there are representatives that are appointed, both by government and civil society organizations. The latter case is more common when the conference also includes representation by workers concerned with the policy area under discussion. At the state and national levels, elected and appointed representatives get together along with the other "participants" (observers, invited guests, members of the organizing committee, ministry or state secretary, among others). All of them take part in the deliberation, and may express opinions, make points and claims, and present arguments, but not all of them can prioritize guidelines in the working groups, nor vote in the final plenary; those tasks are reserved for the "representatives" no matter whether they were elected in the local level or appointed at a previous stage. "Participants" and "representatives" have an equal share of *isegoria*, the right to have a voice, and thus deliberate. Representatives, however, are those participants that may not only deliberate but also vote.

Notwithstanding this undeniably representative dimension of such a participatory experiment, what matters most to the claims made in this chapter are the eventual impacts on the conventional institutions of political representation, contributing to more responsive and democratic lawmaking and policymaking, as well as to more inclusive representation, as we will discuss in the next sections.

Impacts on Lawmaking

The impact of national policy conferences in the legislature is a growing reality. Conference final reports' policy guidelines prompt legal action by the Congress, and their effects on lawmaking can be measured by the number of bills proposed and statutes enacted, as well as by the content they address. From 1988 to 2009, 19.8 percent of all regular bills proposed by the Congress were substantively consistent with the national conferences' policy guidelines, and the same is true for 48.5 percent of the constitutional bills.[4]

As for approved legislation, 7.2 percent of all statutes and 15.8 percent of all constitutional amendments enacted by the Congress from 1988 to 2009 can be said to deal with the specific issues deliberated in national policy conferences. This impact may seem low, but it is very significant given the high absolute number of pieces of legislation produced by the Congress and the extended period of the time analyzed (21 years). One should also keep in mind that 73 percent of all national conferences held between 1988 and 2010 have taken place since 2003. This suggests that although the Congress has demonstrated a high degree of productivity over the years, this may be further expanded by the national conferences—not only quantitatively but qualitatively as well.

Beyond setting the congressional agenda and influencing policy preferences and choices, national conferences also seem to improve and increase the deliberative component of lawmaking since they have a larger effect on bills proposed rather on statutes approved, which points to a qualitative (increasing on variety) rather than quantitative (timing of consent achievement) impact on the legislature. Moreover, the significant number of constitutional amendments whose content coincide with the guidelines of national conferences points to their unanticipated legitimacy and potential to alter institutional design.

In the entire sample of legislative activity whose content is substantively convergent with national conference guidelines over a 20-year time frame (1988–2008), 85.2 percent of the bills presented to congress (including 91.6 percent of the constitutional bills), 69.2 percent of the enacted statutes, and 66.6 percent of the amendments to the constitution were approved in the first six years of Lula's presidency (2003–2008). Although it is reasonable to expect that the impact on the legislature will grow commensurate with the increase in the quantity and frequency of national conferences during Lula's mandates, and even though bills and constitutional bills become inactive if not voted upon or reintroduced in a new legislative season, it is evident that both the increase in participation and the impacts on representation occurred after Lula took office. In short, policy-making and decision-making have been significantly altered in Brazil since the Workers' Party came into power.

The impact of the national conferences on the legislature constitutes an effective political process that runs parallel to the electoral logic followed by political parties. The normative policy guidelines that arise from national conferences are apparently well supported by political parties (as they propose bills that are congruent with the content of conference guidelines)—and by parties that are and are not in the government coalition, and belonging to different positions in the right-left continuum. The parties that compose the PT coalition seem to be no significantly more supportive of bills convergent with national conferences' guidelines than other opposition parties such as the Brazilian Social Democracy Party (PSDB) (Pogrebinschi, 2012b). This suggests that these participatory endeavors point to a way of overcoming the traditional ideological channeling of interests, and the party structure that typically constrains them.

So far no data have shown how political parties may make themselves present at national conferences through their supporters, and thus try and influence the policy guidelines that are deliberated and approved, which might indicate an undesirable partisan dimension to the process. Not all Brazilian political parties are, however, enthusiasts or display support of the national conferences. Despite the fact that PSDB representatives are among those in the Congress that support bills that are congruent with national conferences policy guidelines (Pogrebinschi, 2012b), PSDB is definitely not a supporter of such participatory experiments in principle or practice. During the 2010 presidential elections, its candidate took a public position against the national conferences, while the year before, when this same politician was then the governor of Sao Paulo, he tried to prevent the organization of the sub-national (or state-level) stage of the National Conference on Communications in the country's largest federated state.

In any event, one can suppose that political parties have incentives to propose and support policies that have been fully deliberated in the public space. National conferences generate policy guidelines that have been thoroughly deliberated in all Brazilian states, and by those groups directly concerned with the issue at stake. Thousands of people are involved at all levels of the deliberative process, and even if they have not been successful in electing in the previous balloting a congressperson who would usually be willing to represent their interests and demands, other representatives usually not aligned with such interests and demands may have an incentive to support them so as to gain votes in the next election. In this way, national policy conferences seem to function as a sort of retrospective vote, allowing for what Mansbridge (2003) calls "gyroscopic representation" or "surrogate representation."

Congress has thus shown itself responsive to the inputs that come from the public sphere. Even if the numbers displayed above only demonstrate a congruence among national conferences' policy guidelines and the legislation produced, and thus cannot rigorously prove that congressmen have been influenced by social participation (as opposed to lobbying from interest groups), it is clear that the legislature has aligned itself with civil society's demands, and that both have been increasingly sharing a policy agenda.

This latter point should suffice to put to rest one of the main criticisms (especially by one of the country's main newspapers and the oppositional PSDB)that has been made in Brazil regarding the national conferences, which is that the PT government uses them for the cooptation of civil society. I posit that the active role that civil society organizations have been playing in national conferences should not be understood as a form of cooptation that undermines social movements or empowers only few of them. Conversely, what is at stake is a form of cooperation among social and political actors that goes beyond electoral bounds and party compromises, allowing for an unprecedented closeness of the state and civil society. The latter has been effective in proposing new areas of policy to be deliberated by national conferences. Even though most conferences are summoned to convene by the executive branch, some result from civil society's demands (which are almost always promptly responded by the government), and some result from joint deliberations of the government and civil society's representatives on the national policy councils. This cooperation is ultimately what defines which policy areas and issues will be given priority and become the object of national plans and programs to be implemented in Brazil. Once the executive accepts and supports civil society's proposals, it is not only acting responsively to social demands, but it also allows the policy agenda itself to be defined in the social sphere. The national conferences on public policy should therefore not be understood merely as a device to give legitimacy to Brazilian governments to implement their preferred policies. Rather, through national conferences civil society has been enlarging policy areas and bringing up new issues for policymaking, as will be shown in the next section.

Impacts on Policymaking: Enlarging the Representation of Minority Groups through Participation

National policy conferences have been decisive in increasing the participatory and deliberative design and implementation of national-level public policies in general, as well as areas where there were no national policies being implemented by the executive in particular. This is particularly true for policies related to the interests of minority groups that have long demanded recognition of their rights and sought political representation.

Some of the newest and most innovative policy areas and issues brought forward by civil society at national conferences are concerned with the interests and rights of social and cultural minorities. Since 2003, Brazil has held national conferences on policies for women, seniors, indigenous peoples, racial equality, people with disabilities, and the LGBT community. Minority groups take advantage of the conferences to shape their concerns and frame their identities, turning participation into representation while being successful in (a) having their demands translated into public policies implemented by the executive despite not otherwise having the resources for lobbying or advocacy, and (b) having these demands enacted as law absent previous engagement with political parties.

It is fair to say that national public policy conferences have established themselves as spaces in which social and cultural minorities are able to progressively transform themselves into political majorities. Of all the national conferences held from 1988 to 2009, 20 specifically involved deliberations concerning minority groups—17 of which took place between 2003 and 2009. There have been an additional 11 conferences on human rights, which always include discussions on policies related to women, people with disabilities, senior citizens, indigenous peoples, children and adolescents, ethnic and racial minorities, and the LGBT community. In fact, many of the demands initially presented by minority groups in national conferences on human rights are taken up by the specific national conferences for each of those minorities, while, inversely, several demands presented by minority groups in specific national conferences for minorities are presented once again in national human rights conferences. Furthermore, since many of the policies demanded by minority groups, in spite of their often very specific character, demand actions that span across different fields of action and issues, these groups are also present—through civil society representatives—in national conferences in which various other issues such as healthcare, education, and social assistance are discussed. Added together, the conferences focused specifically on minorities, and 35.6 percent of all national conferences held between 1988 and 2009 concentrated on human rights in general.

As I have argued elsewhere (Pogrebinschi, 2010a and 2010c), minority groups not only are able to rely on a significant number of national conferences in which public policies targeting them are the specific object of deliberation but also have succeeded in advancing a considerable number of normative guidelines in their final resolutions. In addition to the fact that

18 percent of the policy guidelines that originated from national conferences between 1988 and 2009 dealt exclusively with demands by minority groups, one can also reasonably assume that a significant portion of the 26.7 percent of the guidelines that originated in national human rights conferences take into account the demands of minority groups that actively participate and are represented by civil society organizations that are traditionally active in debating these issues. In other words, since the guidelines that come out of the national conferences evidently inform parliamentary activity, a high percentage of the proposals passed on to the Congress deal with demands made by minority groups. The concrete impact in terms of actual legal inclusion of proposals from minority groups is an issue yet to be addressed, as is also the case of the redistributive effects of the policies designed accordingly to the demands brought up by those groups in national policy conferences.

It is by focusing on national conferences' impact on the executive branch that one can observe how policymaking has been contributing to the inclusion and political representation of minority groups. Considering only the presidential decrees issued since 2003, one notes a very significant increase starting in 2006. With the exception of "rights of children and adolescents," the first national conference to specifically address a minority group's interests was held in 2004 (on policies related to women), followed by another in 2005 (on racial equality), three in 2006 (on policies related to seniors, people with disabilities, and indigenous peoples), and an average of three each year until 2009. Graph 3.3 displays how executive decrees have increased following the increased frequency of national conferences focused on minority group's issues. In 2003, when national conferences only addressing human rights of children and adolescents took place, 12 presidential decrees relating to those issues were issued. In 2009, after each minority group had its

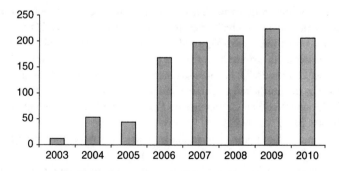

Graph 3.3 Presidential decrees on minority and human rights issues (2003–2010)

own issue-specific national conference, the number of presidential decrees that matches conferences' guidelines increased to 224.

However, the major impact of the national conferences on policymaking is qualitative. Several policies were made in Lula's government with the clear and explicit intent of fulfilling the civil society's demands contained in national conferences' guidelines. One of the most well-known examples is the so-called National Program for Human Rights 3 (known as PNDH3). This lengthy national plan, which contains among other things policies for all manner of minority groups, became binding after the publication of a presidential decree at the end of 2009. The policy's 25 guidelines, 81 strategic objectives, and hundreds of action steps reflect the demands of around 55 national conferences held during the Lula presidency, especially those related to minority groups' and human rights issues.

Several other important presidential decrees were issued, many of them bringing to life national policy plans for the first time in areas that have never before been specifically addressed by federal policymaking. This is the case, for example, of policies related to women. Although women have in one way or another been considered in different policies over the years, they have never had specific policies that addressed them as a group, let alone a public program that intended to provide a national framework for issues of concern to women to be implemented in each and every state of the country. Most importantly, women had never taken part in the drafting of such a program. This changed with the March 2005 presidential decree that enacted the First National Plan for Policies for Women, which explicitly states in its introduction that it was the result of the First National Conference on Policies for Women, which, the National Plan states, "established itself as a watershed in the affirmation of the rights of women, and mobilized throughout Brazil approximately 120 thousand women, who directly participated in debates and presented proposals for the elaboration of a National Plan of Policies for Women." As participation began to be institutionalized in Brazil and the women's movements received a new impetus, a Second National Plan on Policies for Women was issued by presidential decree in March 2008. This latter plan declares in its introduction that the plan is the "result of the mobilization of almost 200 thousand Brazilian women, who participated throughout the country in the municipal and state Conferences, and elected 2,700 delegates to the Second National Conference on Policies for Women which took place in August 2007."

National policy plans were similarly drafted for Afro-Brazilians, people with disabilities, and senior citizens. This illustrates the potential that policy guidelines formulated at national conferences on minorities and human rights have for being converted into public policies formulated and implemented by executive branch at the federal level. Even though the main scope of national conferences consists of providing content for the formulation of national policies, national plans and programs that incorporate the demands voiced by minority groups are complemented by several other decrees regulating them, and their scope has been both broadened and specified by a wide array of normative acts of the federal public administration that privilege sectorial policies and specific actions that aim to turn the deliberations of the national conferences into reality.

A precise measure of how much national conferences are able to shape the public policy agenda in Brazil certainly requires a more rigorous analysis. However, there is no doubt that, based on the data presented above, these nation-wide participatory practices strongly impact on the actions of the executive branch, which, on its part, has become increasingly responsive to the demands of minority groups, and, equally importantly, has been redesigning itself institutionally, particularly with regard to the way it formulates, implements, and oversees public policies.

National public policy conferences are thus participatory and deliberative experiences, which not only give minority groups a voice but also make them heard in Congress. Even when these groups are not able to elect their candidates, national conferences may provide them with an opportunity to have their interests represented in the legislative branch. The legitimizing force of a bill strongly supported by a national conference can function as a form of retrospective representation, which applies to situations in which members of Congress are presented with incentives that may eventually compel them to transcend party agendas or the priorities of traditional constituencies, and to come to the defense of demands presented in national conferences and thereby gain new supporters or reestablish severed ties with former ones. National conferences are thus capable of achieving political representation for minorities that would otherwise not be able to construct party majorities.

Participatory democratic practices such as national policy conferences therefore make it possible to represent the interests of minority groups in the Congress even when they are not being defended in traditional party platforms. The guidelines for public policies contained in the final resolutions produced at national conferences initiate legislative activity in the legislature, offering members of Congress a broad menu of demands directly formatted according to the preferences of civil society in a nonelectoral setting—one that is more independent of party influences, thus circumventing the need to appeal to the media or other forms of interference in the formation of citizen opinion and will. Policy guidelines originating in national conferences are imbued with a strong assumption of popular legitimacy that allows them to overcome the traditional logic of interest distribution. This may prompt a major party to represent a previously unrepresented interest, one hitherto unrepresented by any party or supported by a minor party. The manner in which national policy conferences have been serving the interests of minority groups demonstrates how participatory forms of democracy are able to express themselves as representation.

Participation as Representation

National conferences on public policy are more than simply practices pertaining to "informal representation" (Castiglione and Warren, 2006) that reproduce somehow the logic of representation: They are participatory experiments that strengthen formal political representation and potentially reinforce the functions and activities of traditional political institutions, such as the legislature and the political parties. In this sense, national policy conferences allow a new participatory element that constitutes the concept and practice of political representation, as evidenced by the genesis of the former and the history of the latter.

Participation has long been a part of the grammar of representation, whether through universal suffrage, proportionality in electoral systems, mass political parties, and even in the activity of lobby and interest groups. Deliberation, too, has long been part of the repertoire of political representation, whether in the procedures adopted for the formation of public opinion that characterize political campaigns and party mobilization preceding elections, in the identification and stabilization of preferences set in motion by voting systems during elections, or, finally, in parliamentary deliberation—both in the more restricted realm of commissions or in the broader congressional floor deliberation. Hence, participation and deliberation can be understood as constitutive elements of political representation; rather than be seen as an attempt to add new semantic content to replace old concepts of political representation, they are a distinct means of putting political representation into practice.

If the widely propagated crisis of political representation is nothing but another one of its historical metamorphoses, the practices of participation and deliberation that have evolved expressively in civil society in the last two decades are actually expressions of a shift in the nature of representative democracy. To the extent that representation's legitimacy increases as it deepens, its institutions are consolidated by redesign.

National conferences on public policy consist of a participatory practice marked by peculiarities that further contribute to their comprehension as an instance that strengthens political representation within the formal institutions of the state. First, they are summoned, organized, and held by the executive. Second, they are jointly organized by the state and civil society, as the latter is already active in different national policy councils or in the various working groups established by ministries and secretariats.[5] Third, they are summoned by the executive with the manifest intent of providing guidelines for the formulation of public policy, with a particular focus on the elaboration or revision of national policy plans concerning several fields, sectors, and groups of civil society. Fourth, they consist of participatory experiences that are national in scope and range, which ensures the universal validity of the definition of the policies deliberated and the reconfiguration of the proportionality of any party interests present.

Most national policy conferences are not yet sustained by laws, and thus depend, along with the implementation of their results, on the political will of federal governments. As discussed earlier in this chapter, the occurrence of the national policy conferences seems to depend heavily on the Workers' Party. Despite the party's overt intentions to institutionalize them as a part of a larger national participatory system and as a consequence of its method of governance (Pogrebinschi, 2012a), the national conferences are so far not enforced by law, and therefore are not binding. Even though after at least 12 years of PT government the recurrence of the national policy conferences may help to create a participatory culture in the country and to compel civil society organizations to rely on them, an eventual victory of another party in an upcoming election may simple rule the national policy conferences out of the political landscape.

Nonetheless, one may say that a certain degree of institutionalization has been so far achieved. As part of the process of formulation and oversight of executive public policy, and, therefore, as part of its structure, the national conferences generate consequences that have impact on the agenda of the legislative, which can choose to use them as an informational source, as mechanisms of legitimization, or as deliberative input for its representative activity. They are thus certainly an example of a "participatory institution" (Avritzer, 2009), alongside other participatory practices and deliberative experiences that have been undergoing institutionalization in Brazil despite the absence of legal backup, from participatory budgets at the local level to policy councils at the national level.

Yet, more than this, I argue that national conferences should be taken as representative institutions—not because they simply internally engender the representative logic (by means of election of delegates and majority voting, among other features) and sustain some "informal" mode of representation. Rather, they consist of a more complex structure of political representation within the state and its institutions that include the participation and deliberation of civil society in a more direct and less mediated fashion, as compared to traditional mechanisms of accountability (through elections), and the preferences they express (that of political parties).

Despite the suspicion raised by the assumption of the eventual formation of consensus in civil society, the extent of its autonomy when acting within the state, the disputes for hegemony in different political projects, and social movements that characterize it, among other factors, the fact is that national conferences on public policy consist of very effective forms of political mediation and are therefore apt to redefine the liberal democracy model by redefining the relationship between civil society and the state. Brazil puts into practice what scholars of democracy and democratic policy-making processes attempt to do through participatory innovation: bring state and society into closer proximity.

Such approximation is verified not only when the state draws civil society within itself, employing national conferences as a participatory component of governmental policy-making processes in all spheres of the federal executive branch and public administration, but also when it is receptive and responsive to their demands by converting them into legislative proposals and acts by government ministries or agencies. Thus the national conferences are a deliberative component of political representation as it is exercised in the Congress. The interplay of participation/deliberation and representation, and the dynamics between civil society and the state that this sets in motion reveal national policy conferences as new forms of political mediation that can potentially deepen democracy in Brazil. Far from replacing political representation or menacing established representative institutions, the national policy conferences appear to strengthen both and allow for a more democratic and responsive government—one that I call as a pragmatic democracy (Pogrebinschi, 2010b).

Notes

1. This pattern has been closely sustained during the first year of mandate of his successor Dilma Rousseff's (also from the Workers' Party), when eight national policy conferences took place in 2011.
2. This statement was made on August 20, 2010, by Minister Luiz Dulci in an official address to the press. The full statement is available at: http://www.secretariageral. gov.br/noticias/ultimas_noticias/2010/08/20-08-2010-nota-a-imprensa-resposta-do-ministro-luiz-dulci-as-declaracoes-de-jose-serra. Accessed: July 23, 2012.
3. The information is available in the general-secretary of the presidency's website: http://www.secretariageral.gov.br/noticias/ultimas_noticias/2012/01/10-01-2012-conferencias-mobilizaram-2-milhoes-de-pessoas-em-2011. Accessed July 23, 2012.
4. A constitutional bill is a proposal presented by members of Congress to amend some aspect of the constitution.

5. The national policy *councils* have also been highly institutionalized during Lula's government and are often confused with the national policy *conferences;* however, the two participatory experiences work in different ways. While the conferences are summoned to convene and are held in a determinate period of time through several stages until it scales up to the national level, the national policy councils are permanent institutions that work within the structure of the federal executive branch, usually housed at ministries, special secretariats, or the presidency itself. As occurs with most of the conferences, the councils are composed of half by representatives from government and half from civil society. While participation in the conferences is entirely open and free at the local level while the delegates that will attend the subsequent stages are elected or appointed, participation in the councils depends on a public process of selection of national-level representative entities from civil society that will have a seat on it for a two-year mandate (on average). While certain conferences have engaged over 500,000 people from the local to the national level, the councils have a permanent body of up to 60 members. As for the aims and purposes, the conferences are summoned with the goal of deliberating and providing guidelines for policymaking in certain predefined areas and issues, while the national councils ordinarily meet every two months (or whenever a need arises) and deliberate on issues brought up by their members or government or civil society. As for the nature of the deliberations, although the national conferences' final reports are normative as described above and are seriously taken into consideration by policymakers, they are not binding; however, the councils have competence to issue normative acts called resolutions, which may contain administrative acts and policies. The councils take an active part in the organization of several conferences, and they also implement and monitor some deliberations to ensure the approved policy guidelines are followed. Brazil currently has around 33 operating national policy councils—18 of them created between 2003 and 2010, and 15 significantly reformulated in the same period so as to contemplate civil society's demands and further its inclusion and participation.

References

Avritzer, Leonardo. (2009). *Participatory Institutions in Democratic Brazil.* Baltimore: Johns Hopkins University Press.

Barber, Benjamin. (1984). *Strong Democracy. Participatory Politics for a New Age.* Berkeley: University of California Press.

Bohman, James. (1996). *Public Deliberation. Pluralism, Complexity, and Democracy.* Cambridge: MIT Press.

Castiglione, Dario e Warren, Mark. (2006). "Rethinking Democratic Representation: Eight Theoretical Issues." Manuscript prepared for delivery at the Centre for the Study of Democratic Institutions, University of British Columbia.

Cohen, Joshua. (1989) [1997]. "Deliberation and Democratic Legitimacy." In: Bohman, James and Rehg, William (eds). *Deliberative Democracy. Essays on Reason and Politics.* Cambridge: MIT Press.

Dryzek, John S. (2000). *Deliberative Democracy and Beyond.* Oxford: Oxford University Press.

Fishkin, James. (1991). *Democracy and Deliberation: New Directions for Democratic Reform.* New Haven: Yale University Press.

Fung, Archon and Wright, Erik Olin. (2003). *Deepening Democracy: Institutional Innovations in Empowered Participatory Governance.* London: Verso.

Geissel, Brigitte. (2009). "How to Improve the Quality of Democracy? Experiences with Participative Innovations at the Local Level in Germany," *German Politics and Society,* Issue 93, Vol. 27, No. 4 Winter, pp. 51–71.

Gutmann, Amy. (1996). *Democracy and Disagreement.* Cambridge: Harvard University Press.

Habermas, Jürgen. (1998). *Between Facts and Norms. Contributions for a Discourse Theory of Law and Democracy.* Cambridge: MIT Press.

Manin, Bernard. (1996). *Principes du Gouvernement Représentatif.* Paris: Calmann-Levy.

Mansbridge, Jane. (1983). *Beyond Adversary Democracy.* Chicago: University of Chicago Press.

——. (2003). "Rethinking Representation," *American Political Science Review,* Vol. 97, No. 4, pp. 515–528.

Pateman, Carole. (1970). *Participation and Democratic Theory.* Cambridge: Cambridge University Press.

Pogrebinschi, Thamy. (2010a). Relatório Final da Pesquisa "Entre Participação e Representação: as conferências nacionais e o experimentalismo democrático brasileiro." Série Pensando o Direito, Ministério da Justiça, Brasília.

——. (2010b). "Democracia Pragmática". In: *Dados,* Revista de Ciências Sociais, Volume 53, número 3.

——. (2010c). "Participação como Representação. Conferências Nacionais e Políticas Públicas para Grupos Minoritários no Brasil". Paper apresentado no 34° Encontro da Associação Nacional de Pós-Graduação e Pesquisa em Ciências Sociais (ANPOCS).

——. (2012a). "Participação como Método Democrático de Gestão. As conferências nacionais de políticas públicas durante o Governo Lula". Paper prepared to be presented at the workshop *The PT from Lula to Dilma: Explaining Change in the Brazilian Worker's Party.* Brazilian Studies Programme, University of Oxford, January 27.

——. (2012b). "Strengthening Representation through Participation." Paper prepared to be presented at the ECPR Joint Sessions of Workshops, University of Antwerp, Belgium, April.

Sintomer, Yves. (2007). *Le pouvoir au peuple. Jurys citoyens, tirage au sort et démocratie participative.* Paris: La Découverte.

Urbinati, Nadia. (2006). *Representative Democracy: Principles and Genealogy.* Chicago: Chicago University Press.

CHAPTER 4

Constrained Participation: The Impact of Consultative Councils on National-Level Policy in Mexico

Felipe J. Hevia de la Jara and Ernesto Isunza Vera

Introduction

The beginning of the twenty-first century brought good news to Mexico. After 70 years of uninterrupted rule by the Institutional Revolutionary Party (PRI), alternation of power had been achieved, the economy was recovering from the crisis of 1995, and the Zapatista National Liberation Army (EZLN) appeared before Congress following its march into Mexico City. Meanwhile, civil society organizations (CSOs), which had been central to the process of democratization in the 1990s, were accessing public space as actors with significant voice. The agenda of the "government of change" highlighted new ways of relating to civil society. This included creating spaces and mechanisms for communication with CSOs, strengthening transparency and public access to government information, and placing CSO leadership in important government positions in the area of social development as well as in the presidency (Isunza Vera and Hevia, 2006).[1]

The landscape looked quite different when in December 2006, Felipe Calderón assumed the presidency in the wake of contemporary Mexico's most disputed elections, which were tainted by the shadow of electoral fraud (Crespo, 2007), uncertainty surrounding the results, and the weakness of electoral authorities (Crespo, 2008). Calderón began his term in the midst of a political crisis of representation that had polarized civil society (Reygadas,

2007). The country was also facing a security crisis, as drug trafficking and common crime (Benítez, 2009) had produced catastrophic increases in homicides and serious human rights abuses (Human Rights Watch, 2011; Escalante, 2011). To this was added an economic crisis that resulted in a significant fall in the country's gross domestic product (GDP) in 2009 (Centro de Estudios de las Finanzas Públicas, 2010) and growing poverty (CONEVAL, 2011).

In this adverse context, and in stark contrast to the blossoming of participation experienced elsewhere in Latin America in recent decades, the Calderón government's initial proposals did not include mechanisms for enshrining "direct democracy" in the constitution.[2] His strategy for citizen participation was limited to strengthening citizen consultative councils as a means to include citizens in the design, implementation, and evaluation of public policy (Poder Ejecutivo Federal, 2007).

These consultative councils aim to incorporate the voice of experts and citizen representatives in advising authorities in public policy decision-making. Compared to other mechanisms, the councils have some advantages, such as the ability to rely on "expert" participants and their low operating cost. Nevertheless, they are disadvantaged by the difficulty of broadly involving the citizenry to sufficiently incorporate the "broad mosaic of citizen interests, since in order to be dynamic and manageable, they must be small in size" (Font, 2001; Zermeño and Domínguez, 2010: 19). The councils are also subject to "over-representation" of previously organized interests at the expense of the poorer and more vulnerable strata of the population (Cunill, 1991, 1997).

By choosing to foster consultative councils, the Calderón government maintained the tradition of using these spaces as the privileged mechanism for participation. This trend had begun in 1982 when the De la Madrid (1982–1988) government instituted the National System for Democratic Planning (Mexico) (Sistema Nacional de Planeación Democrática), which established democratic planning councils in all states and municipalities (COPLADE and COPLADEMUN, respectively). During President Carlos Salinas Gortari's six-year term (1989–1994), solidarity councils and consultative councils for sectoral policies were created as part of the administration's signature National Solidarity Program (Solidaridad) (Cornelius, Craig, and Fox, 1994). Subsequently, the government of Ernesto Zedillo (1994–2000) implemented consultative councils for a variety of sectors to represent the "voice" of diverse actors, particularly those with specialized information in the field, while retaining decision-making within the governmental sphere. Under President Vicente Fox (2000–2006) these bodies were progressively more formalized through regulations, laws, and, increasingly, in procedural rules, which also coincided with the growing tendency in states and municipalities to establish participatory consultative bodies (Isunza Vera and Hevia, 2006).

Given the government's interest in creating consultative councils, and the fact that some of them have endured, it is surprising how little attention they have received as a subject of study. With some thematic exceptions— like the consultative councils for sustainable rural development—there are few panoramic studies on these bodies that analyze their continued existence or their potential contributions to building democracy in Mexico.[3]

This chapter provides empirical information to fill this gap with an evaluation of the impact of this strategy in contexts, such as Mexico, where civil society is poorly articulated, authoritarian-corporatist forces continue to be powerful, and public space is fragmented (Aziz y Alonso, 2009; Olvera, 2010; Merino, 2010). The questions that guide this reflection are given: Under what conditions do consultative councils influence policies? What type of actors participate? What are the consequences of their design? What impacts do they have on the representational system?

To answer these questions, we chose a descriptive-comparative strategy. First, information was gathered on consultative councils in the federal government. Second, an area of public policy was selected and described (e.g., the environment), focusing on a case that several informants considered successful: the Consultative Councils for Sustainable Development (CCDS). This case was then compared with the rest of the federal-level consultative councils in three critical aspects: institutionalization, representativeness, and quality of impact.

The results show how over time the CCDS, as relatively successful councils in the Mexican context, sought explicitly to incorporate more voices, from national as well as regional groups, in their operations. This created high levels of representativeness and coincided with the participants' interest in expanding the effectiveness of the councils. The subsequent comparison with other federal-level councils indicates that the participation of autonomous voices in deliberative bodies in Mexico continues to be more an exception than the norm, and that the "expansion of voice" is central to generating commitment from the authorities, since it compels them to respond to these bodies despite no formal obligation to do so.

Thus, the chapter's principal conclusion is that creating consultative councils with clear functions and powers, and that involve interested and participatory actors, can be an important innovation in institutional contexts that are traditionally sealed off from participation. By creating conditions for strengthening spaces with some capacity for impact, even if they do not manage to break down structural barriers or transform critical aspects of public policy cycles, they can provide spaces for constrained participation.

How Many State-Society Bodies Exist At the Federal Level?

A review of administrative laws and rules identified 409 bodies affiliated with the Federal Public Administration (Administración Pública Federal—APF) (Hevia, Vergara-Lope, and Ávila, 2011).[4] Of these, 163 (39.5 percent) are state-society bodies, composed of both government and nongovernment actors.[5] The rest of them were 182 intragovernmental entities (44.25 percent) and 64 civil society bodies with no government actors (15.65 percent), such as the Committees for Community Promotion of the Progresa/Oportunidades Program.

These entities are distributed throughout the APF, with particular presence in social development and renewable resources.

The legally mandated functions of these state-society bodies fall into three major types: consultation, decision, and execution. The most common function is consultation, in which they act as auxiliary bodies to agencies or entities and their resolutions are nonbinding on the authorities (63.7 percent), followed by decision functions (27.8 percent) and execution and operation of programs (26.4 percent).

Comparing the functions with the type of bodies reveals important differences. While consultation functions are concentrated in state-society bodies, decision and execution functions are found in state bodies. Thus, there is a clear tendency to concentrate decision-making in government bodies, consultation in state-society bodies, and execution in civil society bodies.

The distribution and classification of these bodies, although relevant, say little about the conditions that allow them to function or not in practice. This requires a specific case analysis that can then be used to compare with other bodies. We chose as our case the CCDS in the environmental sector, which were considered by a number of informants to be the most "successful" cases at the federal level.

How Do State-Society Bodies Work? The Case of the Consultative Councils for Sustainable Development (CCDS)

The CCDS are one of the 93 state-society consultative bodies at the federal level. These councils have specific characteristics that differentiate them from other bodies reviewed in the literature (Rodríguez Caloca, 2008). Their most distinctive features include the time that they have been operating (since

1995, with four generations of councilors), the systematization of their work (publication of white books), and their decentralized management.

Purpose

The complex task of defining and implementing environmental policy in Mexico is the responsibility of the federal government, particularly the Secretariat for Environment and Natural Resources (SEMARNAT). One of its responsibilities is formulating and managing national natural resource policy, ecology, environmental health, water, and environmental regulation of urban development and fishing, as well as promoting civil society and scientific community participation in the formulation, application, and monitoring of environmental policy (Estados Unidos Mexicanos, 1988).

To fulfill its mandate, the SEMARNAT has created multiple consultation bodies, which include the Consultative Councils for Sustainable Development.[6] According to the enabling decree, these councils have the objective of "facilitating the appropriate participation of all sectors of society to promote the protection, conservation and restoration of ecosystems, natural resources and environmental goods and services, in order to create the conditions for their use and sustainable development" (SEMARNAT, 2008a).

To this end, the CCDS are comprised of plural representation for providing voice to "major groups": academics, business, civil society organizations (CSOs), NGOs, women's organizations or groups with a gender perspective, indigenous groups, youth organizations, as well as the executive and legislative branches.

According to prevailing norms, the principal functions of the CCDS are "to consult with the SEMARNAT in the formulation, application and monitoring of the national strategies for environmental policy . . . ; formulate recommendations and periodically evaluate policies, programs, studies and specific actions; make recommendations to improve the legal framework . . . ; issue opinions, proposals and recommendations for specific issues and cases; and provide follow-up to the Secretariat's actions" (SEMARNAT, 2008b). Thus, the fundamental purpose of these councils is to consult with the variety of actors involved in environmental policy, rather than coadministrate specific policies and programs or the monitor public employees.

The operations of the CCDS are essentially a network of state-society mechanisms for participation from a range of fields. At the base are 32 Core Councils, one in each of the Federation's entities, which includes ten councilors, seven of whom are from NGOs (of that of academics, CSOs, women, indigenous, youth, business, and others), and three government representatives (from the executive, federal, state, and legislative branches). The

32 Core Councils are grouped in six Regional Councils, made up of representatives from the Core Councils. Finally, there is a National Council comprised of 56 advisors from the Core Councils as well as the Regional Councils, representatives of the "major groups," and the secretary of the SEMARNAT, who acts as president.

History and Development of the CCDS

The CCDS emerged in the 1990s as the result of a concurrence of four factors: (1) international agreements that enabled public participation in environmental management, especially the 1992 Rio Summit and Agenda 21; (2) the arrival at SEMARNAT of a current of public policy technocrats with sensitivity toward and experience in participatory programs, headed by Julia Carabias; (3) an extensive and diverse environmental movement operating at local levels as well as in national organizations; and (4) the technical/operational and financial support of a multilateral agency (United Nations Development Program—UNDP) that was vital for their operations and sustainability over time.

The creation and implementation of the CCDS did not result from demands and pressures from an environmental movement seeking space for dialogue with the government; nor was it the product of a "sandwich strategy" (Fox, 1993), in which social actors and public employees ally to pressure bureaucracies resisting participation. Rather, these councils came out of a top–down process in which the government set up the mechanisms, which were in turn occupied by diverse actors. The fact that the councils were actively used, and the technical-operational support they received, allowed their continuity over time, making them an exceptional case in Mexico, as much for their durability (at least 15 years and four generations of councilors) as for their processes for institutional consolidation and selection of participants.

Between 1995 and 2010 there were three phases: creation (1995–2000), the challenge of continuity (2001–2007), and decentralization and vertical articulation (2008–2010). In the first phase the mandates contained in the Rio Declaration of 1992 (especially principal 10) and Agenda 21 were key (Bustos and Chacón, 2009; United Nations, 2011; SEMARNAT, 2008a).[7] These declarations, and the potential impact of NAFTA in the environmental sector (Sánchez, 1991), created a favorable international context for environmental policies that incorporate the participation of diverse social groups. This led to reforms in the General Law of Ecological Equilibrium and Environmental Protection (LGEEPA) that were passed in 1988 to guarantee public participation, whether individual or collective, in environmental and natural resource policy.

One of the instruments for participation envisioned in the reforms was the creation of bodies where "public entities and agencies, academic institutions and social and business organizations participate. These bodies will have consulting, evaluation and monitoring functions with respect to environmental policy and can issue opinions and observations they deem pertinent." Additionally, "the obligation to reply (explaining the reasons for acceptance or rejection of recommendations) by the Secretariat" was mandated (LGEEPA, Art. 159). These reforms were the legal basis for the CCDS and other consultative bodies.

The second factor was the government's promotion of the public policy approach developed in the academy headed by Julia Carabias. The team set up by the Program for Comprehensive Use of Natural Resources in Marginalized Indigenous Zones (PAIR) at the Universidad Nacional Autónoma de México (UNAM) inaugurated the recently created Secretariat of Environment, Natural Resources and Fisheries (SEMARNAP) in 1994. Carabias, a left militant with roots in the Popular Action Movement and the Unified Socialist Party of Mexico, was the president of the National Institute for Ecology (Mexico). He had a solid resume as an environmental researcher and activist (Samaniego, 2006). The team had experience in the development of projects that integrated participation as a principal component, which was essential to the Programs for Regional Sustainable Development in marginalized rural regions (PRODERS) (Blauert et al., 2006; Toledo, 2000), especially for fostering participation in the management of protected natural areas (Paz, 2005), and for the creation of the CCDS.

The third factor was the use made of these spaces by the heterogeneous Mexican "environmental movement." As part of the "new social movements" along with feminist and indigenous movements, beginning in the 1970s the environmentalist movement began to gain importance and visibility. The movement had strong ties to the academy and a heterogeneous agenda and modes of action (Gudynas, 1992). Associations such as the Environmental Studies Group (Mexico), the Mexican Ecological Movement, and the Ecological Groups Pact (Mexico) emerged in those years, bringing together artists and intellectuals as well as biologists and ecologists, who began to express their concerns for the environment.[8] In the 1990s those groups were joined by others that promoted efficient resource use or opposed the North American Free Trade Agreement (NAFTA) for environmental reasons, and the demands of indigenous groups and the Zapatista movement also became part of the discourse. Examples such as the Mexican Center for Environmental Law (CEMDA) and Citizen Presence (Mexico) enhanced the heterogeneity of the movement (Vargas-Hernández, 2006).

This diversity of actors was reflected in the use of spaces for participation. While the councils for regional sustainable development were run by indigenous and farmer groups, or by NGOs and local associations, the CCDS included representatives of academic, government, legislative, NGO, and private and social sectors; a representative from each sector for each federal entity in the region sat on the regional councils. Even though the creation of these opportunities for advising and consultation had not been a demand of the environmental movement, once they existed they were utilized. This was unlike other cases of participatory mechanisms created during the same period that did not have a social base, and therefore failed to take root, such as the Councils for Social Participation in Education (Mexico).

The fourth critical factor was technical and financial support from the UNDP, which sustained monitoring of resolutions and recommendations, publication of white books, and support for the personnel who worked to facilitate and promote the regional and national councils.

Thus, on April 21, 1995, the *Official Gazette* published a Resolution (an administrative decision) on the Creation of Consultative Councils for Sustainable Development. These would be consultative bodies for the environmental sector with the idea of "participating as a society in government actions through advice, analysis, evaluation and consulting on issues that affect the conservation of natural resources and the environment to promote sustainable development" (CCNDS, 2000: 11). Two years later, the first generation of councils was established (1997–2000).

This generation focused on institutionalizing the councils by creating internal rules and work agendas, and conducting ordinary and extraordinary meetings. The councils sought the participation of the so-called major groups, following the Agenda 21 guidelines, including the most organized and visible sectors within the environmental sphere: academics, businesspeople, and NGOs, but they also incorporated a more diffuse "social sector" as well as the executive and legislative branches. There is insufficient information on the selection processes for the Consultative Councils in this first generation; informants indicated that it mostly involved the agency's invitation of "notables," people with known backgrounds. Finally, with respect to impact, the white books recognize as progress the presence of diverse actors around the same table; however, the substantive impact and the actual means of influence remained unclear (CCNDS, 2000). In this first phase council members focused on institutionalization and representativeness of the councils more than on their potential impact.

The second phase posed the challenge of continuity (2001–2007). The change of government and the arrival of a new administration to the Secretariat was a challenge for the councils. Despite legal authorities that guaranteed the existence of the councils, they faced the tradition of "reinventing" the administration with each change of government. A new president as well as a new political party meant that this rupture would be even greater. Nevertheless, after more than a year without operating, on November 21, 2002, the original resolution was renewed and the second generation of advisors went to work (2002–2004).

According to our informants, a significant force for continuity was the UNDP's project Public Spaces for Social Coordination for Local Sustainable Development (Mexico) and the interest taken by the Coordinating Unit for Social Participation and Transparency (UCPAST). Indeed, rather than oversee the disappearance of spaces for participation, the new government's expectations were that they would have to open up and multiply. At the same time, the citizen's agenda together with the change of political party in power led to the Federal Law for Transparency and Public Access to Government Information, which was also part of the environmentalist agenda.

In this period there were some changes to the CCDS. Most significantly, representation was expanded, and new Agenda 21 actors were incorporated, such as women, youth, and indigenous people. They also defined minimal selection criteria for appointing participants, such as the requirement for public announcements, so that each major group could select its own representatives. The incorporation of new actors strengthened the nongovernmental presence on the councils, broadening the opportunity for voice to groups that had previously been part of the "social sector." The inclusion of new voices intersected with the concern of some of the advisors about the type of impact the councils were having. The second generation had greater clarity about how the councils were to function, and they consolidated their principal means of influence on the Secretariat: recommendations and requests.

The council generally uses the principal mechanisms of recommendations and requests to impact environmental policy. Nonbinding on the Secretariat, they are approved by the full council and are sent as official letters to the Secretariat's administrative units, which must reply with a reasoned approval or rejection. If the council does not agree with the response, it may send a new recommendation. According to its white book, between 2002 and 2004, the National Council issued 133 recommendations involving 127 resolutions. Of these, 45 proposed a concrete policy, program, or action. In these cases, the Secretariat complied with 24 recommendations. Thus, according to the National Council, 53 percent of the recommendations had effective impact. Of the 34 requests issued by the National Council, 52 percent (18 cases) were translated into a concrete policy, program, or action (CCNDS, 2004).

Another feature of this phase was the 2005 integration of a third generation of councils under the same rules. This generation continued its focus on enhancing impact on environmental policy and the councils' powers. In the white book for this generation 108 recommendations were reported, of which 14 percent related to legal procedures and 14 percent dealt with international issues. The recommendations involved 146 actions with a 96 percent response rate—thus, the majority received attention.

Nevertheless, they also identified limitations: the councilors indicated that they "did not manage to impact environmental policy to the extent they had hoped" due to lack of coordination in the Secretariat as well as problems within the councils themselves, such as lack of communication and comprehensiveness in the work commissions, the apathy of some advisors, lack of knowledge of legal and administrative concepts, and the difficulty of establishing technically and politically viable recommendations (CCNDS, 2007).

The third phase was characterized by decentralization and vertical integration (2008–2010). During this phase Core Councils were established in each of the Republic's 32 entities. In this period, new forms of selecting regional and national councilors were instituted to create a rising structure of representation. In 2008, the Core Councils began to elect their own representatives to the Regional Councils, who in turn elect their representatives to the National Council. Thus, a state advisor might also simultaneously be a representative at the regional and national levels.

Like other decentralization processes in Mexico, the purpose of Core Councils in each entity is to respond locally to problems that had previously been addressed in the regional and national councils. The Core Councils have the additional advantage of working directly with the SEMARNAT delegate in each entity, which facilitates their advisory role, since they have a direct counterpart in the Secretariat.

The fourth generation of councilors took office in 2008–2011 and they were able to benefit from the accumulated experience. For example, at the beginning of their service all the councilors were trained on specific issues (how to write recommendations, how the SEMARNAT operates, etc.) and civil society organizations offered general training on democracy and participation. Their work took place within a comprehensive strategy for citizen participation.

Part of the improvements in council operations and training for new members were instigated by several former council members who went on to take positions in the federal or state administrations.[9] For example, Mateo Castillo Ceja was a member of the National Council in the 2002–2004 group as an NGO representative (from the Advisory Council to the North American Agreement on Environmental Cooperation). In 2007 he was appointed as the leader of the Secretariat's Participation Unit, becoming the architect of the changes during this period, which included a national strategy for citizen participation in the sector (SEMARNAT, 2008c).

The results from this generation remain to be seen. These consultative bodies now enjoy solid institutionalization, including a selection system used on multiple occasions in regions, states, and the National Council, as well as a mostly stable system for recommendations and requests. Hundreds of people have directly participated on the councils. Yet many citizens remain frustrated by the weak influence of these spaces. An advisor (José René Córdova) summarizes it:

> The principal function of the CCDS is informational, neither from the Secretary to the Council nor vice versa is there any binding obligation in any sense, the only power the councilors have is the force of their arguments and the soundness of the arguments that they provide. Do not misunderstand this recommendation, since this is an important space that should be used to make a record of our concerns and to advocate decisions that will be taken by the other side.

> (Córdoba, 2010)

Selection of Participants

Councilors are elected through public announcements "by major group" (women, indigenous people, academics, businesspeople, NGOs, etc.) in the 32 federal entities. Each Core Council selects seven NGO regular advisors and seven substitutes (from each of the "major groups") and three government representatives and substitutes (a delegate from the SEMARNAT, a representative from the state executive, and another from the legislature). Each major group nominates candidates via public notice 15 days prior to the election. The notice must be published in at least one newspaper with national and state circulation.

The regional councils are made up of representatives from the Core Councils according to the number of states in the region. For example, the southern region (Chiapas, Guerrero, Oaxaca, and Veracruz) has 16 members, four from each Core Council.

Finally, the National Council is made up of the president, who is the head of the Secretariat; a technical secretary, designated by the president; 16 representative members from the "major groups" invited by the secretary of the SEMARNAT; a senator and a deputy from the environmental committees; the six presidents of the Regional Councils; and 32 member representatives from the Core Councils.

Unlike other councils, such as the Brazilian public policy councils, there is no civil society–government parity, since the Mexican system grants greater representation to civil society in the Core Councils and, as a consequence, in the regional and national councils. Nevertheless, especially in the national council, privileges are reserved for the Secretariat, since it names 32 percent of the membership (it invites the 16 representatives of major groups) and it holds the presidency and the technical secretariat, creating the paradox that the advisee is simultaneously the president of the advisory body.

The selection of participants in the Core Councils defines this vertical-ascendant system of representation, since they make up the Regional Councils and a good part of the National Council. Our informants indicated that these procedures still have some problems, sometimes because of members' interest in maintaining themselves in the position (and thus failing to disseminate the announcement for elections) and in other instances because of logistical problems. Although the selection of representatives from "major groups" is legally mandated to be autonomous, the procedure is conducted by the Participation Unit of the Secretariat, which is responsible for publishing the electoral notice and validating the process. According to the head of the unit, more than once they have received complaints from organizations that did not find out about the process or that, because they take place in all the state capitals simultaneously, were unable to reach the electoral events.[10]

Operations, Types of Communication, and Decisions

Every council (national, regional, and core) has a calendar of between four and six ordinary meetings in which attendance is taken, the minutes of the previous meeting are approved, and an agenda is presented. An analysis of the available minutes shows that the agendas for the Core Councils include presentations of current issues, information on members' participation in various communication and advisory forums, agencies or officials invited to speak about a particular issue, review of previous resolutions, and decisions on new resolutions (and those responsible), which are numbered and incorporated into a log, thus allowing members to follow the progress of each issue in subsequent meetings.

For example, at the Veracruz Core Council meeting on October 18, 2010,[11] the delegate from the Federal Ombudsman's Office for Environmental Protection (PROFEPA) reported on the progress of investigations into several environmental complaints made to the council. One of the resolutions was a visit by the members to inspect lands related to two of the complaints. However, the issues dealt with at the meetings most frequently reflect certain characteristics of these councils.

One such issue was the report on the destructive effects of hurricane Karl, which battered the area in September 2010, affecting low-income housing constructed in irregular zones (as it evaporated lagoons with zoning variances for the construction of social housing). On this issue, the SEMARNAT requested that the academic and NGO members provide a technical assessment to modify the projects for land-use changes. The delegate requested that the membership pressure the legislature to introduce legislation regulating coastal land-use planning.

The second was a complaint, principally from the academic and business members, about the Veracruz state government's agreement with an unknown contractor for the creation of a land-use plan for the central zone, which they did not hold in high regard. In this case, the council sought to act as a subject with its own voice in undertaking a critical action to preserve the state's environment. More than the sum of their voices, the members spoke "on behalf of the Council" to request meetings with the state government and consulting group.

These cases illustrate two significant characteristics of the decision-making process in these councils that we analyze in greater detail in the conclusions: first, the effort to become "social subjects," transcending the communicative character of the space for interaction, and second, the difficulties of having an impact as a council on environmental policies that are the state's responsibility.

Comparing the CCDS with Other Consultative Councils: Glass Half-full or Half-empty?

What lessons can we learn from the CCDS case? How can we compare this with other cases? Are the diversity of voices and the effort to have an impact an exception or the norm? In this section we compare the CCDS with the data obtained in a survey taken at the end of 2008 of 81 members in 47 bodies affiliated with the Federal Public Administration (Hevia, Vergara-Lope, and Ávila, 2009) with respect to three variables: institutionalization, representativeness, and impact.

Institutionalization

The degree of institutionalization in the creation and operations of these bodies is notable. One factor in the CCDS innovations is their constant institutionalization. The CCDS are supported by a solid legal framework that is regularly updated, in which every council has the authority to make internal rules that regulate their operations, including monitoring mechanisms for the resolutions and recommendations.

The relatively high levels of institutionalization of the CCDS are shared by the majority of the councils, although there are important variations.

According to those surveyed by Hevia, Vergara Lope, and Ávila, the majority of members know that the body in which they participate has a legal basis (80 percent have internal regulations) and 70 percent believe that the norms are followed. But of the 81 members interviewed, only 51 percent thought powers were well specified and 11.4 percent thought they were poorly specified. Similarly, for the description of functions, 54.3 percent of the respondents thought they were clearly described, while 37.1 percent deemed them "more or less" described.

With respect to the general operations of the councils, 71 percent of the 81 members surveyed indicated that the meetings are scheduled annually and, in general, do take place, along with some extraordinary meetings. According to the 81 members, in 2008 an average of 5.73 meetings were planned (SD = 4.1; max. 21, min. 1), and 5.82 took place (SD = 4.7), a high correlation between meetings that were planned and ones that were actually conducted ($r = 0.89$, $p < 0.01$). Regular member participation at these meetings is at an acceptable level, since 81 percent of the membership that is obligated to attend does so regularly, although only 40 percent agree that the regular members always attend.

As for the power to call a meeting, the CCDS are part of a small group of bodies (34 percent) in which the members indicate that in effect they can call a meeting, as opposed to the remaining 57 percent who thought that only government actors have this right.

Finally, the CCDS are part of the elite group of councils that have an operating budget, which is only true for 4 percent of the bodies surveyed. Twenty-three percent of the participants did not know if their council had a budget. Of the remaining 77 percent, the overwhelming majority (96 percent) reported they did not have a budget to support their operations.

The vertical structure of the CCDS further differentiates them from the rest of the national councils, including those that have an innovative "architecture" for participation, such as the National Institute for Women (Mexico), which has a government board that coadministers with an equal number of directors from both civil society and the state, although they are not articulated with their respective institutes in the states and municipalities (Hevia, Vergara-Lope, and Ávila, 2011). Indeed, the direction of the vertical structure (bottom–up) is the opposite of one of the most cited examples of participation in Mexico: the Federal Electoral Institute. In that case, the "cascading appointment system" for the members of local and district councils by the nine members of the general council is based on the opposite logic: the national members elect the local ones, who in turn elect the district members (Aziz and Isunza Vera, 2007).

Representativeness

Another important variable is the criteria for selection of members of state-society bodies. If, as in the case of the CCDS, the goal is to assure the presence of the greatest diversity of significant "voices" in a field of public policy, the criteria and mechanisms for selecting the representatives are critical. As the most recent literature demonstrates, the procedures for participation should be considered with respect to the impacts, criteria, and arguments for representation (Dowbor, Houtzager, and Serafim, 2008; Isunza Vera and Gurza Lavalle, 2010).

The CCDS units select their members through public invitations for candidates, but some of the National Council participants are invited by the president of the council, who is also the head of the Secretariat. Selection by invitation seems to be the norm in federal consultative councils in Mexico. Asked if there are clear criteria for selecting members, the majority of the 81 respondents from various bodies (54 percent) thought that there are not, and as shown in Table 4.1, only 28.6 percent of the councils use public competitions to identify participants.

In addition to this indicator of reduced autonomy, the membership has limited capacity to choose the leadership of these bodies. For example, 17 percent of the 81 participants surveyed reported that there are no clear criteria for selecting the president of the body, and 57 percent believed that the appointment was made by the affiliated agency, which is the policy followed in the national CCDS and for some key positions in the Core Councils (such as the secretary, who is always the Secretariat's delegate). Thus, even innovative bodies, such as the CCDS, do not escape the limiting logic of procedures for constituting the councils.

Another important difference between the CCDS and other federal consultative councils is that the CCDS include the "major groups," which assures representation of diverse social actors: CSOs, business people and academics, youth, women, and indigenous people. According to surveyed participants

Table 4.1   Criteria for member selection

Member selection	Percentage
Appointment from the agency	22.90
Invitation from the agency	45.70
Public competition	28.60

Source: Based on data from Hevia, Vergara-Lope, and Ávila (2009).

in the other councils, nongovernmental representatives are mostly from civil society organizations (52 percent), followed by trade and business associations (25 percent), and academics and experts (23 percent). However, asked if the bodies have adequate nongovernmental representation, 86 percent thought they did not. The efforts to expand representation in the CCDS reflect the struggles for recognition by social actors involved in the environmental field.

Finally, according to the survey, the renewal period for the councils averaged 2.48 years (SD = 0.7; max. 3; min. 1). Notably, 34 percent of the members did not know or did not respond, which indicates important gaps in the understanding of the councils' operations.

Quality and Impact

Despite having high levels of institutionalization and information, a workgroup-based mechanism for operations, as well as clear criteria for selecting members, the majority of the surveyed participants (including those in the CCDS) thought that the bodies do not fulfill their mandates and have little or no impact on the policies they engage. They also believed that the impact that the bodies have on developing CSO activities and citizenship participation in general was "modest," even though they reported that the contributions of nongovernmental actors were significant.

The survey asked participants about the amount of information available to them, a critical aspect of impact. In response, 65.7 percent reported that they always had the relevant information in advance of dealing with issues, and only 8.6 percent indicated they never had this information. Only 6 percent of members reported receiving regular training on how to carry out their work on the councils, and 51 percent had not been trained. Of course, the CCDS did not receive training until the fourth generation of members. A large majority indicated that the councils operated by creating work groups or commissions. According to 37.1 percent of respondents, work groups were always established, whereas only 8.6 percent indicated that this practice was not employed, as in the case with the CCDS.

The majority of bodies, like the CCDS, have instruments to track resolutions and recommendations. According to 88 percent of respondents, the bodies use such mechanisms, generally the taking and approval (in the next meeting) of minutes (91 percent), although only 43 percent reported that the minutes are made public.

With respect to publicity given to their work, only 50 percent of respondents perceived that their council disseminates information about results to the general public. About 54 percent of respondents believed the councils fulfilled their mandates in most or all aspects, whereas 46 percent thought they did so in some or no aspects. According to survey respondents, the impact of these bodies on policy is positive but limited. Although 32 percent thought that they contributed "a lot" to policy formation and policy implementation, 17 percent indicated they contributed "nothing," and 30.9 percent reported "little" contribution.

Finally, only 22 percent thought that the councils had "a lot" of impact on citizenship participation, compared with 12.3 percent who indicated they had "none," and 38 percent who reported "little" such impact. This perception of limited impact, which is shared by the CCDS and other surveyed council members, appears to be the principal characteristic of these models for participation in Mexico.

Conclusions and Discussion: Constrained Participation in Mexico

Four central points emerge from this discussion about state-society consultative bodies' contribution to democracy and the conditions for their development. First, the most salient problems with these bodies in Mexico are not with their institutionalization or membership selection, but in the degree of impact they have on the policy-making process. Looking at one of the most developed cases at the federal level showed that after 15 years in operation and adopting of complex procedures for implementation and selection, the CCDS have a relatively minor role in the development of public policy: although they seek to become "social subjects," they continue to operate as spaces for interaction without the capacity of coadministration and little capacity for impact. If this is the case in councils that enjoy official support, operating funds, and the inclusion of representatives from relatively strong organizations and movements, it is imaginable that in other instances the councils have even less impact on public policy, as evidenced by the survey results.

Second, the "high-level of institutionalization/low-level of impact" nature of the councils reflects the dynamics of state-society relations in Mexican public life of recent decades, in which simulation is part of the governmental ethos (Sefchovich, 2008). As illustrated by the CCDS case, the capacity for impact of these bodies is constrained from the very moment of their establishment. Although this fact may be questioned by some social actors, it has consensus support among the political class and governmental actors.

The postrevolutionary tradition, which reduced interest representation to nonplural, noncompetitive state-corporatist entities, was only partially modified by the opening up of the party system; it has not developed toward the creation of new state-society relations that incorporate mechanisms for participation beyond elections for governments and legislatures or mechanisms for influence beyond information and consultation. Coadministration and citizen control of public policy outside of corporatist entities did not emerge in the classical postrevolutionary period or in the neoliberal period of the Institutional Revolutionary Party (PRI) and National Action Party (PAN) governments. The state apparatus remains sealed off from civil society influence, and thus continues to limit participation to information, and in the best case, consultation, as reflected in the regulatory framework as well as the corporatist and neoliberal political projects (Dagnino, Olvera, and Panfichi, 2006).

Third, constrained participation and hermetic government entities do not invalidate the efforts by social actors to influence the process. To the contrary, they continue to use these spaces even though they do not fully trust the results. If they are so constrained, why do thousands of Mexicans participate in them? The CCDS case leads to this hypothesis: despite the constraints on these councils (in legal terms and in terms of the relationship dynamic), they have an oversight mechanism that influences the public policy process—the reputational cost of refusing to comply with the recommendations of "citizenized" councils. In the case study, this mechanism works because of double process: the appropriation of state-society spaces by actors committed to a policy that promotes citizen participation to influence public policies, and additionally, the commitment of state officials responsible for policy to supporting the participation initiatives.

As the social accountability literature shows (Isunza Vera and Gurza Lavalle, 2010; Isunza Vera and Olvera, 2006; Peruzzotti and Smulovitz, 2002), although the recommendations are nonbinding, they do affect public policy decisions and procedures, since they are issued by a body that has social legitimacy and recognition. The effort to transform these spaces into "social subjects" can be seen as seeking society's recognition for "speaking in its name" through presumptive or virtual representation (Gurza Lavalle, Houtzager, and Castello, 2006). Through their legitimacy as representative of certain social groups, the influence of the councils increases.

This reasoning requires that participants seek to transform the council into a legitimate actor, the place for making demands "from outside," like traditional social movements. Thus, it is critical for government actors to promote the councils in this way. If the authority does not pay attention to its Consultative Council, it will disappear, de facto or de jure. It is therefore surprising that the CCDS have enjoyed longevity in the Mexican context: several federal administrations have kept their commitment to the social participation strategy in the environmental sector, listening to (and sometimes following) the recommendations of the CCDS. The Secretariat's Participation Unit, which is responsible for advocating attention to the Consultative Councils' recommendations within the agency, understands that the result of its efforts will determine whether or not the councils disappear; if they become irrelevant in influencing public policies, social actors may abandon them.

Finally, how do these councils contribute to the strengthening of democracy? What would happen if they did not exist? In our opinion, these mechanisms contribute a fundamental component for democracy building in the development of new dynamics and actors and their consequences. Like participatory processes in the paradigmatic case of Brazil, these councils, as state-society entities, have become schools for citizenship where the social and state actors establish dynamics outside state corporatism, despite the constraints on participation and the desire for greater influence. These consultative bodies are not only a kind of "training" to build the skills of potential participants in future entities that would have social control and involve in coadministration, they also serve as a laboratory for those entities, by testing limitations and identifying problems. For the state actors, the councils are learning spaces, providing innovative solutions for administrative changes to processes of reform of the state.

As illustrated in the case of Brazil, addressed in chapters 3 and 5 of this book, change in state-society dynamics and the emergence of extensive participatory processes did not depend only on the strength of social movements. In addition, state capacity to implement proparticipation policies and the tradition of state-society relations rooted in the twentieth century, at least from the time of the *Estado Novo*, were also central. Consultative councils (e.g., in health), appeared at that time and the practices for communication developed between the state and social movements lasted for the medium term, culminating in recent participation that flourished at the end of the 1990s and into the twenty-first century.

In sum, the creation of Consultative Councils with clear functions and responsibilities, as well as with interested and participatory actors, may not initially break through structural barriers to transform critical aspects in public policy cycles. However, they can in fact be an important innovation where state authorities have been traditionally sealed off from participation. This is achieved by creating conditions for strengthening spaces with some possibility of influence via the construction of social actors with the capacity to dialogue with the government and plan future reforms of the state.

Notes

1. As for spaces for interaction, the most important laws were the General Law for Social Development and the Federal Law for Promoting Civil Society Organization Activities, both passed in 2004; with respect to transparency, the implementation of the Federal Law for Transparency and Public Access to

Government Information and the creation of the Federal Institute for Access to Public Information were critical; and civic initiatives promulgated by the federal government include the civic current before the Institute for Social Development and the Progress/Opportunities program (Hevia, 2011). However, the Fox government's implementation was very far from the political, economic, and social expectations that were generated, exacerbating political polarization (Aziz, 2007).

2. As recently as the end of 2009, a proposed political reform that did not pass was the popular legislative initiative as the only mechanism for direct democracy to be included in the constitution.

3. Some of these exceptions are rural development (Cartagena, 2005; Fox, 2007) and planning councils (Flores, 2005).

4. This section is based on information from Hevia, Vergara-Lope, and Ávila (2009), especially Chapter 2.

5. The state-society bodies include 33 intrastate entities that are legally allowed to invite specific nongovernmental actors to meetings, generally without a vote, but with voice.

6. Specifically, these are National Council for Environmental Education for Sustainability; National Council for Natural Protected Areas; National Advisory Council for the Meso-American Biological Corridor; National Forestry Council; Advisory Council on Climate Change; National Technical Advisory Council for the Conservation and Sustainable Use of Wildlife; National System to Combat Desertification and Degradation of Natural Resources; National Committee for Priority Wetlands; Committees for Regional Ecological Planning; and Consultative Councils for Mining Areas (SEMARNAT, 2008c).

7. This principal was subsequently ratified at the Summit for Sustainable Development in 2002 and in the Millennium Declaration of 2005.

8. At this time the National Ecological Alliance was also formed. It came out of the Mexican Green Party at the end of the 1980s, which in 1991 became the Mexican Ecological Party. In 1993, it became the Mexican Green Ecological Party, which currently has an agenda quite removed from environmental themes.

9. There were similar cases in Durango, Oaxaca, and YucatánYutacan, where Consultative Council members subsequently became part of the state or federal administration.

10. For example, in Quintana Roo, the meeting took place in the capital, Chetumal, but most of the organizations are based in Cancún, and they did not find out about the election, thus missing the opportunity to participate in the selection of the new membership.

11. The research team attended this meeting, and the paragraphs below are based on the research notes and interpretations of the researchers.

Bibliography

Aziz, Alberto. 2007. "El retorno del conflicto. Elecciones y polarización política en México". *Desacatos* 24: 13–54.

Aziz, Alberto, and Jorge Alonso. 2009. *México una democracia vulnerada*. México: CIESAS; Miguel Angel Porrúa.

Aziz, Alberto, and Ernesto Isunza Vera. 2007. "La crisis del modelo electoral mexicano: financiamiento, medios, instituciones y política social". *Foro Internacional* XLVII (4): 740–784.

Benítez, Raúl. 2009. "La crisis de seguridad en México". *Nueva Sociedad* 220: 173–189.

Blauert, Jutta, Martha Rosas, Salvador Anta, and Sergio Graf. 2006. "¿Espacios para la deliberación o la toma de decisiones? Lecciones para la participación y las políticas en consejos ambientales en México". In *Democratización, rendición de cuentas y sociedad civil: participación ciudadana y control social*, ed. Ernesto Isunza Vera y Alberto Olvera, 601–642. 1st ed. México D.F.: Miguel Ángel Porrúa; CIESAS; Universidad Veracruzana.

Bustos, Carlos, and Galia Chacón. 2009. "El desarrollo sostenible y la agenda 21". *Telos* 11 (2): 164–181.

Cartagena, Ruth. 2005. "Participación social y toma de decisiones en los consejos municipales de desarrollo rural sustentable de los Altos de Chiapas". *Gestión y política pública* XIV (22): 341–402.

CCNDS. 2000. *Libro Blanco Consejo Consultivo Nacional. Por la consolidación de la política ambiental mexicana*. México: Consejo Consultivo Nacional de Desarrollo Sustentable; SEMARNAP.

———. 2004. *Consejos Consultivos para el Desarrollo Sustentable. Consejo Nacional. Libro Blanco, segunda generación*. México: SEMARNAT; PNUD.

———. 2007. *Consejo Consultivo Nacional de Desarrollo Sustentable. Libro Blanco. Generación 2005–2007*. México: SEMARNAT; PNUD.

Centro de Estudios de las Finanzas Públicas. 2010. "Principales indicadores económicos". http://www3.diputados.gob.mx/camara/001_diputados/006_centros_de_estudio/02_centro_de_estudios_de_finanzas_publicas/03_bancos_de_informacion/01_estadisticas_historicas/01_indicadores_macroeconomicos_1980_2010/01_principales_indicadores_economicos. Accessed: March 23, 2012.

CONEVAL. 2011. "CONEVAL Evolución de las dimensiones de la pobreza 1990–2010". http://www.coneval.gob.mx/cmsconeval/rw/pages/medicion/evolucion_de_las_dimensiones_pobreza_1990_2010.es.do. Accessed: July 6, 2012.

Córdoba, José René. 2010. "Cómo ser consejero de la SEMARNAT sin morir en el intento". *CCDS*. http://0305.nccdn.net/4_2/000/000/00b/f11/rene_cordova.pdf. Accessed: June 13, 2012.

Cornelius, Wayne A., Ann L. Craig, and Jonathan Fox. 1994. *Transforming State-Society Relations in Mexico: The National Solidarity Strategy*. La Jolla, CA: Center for US-Mexican Studies, University of California, San Diego.

Crespo, José Antonio. 2007. "Empate, conflicto, incertidumbre". *Desacatos* 24: 181–194.

———. 2008. *2006: hablan las actas: las debilidades de la autoridad electoral mexicana*. México: Random House Mondadori, S.A.

Cunill, Nuria. 1991. *Participación ciudadana: dilemas y perspectivas para la democratización de los Estados latinoamericanos.* Caracas: CLAD.

———. 1997. *Repensando lo público a través de la sociedad.* Caracas: CLAD.

Dagnino, Evelina, Alberto Olvera, and Aldo Panfichi, eds. 2006. *La disputa por la construcción democrática en América Latina.* 1st ed. México D.F.: Fondo de Cultura Económica; Universidad Veracruzana; CIESAS.

Dowbor, Monika, Peter P Houtzager, and Lisandra Serafim. 2008. *Enfrentando os desafios da representação em espaços participativos.* São Paulo: CEBRAP; IDS.

Escalante, Fernando. 2011. "Homicidios 2008–2009. La muerte tiene permiso". *Nexos* 397: 36–49.

Estados Unidos Mexicanos. 1988. *Ley General del Equilibrio Ecológico y la Protección al Ambiente.* México: Latest reform published DOF, August 20, 2011.

Flores, Arturo. 2005. *Local Democracy in Modern Mexico: A Study in Participatory Methods.* London: Arena Books.

Font, Joan. 2001. *Ciudadanos y decisiones públicas.* Barcelona: Editorial Ariel.

Fox, Jonathan. 1993. *The Politics of Food in Mexico: State Power and Social Mobilization.* Ithaca, NJ: Cornell University Press.

———. 2007. *Accountability Politics: Power and Voice in Rural Mexico.* New York: Oxford University Press.

Gudynas, Eduardo. 1992. "Los múltiples verdes del ambientalismo latinoamericano". *Nueva Sociedad* 122: 104–115.

Gurza Lavalle, Adrián, Peter P Houtzager, and Graziela Castello. 2006. "Democracia, Pluralização da Representação e Sociedade Civil". *Lua Nova* 67: 49–103.

Hevia, Felipe. 2011. *Poder y ciudadanía en el combate a la pobreza. El caso de Progresa/Oportunidades de México.* Brussels: PIE Peter Lang.

Hevia, Felipe, Samana Vergara-Lope, and Homero Ávila. 2009. *Construcción de línea base para posteriores evaluaciones de impacto sobre la inclusión de las Organizaciones de la Sociedad Civil (OSC) en instancias públicas de deliberación. Informe final de investigación.* México: CIESAS; INDESOL.

———. 2011. "Consejos consultivos y otras instancias públicas de deliberación". *Perfiles Latinoamericanos* 38: 65–88.

Human Rights Watch. 2011. *Ni seguridad ni derechos. Ejecuciones, desapariciones y tortura en la "guerra contra el narcotráfico" de México.* Washington, D.C.: Human Rights Watch.

Isunza Vera, Ernesto, and Adrián Gurza Lavalle, eds. 2010. *La innovación democrática en América Latina: tramas y nudos de la representación, la participación y el control social.* 1st ed. México D.F.: CIESAS; Universidad Veracruzana.

Isunza Vera, Ernesto, and Felipe Hevia. 2006. *Relaciones sociedad civil-estado en México: un ensayo de interpretación.* Cuadernos para la democratización 2. Xalapa: CIESAS; Universidad Veracruzana.

Isunza Vera, Ernesto, and Alberto Olvera, eds. 2006. *Democratización, rendición de cuentas y sociedad civil: participación ciudadana y control social.* 1st ed. México D.F.: MA Porrúa; CIESAS; Universidad Veracruzana.

Merino, Mauricio, ed. 2010. *¿Qué tan público es el espacio público en México?* México D.F.: FCE; CONACULTA; Universidad Veracruzana.

Naciones Unidas. 2011. "Agenda 21". http://www.un.org/esa/dsd/agenda21_ spanish/. Accessed: July 6, 2012.

Olvera, Alberto, ed. 2010. *La democratización frustrada. Limitaciones institucionales y colonización política de las instituciones garantes de derechos y de participación ciudadana en México*. México: CIESAS; Universidad Veracruzana.

Paz, Fernanda. 2005. *La participación en el manejo de áreas naturales protegidas: actores e intereses en conflicto en el corredor biológico Chichinautzin, Morelos*. 1st. ed. Cuernavaca México: Universidad Nacional Autónoma de México Centro regional de Investigaciones Multidisciplinarias.

Peruzzotti, Enrique, and Catalina Smulovitz, eds. 2002. *Controlando la política: ciudadanos y medios en las nuevas democracias latinoamericanas*. Buenos Aires: Temas.

Poder Ejecutivo Federal. 2007. *Plan Nacional de Desarrollo 2007–2012*. México: Presidencia de la República.

Reygadas, Rafael. 2007. "Las organizaciones civiles: entre resistencia y reforma". *Metapolítica* 11 (56): 53–57.

Rodríguez Caloca, Sergio. 2008. *Los consejos consultivos, consideraciones desde la sociedad civil*. México: Incide Social AC.

Samaniego, Fidel. 2006. "Julia Carabias Lillo, ecologista de una sola pieza". *El Universal*, March 12. http://www.eluniversal.com.mx/nacion/136103.html. Accessed: July 6, 2012.

Sánchez, Roberto. 1991. "El tratado de libre comercio en América del Norte y el Medio Ambiente en la frontera norte". *Frontera Norte* 3 (6): 5–28.

Sefchovich, Sara. 2008. *País de mentiras: La distancia entre el discurso y la realidad en la cultura mexicana*. México: Océano.

SEMARNAT. 2008a. *Programa Sectorial de Medio Ambiente y Recursos Naturales*. México: SEMARNAT.

———. 2008b. *Acuerdo mediante el cual se crean el Consejo Consultivo Nacional, seis Consejos Consultivos Regionales y treinta y dos Consejos Consultivos Núcleo para el Desarrollo Sustentable*. México: DOF March 14, 2008.

———. 2008c. *Estrategia Nacional para la participación ciudadana en el sector ambiental*. México: SEMARNAT.

Toledo, Carlos. 2000. "Los programas de desarrollo regional sustentable en regiones campesinas marginadas". In *Del círculo vicioso al círculo virtuoso: cinco miradas al desarrollo sustentable de las regiones marginadas*, ed. Carlos Toledo y Armando Bartra, 17–55. México: Plaza y Valdés; SEMARNAP.

Vargas-Hernández, José G. 2006. "Nuevos movimientos sociales ambientales en México". *Revista Venezolana de Ciencias Sociales* 10 (001): 37–54.

Zermeño, Martha Fabiola, y Moisés Domínguez. 2010. *Fortalecimiento institucional desde un enfoque de derechos y equidad de género para el desarrollo social en el Distrito Federal*. México: PNUD.

CHAPTER 5

Learning to Be "Better Democrats"? The Role of Informal Practices in Brazilian Participatory Budgeting Experiences

Françoise Montambeault

Introduction

Participatory democracy, or the direct involvement of citizens in the democratic decision-making process, is an idea that has become increasingly important among both political theorists and practitioners. Two main positive outcomes have been associated with institutionalized participatory practices. First, some suggest that they increase policy efficiency and governmental effectiveness—or more broadly good governance. According to this view, citizens who are directly affected by policies are likely to not only have a better knowledge of local needs but also become invested in the projects to which they have contributed and become effective accountability agents (Ackerman 2003). Second, some political theorists argue that including citizens in the decision-making processes has the potential to widen the public sphere and empower ordinary people from traditionally excluded groups (Fung and Wright 2003; de Sousa Santos 2004; Dagnino, Olvera, and Panfichi 2006; Cornwall and Coelho 2007). As such, the Brazilian model of direct participation and deliberation over budgets and public spending through participatory budgeting (PB) institutions has often been cited as one of the most promising institutional innovations (de Sousa Santos 1998; Avritzer 2009; Abers 2000). It is a formal space created to give voice to the formerly excluded (Hirschman 1970), through which the inclusion of citizens in every step of the local democratic governance process is the most thorough, extending from decision-making to policy implementation and monitoring.

From a democratic deepening perspective, it is mostly the second argument that calls our attention. One of the various ways the notion of empowerment has been operationalized is of particular interest: the idea that participatory democracy becomes a "school for democracy," an institutional space for citizenship learning and for citizens to become better democrats. In a context traditionally marked by state-led social exclusion, PB not only gives an institutional channel for citizens to voice their concerns and demands to local officials but also educates them to exercise this voice. This move is especially important because, prior to their involvement, ordinary citizens who aim to be empowered often lack the political knowledge and skills often associated with better deliberative processes and policy outcomes. While the relationship between individuals' participation and citizenship learning has been well defined theoretically (Pateman 1970), little attention has been devoted to study this phenomenon empirically. Although the existence of genuinely deliberative institutional features is often cited, the conditions under which democratic knowledge, skills, and attitudes are more likely to develop among participants remain largely overlooked.

To what extent is PB contributing to citizenship learning among its participants in Brazil? How do formal institutions of deliberation interact with actual practices, both formal and informal? How does this interaction affect citizenship learning? Due to a wide variety of experiences with PB across the country, Brazil is an excellent case study for an insightful comparison that will offer responses to these questions. While in cases such as Porto Alegre, PB institutions have created a space for democratic citizenship learning among participants, the causal relationship is not so straightforward. In many cases, traditional and nondemocratic ways of doing politics (i.e., paternalism, clientelism) are shared by participants and politicians alike; in such circumstances, citizens are led from above, "accompanying" politicians and helping them to achieve their mandate. Along with Helmke and Levitsky, I argue that informal practices are central to the analysis of PB learning outcomes as they "shape the way formal democratic institutions work," sometimes reinforcing and at other times subverting them (Helmke and Levitsky, 2004: 2). Based on a comparative analysis of the cases of Belo Horizonte, Porto Alegre, and Recife, I show that in addition to the formal opportunities provided by the PB cycle, the divergent nature of informal practices prevalent among both state and society actors has the potential to either circumvent or reinforce the aim of formal institutions, also contributing to shaping social learning outcomes. Thus, it is important to pay greater attention to them in the analyses of participatory institutional reforms in Latin America.

Participatory Budgeting in Brazil

The Brazilian PB model, an initiative of the *Partido dos Trabalhadores* (PT, Workers' Party),[1] is one of the flagship participatory democracy programs aimed at including ordinary citizens in the municipal governance process, giving them a voice in local decision-making and in the definition of collective policy priorities through face-to-face deliberation and cooperation with the municipal government. Emerging in Porto Alegre in 1989–1990 (Abers 2000; Baiocchi 2005; Avritzer 2002), PB, which was adopted by both PT and non-PT municipalities, soon became widespread across Brazil (Wampler and Avritzer 2005). The success of PB in Porto Alegre provided a "demonstration effect" (Wampler and Avritzer 2005), prompting local leaders from a diversity of political parties to implement PB as a resource allocation mechanism that empowered traditionally marginalized urban populations and sustained efforts to "urbanize" the *favelas* (shanty towns).

The structure of the process and the percentage of the municipal budget that is subject to citizen deliberation differ slightly between cities, but some common characteristics are observable. PB is organized on a regional basis: the city is divided into several administrative regions, to which a certain budget is allocated for deliberation in meetings held at the neighborhood and then at the regional level before being included into the broader municipal budget proposal. In most cases, PB is done on an annual basis (with some exceptions, as in Belo Horizonte, where it is a biannual process), through a series of participatory meetings that follow the different dimensions of the budgetary and policy-making cycles and that entail different types of participation and deliberation processes at the neighborhood, regional, and citywide levels (see Graph 5.1). The projects that are submitted through the PB process are generally small scale and related to municipal infrastructure. Examples of regularly approved proposals include street paving, street lighting, water sewage, sanitation infrastructure, public parks, health centers, primary schools, and playgrounds. The projects are generally located at the neighborhood level, except in cities where there are thematic assemblies held parallel to the regional ones, where gender, cultural, health, or racial issues are discussed at a more general level.

Prior to the final deliberations among PB council members that will lead to the adoption of the final investment plan, some cities also organize what is

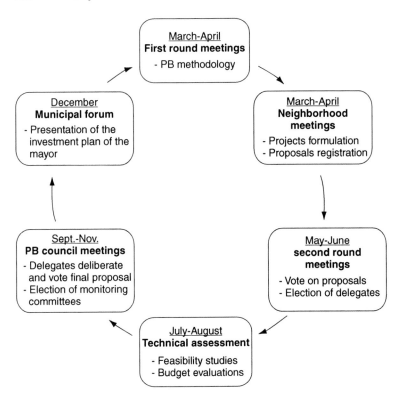

Graph 5.1 Example of participatory budgeting cycle

called the "Caravan of Priorities," during which delegates take part in a tour of the city in order to give them a better understanding of their counterparts' projects, and of the city's needs. After the discussions and vote of the PB Council, the municipal plan is approved by the local government, and then made public in large assemblies organized by the mayor's office to disseminate the results of the deliberative process.

PB is now a quite important phenomenon in Brazil as its institutions formally give a voice to ordinary citizens—especially the poor and traditionally marginalized—who take an active part in the formulation, design, and implementation of urban development policies and projects. Such a deliberative process is argued to have an impact not only on social inclusion and empowerment but also on democratic learning. Before looking empirically at concrete experiences to assess the validity of this claim, we shall first turn to the theoretical foundations of the relationship between participation, deliberation, and democratic learning.

Learning to Be Better Democrats: The Role of Deliberative Institutions

The focus on citizen participation is not new to democratic theory. Classical democratic theorists often praised citizen participation in small-scale and face-to-face democratic decision-making processes for its educative functions, and this has been revived in the associated notion of deliberation. More recently, radical, participatory, and deliberative democrats have brought back the idea of direct citizen participation in democratic decision-making processes at both the individual and collective levels, as expressed by Mansbridge's assertion that "participation does make citizens better" (1995). Following these theoretical assumptions, deliberative institutional experiences have been argued to have the potential to be "schools of democracy." How has this theoretical relationship been articulated in "real world" participatory experiments? What is the alleged relationship between deliberative institutions and democratic learning in practice?

Participation, Deliberation, and Democracy: Theoretical Foundations

From Aristotle to Rousseau, several classical political theorists have made citizen participation a central feature of good democracies. However, it is Alexis de Tocqueville who, in his study of participation in New England town halls, first made the claim that participation had an educative power that could transform individuals, developing one's character and commitment to the common good, making it their own. As he explained, "it is by putting citizens in charge of the administration of small affairs [. . .] that you interest them in the common good and that they realize that they always need each other to generate it" (Tocqueville, 1981 [1835]: 133). Participation in decision-making processes thus allows citizens to hear about each other's needs and to reflect upon their own concerns as members of a community, transforming their understanding of the world. This idea that participation has an impact on the formation of individuals' rationality was further reinforced by the writings of John Stuart Mill, who posited that participation is "taking them [the free people] out of the narrow circle of personal and family selfishness, and accustoming them to the comprehension of joint interests, the management of joint concerns—habituating them to act from public or semi-public motives and guide their conduct by aims which unite instead of isolating them from one another" (Mill, 1960 [1873]: 112). While de Tocqueville's contribution mostly emphasized the educative function that active participation had on individuals, Mill was mostly concerned with the social aspect of individual learning and its effect on government stability (Mansbridge 1995), highlighting more generally the potential of such individual and collective citizenship learning for deepening democracy and making citizens "better democrats."

Several contemporary participatory democrats, building upon the lessons of classical theorists, also emphasized the educative effect of citizen participation, and have interrogated the types of faculties that individuals need to develop for democracy to flourish. In this vein, Carole Pateman (1970) argues that if participation contributes to the development of individual capacities among participants, the goal of its educative function should be democracy itself. As she specifies, participation and democracy are not only related; they are inseparable: "for a democratic polity to exist it is necessary for a participatory society to exist," adding that participation refers to "(equal) participation in decision making" (Pateman 1970: 43). She argues that it is mostly a sense of political efficacy that people learn from participation, as democracy requires "confidence in one's ability to participate responsibly and effectively" to the collective endeavor (Pateman 1970: 28). Going further in explaining the benefits of participation for democracy, Mansbridge argues that "participation in small face-to-face democracies can help citizens develop a better understanding of their real interest" (Mansbridge 1980: 292), as participation has the function of revealing "whether one's interests complement the interests of others in the polity or conflict with them" (Mansbridge 1995: 6), providing a better understanding of the community for which the common good is collectively defined. This position is reinforced by the writings of deliberative democrats, who focus on deliberation—a type of citizen participation defined as an open and public discussion among equal participants, which finds its legitimacy in the giving of defensible reasons, justifications, and explanations for public decisions—as the main feature enabling democratic learning among citizens. In fact, according to them, good deliberation helps citizens develop a better understanding of their interests in relation to the common good (Held 2006), which in turn increases the reasonableness of the deliberative process and policy outcomes.

Thus, the theoretical relationship between participation, deliberation, and democratic learning is not such that increased citizen competence contributes to an increase in participation in other spheres of the political arena, as Putnam and social capital scholars argue (Putnam 1993). Instead, participation—and more specifically deliberation—contributes to the development of democratic skills, consciousness, and attitudes among participants (Elkin and Soltan 1999), and contributes to shaping their broader understanding of politics and of the community within which their interests are defined, both individually and collectively.

Taking Deliberation to the "Real World": Deliberative Experiences as Schools of Democracy

The idea of a positive relationship between participation, deliberation, and citizenship learning has also been taken up by students and proponents of deliberative democracy reforms, who have further developed the indicators of democratic learning encouraged by participation. For them, the institutionalization of participatory processes that include ordinary citizens has become a cornerstone for the articulation of the causal relationship between participation and democratic citizenship learning. Because they codify and institutionalize a new set of practices and transform collective expectations, institutions such as PB become "schools of democracy and citizenship." Not only do they generate political knowledge and skills among participants, but they also contribute to the quality of the whole polity by making citizens better democrats, developing a better understanding of their roles as members of a society, of their "real" interests in relation to the common good.

Besides generating political knowledge among participants about decision-making processes and the local bureaucracy, policy issues, political parties, and politicians, there are two principal ways that deliberative experiments function as schools of democracy. On the one hand, participants can become better citizens at the *individual* level, learning democratic skills: how to communicate more effectively; to listen to others more carefully; to negotiate among themselves, with politicians, and with bureaucrats; to formulate demands; to organize and mobilize; and so forth (Schugurensky 2007). If deliberation is more likely to succeed when participants have some experience with the process, there is a learning curve associated with the participatory process, and deliberation itself contributes to the education of participants. This is especially important in the context of PB in Brazil, which seeks the inclusion of the poorest and traditionally most marginalized sectors of the population, who often initially lack the basic skills and self-confidence to effectively communicate in a deliberative forum. The example of Porto Alegre is illustrative. As Baiocchi's study shows, years of participation in the process is "a powerful predictor of whether people will talk" (2003: 51), which suggests that there is an educative component intrinsic to the participatory process. But, as he further highlights, this is also explained by certain didactic institutional features specific to the PB model that make this "natural" participatory learning "more or less available to all" (2003: 53).

On the other hand—and this is what is of central interest to us here—participants can also become better citizens at the *collective* level, developing democratic attitudes toward the governance process and, more broadly, toward the political. Such attitudes are closely associated with a renewal of shared "understandings" of the world, of the political sphere, and of the common good, which has an impact on the quality of democracy itself (Pateman 1970). In fact, collective deliberation has the potential to lead to the development of an active and reasonable citizenry, "capable of genuinely public thinking and political judgment and thus able to envision a common future in terms of genuinely common goods" (Barber, 1984). This argument starts from the assumption that citizen preferences are not fixed; they are objects of transformation through the participatory process. In fact, it gives citizens the opportunity to become better democrats, for whom rational individual political preferences are embedded and intertwined with the interests of the community to which they belong rather than being motivated by personal interest maximization. As explained by Fung and Wright, "by seeing that cooperation mediated through reasonable deliberation yields benefits not accessible through adversarial methods, participants might increase their disposition to be reasonable and to transform narrowly self-interested preferences accordingly" (2003: 32). Moreover, because the institutions of deliberation change the formal rules of the game for decision-making in relation to resource distribution—emphasizing collective deliberation, state-society cooperation, and transparency—they also contribute to the transformation of shared expectations about both citizens' and state actors' respective roles and shared spaces in the political process.

While developing democratic skills and knowledge is probably essential to ensuring the democratic quality and fairness of deliberative processes' policy outcomes, such competences say less about the impact of PB on the quality of democracy itself, that is, on the shared expectations about democracy and on the rationales behind citizens' political preferences and behaviors. I therefore contend that in order to measure the impact of PB on citizenship learning and the deepening of democracy in Brazil, we should look more specifically at the general understanding participants have of the common good and of their role in the democratic process, at the attitudes participants develop toward the participatory process, and at the political preferences and behaviors that these attitudes ultimately influence.

Institutional Design: A Variable Held Constant across Brazilian Cases

As highlighted by several empirical analyses of deliberative and participatory reforms, institutional design is a central element to take into account in explaining their democratic learning potential. In fact, although participation and deliberation can theoretically be self-sustaining because of their intrinsically educative functions, as Pateman argues, formal institutions featuring specific mechanisms designed to encourage and promote this path to learning are conducive to realizing this potential in practice (Baiocchi 2003). How should participatory deliberation be designed to become schools of democracy?

According to Fung and Wright (2003) and Abers (2009: 143), to achieve this objective formal deliberative institutions' design should follow three main principles. First, Fung and Wright argue that deliberative institutions should be oriented toward practical goals and policies, often delivering goods to traditionally excluded sectors of the population. Abers goes even further by proposing that these institutions involve the collective definition of the common good and not only implementation of a set of predesigned policies. Second, both Fung and Wright and Abers emphasize that the participatory processes should establish new channels for bottom–up participation of those most affected by the selected issue area, and motivate traditionally excluded populations, who are otherwise not politicized and organized, to formulate demands and exercise some form of control over the government's decisions. Third, these authors highlight the necessarily deliberative nature of participatory mechanisms. As Fung and Wright argue, they should lead to deliberative solution generation, a process through which participants "listen to each other's positions and generate groups' choices after due consideration" and by which they find reasons for collective action (2003: 17). Abers adds that they should involve effective deliberative power for participants and effective citizen control and enforcement capacity over collective decisions.

In both theoretical and practical terms, the design of PB institutions in Brazil, though with slight variations across cities, generally followed these principles, becoming an ideal institutional setting for democratic and citizenship learning at the local level. First, PB is clearly oriented toward the collective definition of the common good, especially with regards to practical concerns such as sanitation, urbanization, and access to basic services for populations for which access has traditionally been denied—mostly *favela* dwellers and the urban poor. Second, PB is a process open to ordinary people. Participants in PB cycles are self-selected, which means that they decide if they want to attend or not, and if they want to contribute to the public debate or not. Moreover, as a program aimed at the "inversion of priorities" and the inclusion of traditionally excluded groups in the urban governance process, PB targets the poorest sectors of the population who are most affected by urban development policies. Finally, PB is fundamentally deliberative. The typical PB process involves three types of citizen-based deliberative meetings: neighborhood assemblies, "thematic" assemblies, and meetings of delegates for citywide coordinating sessions. Concomitantly, popular assemblies, which are the cornerstone of the PB, are held in all neighborhoods prior to presenting proposals for deliberation in PB meetings. Thus, at the formal level, PB institutions in Brazil have all the attributes that would make them ideal sites for developing more democratic attitudes among participants, contributing to making them better citizens.

PB's formal institutions thus can become a school of democracy (Schugurensky 2007; Puntual 2000), a space for democratic citizenship learning where both citizens and the state develop a broader understanding of politics, the common good, and the community they inhabit. While such a positive outcome may be observed in certain cities, studies have highlighted that traditional ways of doing politics often persist alongside the new formal practices of PB. While formal opportunities and institutions for democratic learning are in place, other political practices survive in many cities, in the form of clientelistic politics that give preferential attention to PB leaders affiliated with the party in power, politics that value personal attention by the mayor to particular demands, and paternalistic attitudes toward the process by which the mayor allows the population to "help" him govern (Chávez Texeira and Albuquerque, 2006: 236). What explains such contradictory democratic learning results? If formal deliberative institutions are designed in a way to encourage citizenship learning in Brazil, why do traditional understandings of the political seem to persist in certain cases? While formal institutions can, in theory, have an impact on citizenship learning among participants, analysts should also look at the prevalence of informal institutions and practices at the level of both state and society, which Helmke and Levitsky define as the "socially shared rules, usually unwritten, that are created, communicated and enforced outside officially sanctioned channels" (Helmke and Levitsky, 2004: 5). Because they interact with formal institutions, informal rules are central to the analysis as they also structure the social interactions that take place within formal institutions and therefore shape their learning outcomes. In this case, informal practices—that is, practices governed by informal rules that occur parallel to the participatory process, outside the PB—frame citizenship learning as they influence the nature of the attitudes and behaviors that are developed among participants. As we shall see next, the purpose, and outcome, of formal institutions can be either reinforced or circumvented according to the nature of informal institutions and practices, a question that is too often overlooked in the participatory democracy literature.

Participating to Learn What? Contrasting Brazilian Participatory Budgeting Experiences

A comparative case study of three important Brazilian experiences with PB—Porto Alegre, Belo Horizonte, and Recife—which display divergent democratic learning outcomes despite sharing a similar formal institutional design, reaffirms the need to look beyond formal institutions. The comparison shows that informal institutions matter, shaping social practices and interactions thereby structuring citizenship learning. Considering informal rules means observing actors' often hidden behaviors within PB institutions, the "subtle ways in which actors present themselves in these settings and what may be at stake in doing so [...] particularly for those who have some standing in the community," such as political actors and association leaders (Baiocchi 2005: 21). As the case of Recife demonstrates, the development of new political understandings and of a culture of active citizenship among participants is often impeded by political cooptation strategies deployed by political actors via informal practices of political control over formal processes, as well as by practices used by association leaders to curtail formal mobilization efforts. As a result, there is no change in participants' expectations about how to do politics or how to democratically formulate demands. Informal institutions and the practices associated with them do not, however, necessarily work against democracy and its formal institutions. As indicated by the findings in Porto Alegre and Belo Horizonte, depending on their nature, informal practices observed among leading actors involved in the participatory process can also become complementary to the formal institutions in achieving democratic aims.

Learning to Be Better Citizens: Belo Horizonte and Porto Alegre

As documented by several studies, Porto Alegre's PB program is generally qualified as an exemplary case on many accounts, including its influence on citizenship learning (Abers 2000). Comparing Porto Alegre with the case of Belo Horizonte reveals important similarities in democratic learning outcomes. Belo Horizonte, which is today the sixth largest city in the country with a population of 2.4 million, is the main industrial city of the state of Minas Gerais. Implemented in 1993 by the local PT administration of Patrus Ananias, the PB process in Belo Horizonte is organized over a two-year cycle, and has generated important urban investments in areas of the city mostly inhabited by marginalized groups. In terms of democratic learning outcomes, interview data gathered in 2008 show that, as observed in Porto Alegre, participants have developed a new understanding of their own preferences and interests through participation. More generally, they now share a common understanding of politics and the community that challenges traditional and nondemocratic ways of formulating demands and of interacting with the local government.

One of the first findings highlighted by observers of the pioneering case of Porto Alegre was the change in the traditional and particularistic logic of demand formulation and, consequently, in the privileged channels used to do so. In fact, participating in PB has, according to Abers' observations (2000), contributed to the constitution of bases of "collective identity," of a social energy, which has become the main force driving people's engagement in their community. Baiocchi often heard from participants that as a result of working together to define collective priorities, they have developed a sense of belonging to a larger community that faced common problems. One participant told him, "You participate and you realize that your problems are the same as everyone else's problems, and you work because your problems are the same" (Ana, cited in: Baiocchi 2005: 103). Illustrating this community-building trend among PB participants, Wampler observed that "when participants took the microphone to speak, they did not focus their attention on government officials. Rather, they spoke to their fellow citizens, imploring them to act or vote in a specific way" (2007: 104). This behavior, he suggests, shows that "individuals act as right-bearing members of their community" in the PB process, rather than as individuals pursuing personal interest (2007: 129).

My interviews in Belo Horizonte reveal trends similar to those identified by researchers in Porto Alegre. In fact, I observed an important change in the traditional demand-formulation logic, in that citizens were learning to become partners with the state in governing their communities as collective actors, rather than using particular channels to reach state actors and realize individual demands. In that vein, a PB delegate in the Centro-Sul region explained the change that had occurred in the local governance process: "we are now called up to do things together—to redistribute resources, to govern together, for everyone. That is what's happening" (Delegada OP-BH 1 2008). Another delegate added that the principal gain of PB for Belo Horizonte's citizens is "the creation of this collectivity, of this link, because then you start to know other people. It's better; it has a better quality [than other forms of mobilization]. I think it's the principal gain we've made with PB; [a] communicative people and a participative city are starting to really take form" (Delegada OP-BH 2 2008). In both the cities, community leaders that have traditionally been considered to be political brokers with privileged relationships to political elites have begun to understand their own role as the representative for their community, accountable to community's members. As explained by one delegate:

> The community leader is pointed out as such by a group of people and tries to do something good for his community, for the collectivity without trying to get something in return, or look nice, without hoping to become mayor or

appointed by him, without expecting to get a job out of it. He does so because
he believes in doing so.

(Delegada OP-BH 4 2008)

The development of a sense of community is also observable in public discourse about public policies and in the way both the state and citizens refer
to the projects adopted through PB. Where the mayor and bureaucrats previously spoke about "their projects" or about a given politician's project to
get credit for social and urban development policies, they are now talking
about "our projects," collectively defined with local communities. And citizens are speaking the same language: "our project" and "our community"
(Delegada OP-BH 4 2008) are terms that were generally absent before and
which show the potential of PB to contribute to the construction of an "us,"
of a community.

This renewed democratic understanding of participants' roles as members
of a community also has an impact on the nature of political preferences,
as neighborhood groups learned to identify with wider regional interests,
eventually even cooperating to propose common agendas and proposals for
longer-term planning and policymaking. As a participant told Abers, visits
in other neighborhoods and regions widen the perspective the participants
have about the common good: "You think of yourself as needy, but then you
arrive in that other community and you see people even more miserable, you
realize that your situation isn't that difficult. That you are even privileged"
(Marta, cited in: Abers 2000: 183). As Abers highlights, these manifestations
of community building and collective action for the definition of the common good were becoming "more common, engaging many participants who
had initially entered into the budget process only to obtain specific improvements for their neighborhood" (2009: 163), showing a change in citizenship
attitudes through participation in the PB process.

In Belo Horizonte, participants have learned about their community's
needs and about their relationship with their fellow citizens through the process. The experience of PB often widens their political preferences beyond
personal interest, a change that resonates in their understanding of the common good. According to a delegate from the Pampulha region, PB indeed
raises a collective consciousness among participants:

> The function of PB is to promote the participation of more individu-
> als in the decisions, and from the moment a person starts thinking about
> this, other things start to happen. You often see people coming to the
> COMFORÇAs [elected committees for the oversight of PB projects] with a

> demand from their streets, and suddenly they are thinking about the city dif-
> ferently, taking a different political standpoint [. . .] I think PB can promote
> the strengthening of society.
>
> (Delegada OP-BH 2 2008)

In terms of the nature of demands made for the next PB cycle, one delegate highlighted that the reasons for sustaining a project are no longer directly tied into the immediate interests of the neighborhood:

> The project that we will ask for in the next cycle is the urbanization of the
> neighboring *favela*, so we will not ask for something that will directly bene-
> fit our neighborhood, but rather will attend the needs of this *favela*, which
> ultimately influences our neighborhood as well.
>
> (Delegado OP-BH 7 2008)

And though many point out that citizenship learning remains limited, the process takes time and is a work in progress: "It's still a learning process, but the power of the people multiplies when they are united, when they act together. It's still something that can be improved, but we are moving in that direction" (Delegada OP-BH 3 2008).

What explains this common trend in Porto Alegre and Belo Horizonte? As argued above, in addition to the institutional opportunities provided for citizenship learning with the implementation of PB programs, informal prac-tices surrounding the participatory process also have to be considered. First, in both Porto Alegre and Belo Horizonte, the relationship of political par-ties and politicians—namely the PT—with participants and the associated claim-making process remained mostly mediated within the formal channels of the PB. As Baiocchi highlights, the PT's "relationship to civil society is not an instrumental one, as its reproduction in power does not depend on its direct influence on civil society" (2009: 132). In fact, and contrary to what will be observed in Recife, he concludes that "there was little attempt to control the content of discussions in PB in Porto Alegre, and OP [PB] meetings were far from being party-controlled spaces" (2009: 133). The same was observed in Belo Horizonte, where there is no informal political control over PB meetings, even in the context where a plurality of interests is repre-sented. As explained by a delegate of the Barreiro region, community leaders are not necessarily apolitical, but partisan interests do not come into play in the deliberative process: "the richness of the process, of this discussion, is that it is not a game between the interests of political parties, the PT, PDT, PSDB or the PSL. There is nothing like this. Here, what we have is an interest in the community" (Delegado OP-BH 6 2008).

Second, in both municipalities, civil society's informal practices have played a key role in strengthening formal venues for citizen participation, reinforcing citizenship and democratic attitudes learned through the PB process. Although participation is organized on an individual basis (in that any person can participate in a PB meeting), coordination work is important as proposals have to be supported by groups to become voted onto the priority list, a collective effort that is often organized through neighborhood associations. In many cases, the indirect interventions of activist groups contribute directly to the transformation of preferences among individual participants and to the collective definition of the common good. For example, in Porto Alegre, the organization of regional Popular Councils meetings held parallel to the PB process assured coordination among neighborhoods within a same region, an informal networking exercise that allowed small neighborhoods' interests to be heard and that contributed to raising awareness about the definition of the common good among participants (Baiocchi 2005; Abers 2000). This is also true in Belo Horizonte, where coordination efforts among COMFORÇAs (Comissão de Acompanhamento e Fiscalização da Execução do Orçamento Participativo, Monitoring Committee for the Implementation of Participatory Budgeting) from different regions were important. Delegates and neighborhood associations from the Pampulha and Barreiro regions not only met on a regular basis to discuss PB and collective matters and exchanged advances through their respective blogs, but they were also working together to organize citywide meetings among civil society representatives parallel to the formal process in order to enhance collaboration and the development of common strategies (Delegado OP-BH 6 2008). Thus, as Baiocchi highlights, "deliberation over priorities and projects is not a discrete event that takes place as meetings begin and end. Rather, there is a great deal of work at the edges of the meetings that help official deliberation work smoothly: these include informal discussions and deliberation, the recruitment of new participants and the coordination of activities between neighborhoods" (2005: 86). As Abers argues, these experiences of solidarity and reciprocity are important as they make people conscious of the fact that they can work together in practice and trust each other, thereby reinforcing the prevalence of horizontal ties and the idea that cooperation is the best strategy to achieve collective goals.

Thus, our observations lead to the conclusion that in both Porto Alegre and Belo Horizonte, it is because of the primacy of informal practices of noncontrolled PB channels, collective training through associational work at the local level, and collaboration among citizens from across the city through formal and informal networks that PB has become a "school of democracy." In fact, such practices have contributed to foster the democratic learning goals of formal institutions. In tandem with initial changes in citizens' attitudes toward the governance process, the perception that both community leaders and politicians have of their respective roles in the political process also changed, reinforcing the potential for further citizenship learning. Community leaders began to see themselves as community representatives rather than political brokers. At the same time, politicians have also started to perceive the cycle as a citizenship learning opportunity. Adding to the initial learning effect, the development of such democratic attitudes became self-reinforcing through a demonstration process, as the new "way of doing things" proved to be successful for citizens: they now generally have better access to public resources, and urban development projects are distributed more effectively among the population.

Learning Politics as Usual: *Recife*

Recife, the capital of Pernambuco, has a unique and interesting sociopolitical history characterized by important political conflicts and a significant level of social contention and neighborhood mobilization around land tenure and urbanization issues. The case of Recife's PB program, however, presents a different story of citizenship learning than the two previous cases. In this case, the present form of PB^2 was introduced in 2001 under the leadership of the PT-led municipal coalition of Mayor João Paulo Lima e Silva,. In spite of official local government concern over raising citizenship awareness among the residents of Recife, however, the citizenship learning process observed through my interviews remains limited. While PB has become the main venue for channeling demands for public works in the city, replacing traditional clientelistic relationships with municipal councilors, it seems that participants learn that "politics as usual" remains the best strategy of accessing public goods in PB institutions. Thus, politics is still governed by cooptation, powerful individuals, and particularistic interests.

Looking at the case of Recife, one observation is particularly striking: the sense of belonging to a community and of working for all its members through PB is not as present among participants as it was in Porto Alegre and Belo Horizonte. As a delegate commented, this results in important misunderstandings regarding the delegates' roles in the PB cycle, which have major consequences:

> People think they are lending a hand to the municipal administration; they see it this way, as if they were working for the municipality. But it's not the case. [. . .] I am not lending a hand to the municipality; I am there to observe what they are doing with my money, which is different. Unfortunately, people still do not see it that way and think that they should get something in return.

If there is a mayor that doesn't have a larger vision, he is going to love it, give free transportation and food for everyone because then he will have everyone under his control. This is another big challenge that we face.

(Delegado OP Recife 3 2008)

In fact, many delegates I interviewed see themselves as working for the local government in the communities, and not as representatives of their community. Commenting on her role as a citizen representative, a PB delegate actively working as both delegate and PB coordinator of her region explained, "As a delegate, I am not from the public administration; I am supporting the administration because I share the same ideology, proposals and dreams" (Delegada OP Recife 1 2008).

Contrary to what we have observed in the two previous cases, where political preferences were gradually evolving among participants toward the pursuit of the common good, the main impetus behind participation in Recife is not to work collectively on the definition of the community's common good, but rather to support someone's particular claim or position within the community. The perceptions of delegates and participants in PB meetings are reflected in the type of goods they choose to defend. One delegate, explaining how he was deciding about the projects he would support in the upcoming vote, made it clear that personal interests remained at the center of their strategy:

First, [as candidates for delegates] we have to defend projects that are close to home, because if not, people don't vote. [. . .] The important thing is not only to win the project, but also to elect representatives because through this the other communities will see if yours is important or not. Generally, everyone defends his own project . . . "This is mine, and this one here is mine"—because you did it; you registered it and mobilized.

(Delegado OP Recife 2 2008)

One delegate in Recife's PB meetings expressed the hope that the process would transcend its present function of making political demands, and instead serve to empower citizens to exert control over their own destiny. However, at present, Recife's PB participants—mostly citizens with significant needs—still define their political preferences in individualistic terms:

You can't pretend that people are going there thinking about a social commitment. When you talk about this, those people don't really understand; they understand that this street needs to be paved; they understand about the barrier that will fall and leave them without a house. This they understand.

(Delegado OP Recife 3 2008)

Thus, while participation in community work led participants to transform their political preferences and support each other's claims in Porto Alegre and Belo Horizonte, in Recife PB has become a collective space for the formulation of particularistic demands that may not be oriented toward the achievement of the common good.

What explains the differences in outcomes observed? As we shall see, in the case of Recife, informal practices of cooption and demobilization tend to prevent formal institutions from playing their citizenship learning role. First, if the main political parties and elected politicians mostly remain outside of the process in both successful cases, in Recife, political control over the participatory process is a well-established informal practice. As an influential member of the local administrative team in charge of PB explained, delegates and forum coordinators have a partisan disposition:

> The forums are informally occupied by parties, used for the political struggles as are the other public spaces. The PT has a majority, but the other parties also organize local leaders in the neighborhood where they have their electoral and militant support bases.
>
> (Assesor do Planejamento Participativo 2008)

This view is corroborated by a PB delegate active in his community since the early phases of the PB program and who is now regional coordinator of the PB Forum:

> What I have seen here in the community associations is an important tendency to affiliate with political parties. There is a great incidence of political affiliation and a lot of people do so without really knowing why.
>
> (Delegado OP Recife 3 2008)

However, the political control exercised by political parties over the participatory process, by coopting of participants, remains hidden and informal, as a delegate explains:

> The majority (of delegates) are people who were pushed there by the PT, but this is something that we don't talk about in the forums, because it's an institution and so you can't talk in terms of parties *per se,* but most of the work is done from below by the PT and other political parties like the PCdoB, the vice-mayor's party.
>
> (Delegado OP Recife 2 2008)

One of the main manifestations of such political control is the use of PB delegates by the PT for electoral purposes.[3] The mobilization of many of the

2,400 PB delegates elected by their communities in PT electoral campaigns is a strategy that has been used in the 2004 and 2008 municipal campaigns. Although publicly condemned by PT officials, the predominance of behind-the-scenes informal practices leading to the cooption of PB delegates for political purposes has also been corroborated through denunciations made by several ex-delegates who decided to stop participating in what they call a political mechanism:

> In the beginning, PB was very good because it let social movements define what they wanted for their regions. But the program lost itself a bit in the past seven years as it mixed with politics. Doing so, it seems that it has armed itself with a whole structure to avoid contestation.
>
> (ex-delegate Evódia Lima in an interview with Valor Econômico, cited by: Mandl 2008)

The prevalence of this type of informal practice in which political elites instrumentalize PB institutions thus generates shared expectations about the process among participants that are different from the fundamental aim of PB. Rather than learning that working collectively for the community bene-fits everyone, citizens tend to confirm that democratic citizenship is "politics as usual," and that civic participation is equal to mobilizing for political elites.

Second, in this case, civil society groups' informal mobilization practices have not contributed to the strengthening of the collective action encour-aged by the formal participatory process. Partly because PB sought to break with CSO (civil society organization) leaders' traditional domination over participatory venues, and because of the tensions among civil society actors regarding the PB process (Wampler 2007; Montambeault 2009), there were few coordinated efforts by CSO members to informally pursue PB mobiliza-tional work at the grassroots level. As most community leaders involved in the PB process were associated with the ruling coalition, their mobilizational efforts were mostly oriented toward political support and electoral goals, while the noninvolved CSOs decried the PB process as a whole, attacking its credibility. Both practices generate shared negative expectations about the governance process, based upon the belief that PB was not a democratic venue for citizens to express their demands and monitor the state's decisions, which reinforced the idea that politics as usual—cooptation and contestation—was still the best way to access resources.

Thus, the failure of Recife's experiences to provide opportunities for cit-izenship learning is explained by the prevalence of informal practices of political control and of instrumentalized mobilizational structures that tend to circumvent the educative goals of PB institutions. This reality, at work in parallel to formal mobilization within PB institutions, has reinforced paternalistic, personalistic, and clientelistic understandings of politics among participants, undermining the educational benefits of the practice of deliberation and participation in formal institutions. In fact, as a PB Council (Conselho do Orçamento Participativo, Participatory Budgeting Council) councilor explained in a public meeting organized in 2003 by the organization ETAPAS, Equipe Técnica de Assessoria Pesquisa e Ação Social (Technical Team for Research Assistance and Social Action),

> During the past administrations, I did not understand because people were prioritizing certain streets, as delegates, and the work was not done. Over time, I realized that it was not important to be a delegate, but you needed to have political influence or the public works would not be done. In the new model, I thought things would be different. On paper it is different, but in reality it is not. Regrettably, that's all I can say.
> (Maria da Penha dos Santos, cited by: Barbosa da Silva and Silva 2003: 33)

This rather traditional understanding of politics and political preferences is reflected in the way the principal actors involved in PB see their own roles in the process, which contributes to reinforcing a sense of apathy toward the community. At the same time, politicians see the cycle as an opportunity for them to mobilize support, which contributes to a politicized understanding of the participatory process. The persistent lack of training for participants, as well as the apathy and misunderstandings about PB among the population, thus only contribute to the disempowerment of participants, reinforcing the prevailing conception of participation and, in turn, opening up the possibilities of cooption by political parties and perpetuating traditional ways of doing politics.

Conclusion

PB institutions are a formal space created to give a voice to the excluded, but the way the exercise of this voice has contributed to make citizens "better democrats" has been mixed across cases. Despite some variations among regions within each city, the overall trend in both Belo Horizonte and Porto Alegre has been the development of a new understanding of politics and citizenship by participants. Significant segments of the population have come to see themselves as proper citizens, working with the local government within PB channels on behalf of their community, and many now pursue the common good of the community's members at large through the deliberative process. The opposite has been found in Recife, where politicized interests prevail over the common good. The findings in the three Brazilian cases show that if institutional design has something to do with the potential for participatory deliberative institutions to become schools of democracy, informal institutions also matter. In fact, as we have seen in Porto Alegre, Belo Horizonte, and Recife, informal institutions—and the practices associated with them—can either contribute to or circumvent the aims of formal institutions by shaping the process and, in turn, the nature of citizenship learning and attitudes acquired through it.

The source of informal practices that impede formal participatory processes in Recife should be further investigated. My previous research has shown that these practices arise from specific endogenous political and social context that prevails in the city in which political competition is fierce, and where CSOs' opinions are divided around the question of PB (Montambeault 2009). Depending on the political and social context, political parties and CSOs are motivated by different sets of incentives in participatory institutions. This indicates that, though PB does create institutional channels for citizens to voice their concerns and demands to the local state, it is not a panacea. Its capacity to become a space for actually exercising this voice, become educated to do so, and to generate loyalty to the community through the process is subject to variations and, in certain cases, exit may remain the option considered best by citizens.

Notes

1. The PT is a leftist party that was formed in 1980 from an alliance of radical union leaders and a number of other "radical" groups, such as the "progressive" church, urban social movements, civil and human rights activists, and radical intellectuals and politicians (Keck 1992). This alliance, developed with people who were opposed to and who struggled against the previous authoritarian regime, was also a reaction against the lack of urban worker representation in traditional parties (Nylen 1997).
2. Two other models of participatory institutions were previously attempted in Recife: *Prefeitura nos Bairros,* followed by a light version of PB, which empowered community leaders rather than ordinary citizens (da Silva 2003).
3. Although the political use of PB institutions by PT candidates has been more thoroughly documented by the local media and in my interviews with participants in the field, there is evidence showing that other political parties have also used PB participants and their denunciations of the process's shortcomings in regions where they could secure more popular support (Vereadora 1 2008).

Bibliography

Abers, Rebecca. 2000. *Inventing Local Democracy: Grassroots Politics in Brazil.* Boulder: Lynne Rienner Publishers.

Abers, Rebecca. 2009. State-Society Synergy and the Problems of Participation in Porto Alegre. In *Widening Democracy: Citizens and Participatory Schemes in Brazil and Chile*, edited by P. Silva and H. Cleuren. Leiden: Brill.

Ackerman, John. 2003. Co-Governance for Accountability: Beyond "Exit" and "Voice". *World Development* 32 (3): 447–463.

Assesor do Planejamento Participativo. 2008. Interview with the author. Recife, Pernambuco, July 4.

Avritzer, Leonardo. 2002. *Democracy and the Public Space in Latin America*. Princeton: Princeton University Press.

Avritzer, Leonardo. 2009. *Participatory Institutions in Democratic Brazil*. Baltimore: The Johns Hopkins University Press.

Baiocchi, Gianpaolo. 2003. Participation, Activism and Politics: The Porto Alegre Experiment. In *Deepening Democracy: Institutional Innovations in Empowered Participatory Governance*, edited by A. Fung and E. O. Wright. London: Verso.

Baiocchi, Gianpaolo. 2005. *Militants and Citizens: The Politics of Participatory Democracy in Porto Alegre*. Stanford: Stanford University Press.

Baiocchi, Gianpaolo. 2009. Politicizing the Public: Participatory Budgeting in Porto Alegre. In *Widening Democracy: Citizens and Participatory Schemes in Brazil and Chile*, edited by P. Silva and H. Cleuren. Leiden: Brill.

Barber, Benjamin R. 1984. *Strong Democracy: Participatory Politics for a New Age*. Berkeley: University of California Press.

Barbosa da Silva, Evanildo, and Neide Silva. 2003. *Gestão participativa no Recife: do PREZEIS ao Orçamento Participativo*. Recife, Pernambuco: ETAPAS.

Chávez Teixeira, Ana Claudia, and Maria do Carmo Albuquerque. 2006. Presupuestos Participativos: Proyectos politicos, cogestion del poder y alcance democratico. In *La disputa por la construccion democratica en America Latina*, edited by E. Dagnino, A. J. Olvera and A. Panfichi. Mexico, DF: Fondo de Cultura Economica.

Cornwall, Andrea, and Schattan Coelho, eds. 2007. *Spaces for Change? The Politics of Citizen Participation in New Democratic Arenas*. London: Zed Books.

da Silva, Tarcisio. 2003. Da participação que temos a participação que queremos: O processo de Orçamento Participativo na Cidade do Recife. In *A inovação democrática no Brasil*, edited by L. Avritzer and Z. Navarro. São Paulo: Cortez Editora.

Dagnino, Evelina, Alberto J. Olvera and Aldo Panfichi, eds. 2006. *La disputa por la construcción democrática en América latina*. México, FCE, CIESAS, Universidad Veracruzana.

de Sousa Santos, Boaventura. 1998. Participatory Budgeting in Porto Alegre: Toward Redistributive Democracy. *Politics and Society* 26 (4): 461–510.

de Sousa Santos, Boaventura, ed. 2004. *Democratizar la democracia: Los caminos de la democracia participativa*. México, DF: Fondo de Cultura Económica.

Delegada OP Recife 1. 2008. Interview with the author. Recife, Pernambuco, July 8.

Delegado OP Recife 2. 2008. Interview with the author. Recife, Pernambuco, July 10.

Delegado OP Recife 3. 2008. Interview with the author. Recife, Pernambuco, July 2.

Delegada OP-BH 1. 2008. Interview with the author. Belo Horizonte, Minas Gerais, August 19, 2008.
Delegada OP-BH 2. 2008. Interview with the author. Belo Horizonte, Minas Gerais, August 18, 2008.
Delegada OP-BH 3. 2008. Interview with the author. Belo Horizonte, Minas Gerais, August 22, 2008.
Delegada OP-BH 4. 2008. Interview with the author. Belo Horizonte, Minas Gerais, August 24, 2008.
Delegado OP-BH 6. 2008. Interview with the author. Belo Horizonte, Minas Gerais, August 23, 2008.
Delegado OP-BH 7. 2008. Interview with the author. Belo Horizonte, Minas Gerais, June 25, 2008.
Elkin, Stephen L., and Karol Edward Soltan, eds. 1999. *Citizen Competence and Democratic Institutions*. University Park: The Pennsylvania State University Press.
Fung, Archon, and Erik Olin Wright. 2003. *Deepening Democracy: Institutional Innovations in Empowered Participatory Governance*. London: Verso.
Held, David. 2006. *Models of Democracy*. Stanford: Stanford University Press.
Helmke, Gretchen, and Steven Levitsky. 2004. Informal Institutions and Comparative Politics: A Research Agenda. *Perspectives on Politics* 2 (4): 725–740.
Hirschman, Albert O. 1970. *Exit, Voice and Loyalty: Responses to Decline in Firms, Organizations and States*. Cambridge: Harvard University Press.
Keck, Margaret E. 1992. *The Worker's Party and Democratization in Brazil*. New Haven: Yale University Press.
Mandl, Carolina. 2008. Delegados do Orçamento Participativo viram cabos eleitorais no Recife. *Valor Econômico*, May 6.
Mansbridge, Jane. 1980. *Beyond Adversary Democracy*. New York: Basic Books.
Mansbridge, Jane. 1995. Does Participation Make Citizens Better? *The Good Society* 5 (2): 3–7.
Mill, John Stuart. 1960 [1873]. *Autobiography*. New York: Columbia University Press.
Montambeault, Françoise. 2009. Models of (Un)Changing State-Society Relationships: Urban Participatory Governance and the Deepening of Democracy in Mexico and Brazil. PhD Dissertation, Political Science, McGill University, Montréal.
Nylen, William R. 1997. Contributions of the Workers' Party (PT) to the Consolidation of Democracy in Brazil. In *Latin American Studies Association Congress*. Guadalajara, Mexico.
Pateman, Carole. 1970. *Participation and Democratic Theory*. Cambridge: Cambridge University Press.
Puntual, Pedro. 2000. O processo educativo no orçamento participativo: Aprendizados dos atores da sociedade civil e do Estado. Dissertation, PUC-SP, Sao Paulo.
Putnam, Robert D. 1993. *Making Democracy Work: Civic Traditions in Modern Italy*. Princeton: Princeton University Press.

Samuels, David J. 2000. Reinventing Local Government? Municipalities and Inter-governmental Relations in Democratic Brazil. In *Democratic Brazil: Actors, Institutions and Processes*, edited by P. R. Kingstone and T. J. Power. Pittsburgh: University of Pittsburgh Press.

Schugurensky, Daniel. 2007. "This is Our School of Citizenship": Informal Learning in Local Democracy. In *Learning in Places: The Informal Education Reader*, edited by Z. Bekerman, N. C. Burbules and D. Silberman-Keller. New York: Peter Lang Publishers.

Tocqueville, Alexis de. 1981 [1835]. *De la démocratie en Amérique*. Vol. II. Paris: GF Flammarion.

Vereadora 1. 2008. Interview with the author. Recife, Pernambuco, July 4.

Wampler, Brian. 2007. *Participatory Budgeting in Brazil: Contestation, Cooperation, Accountability*. University Park: Penn State Press.

Wampler, Brian, and Leonardo Avritzer. 2005. The Spread of Participatory Democracy in Brazil: From Radical Democracy to Participatory Good Government. *Journal of Latin American Urban Studies* 7: 37–52.

CHAPTER 6

The Possibilities and Limits of Politicized Participation: Community Councils, Coproduction, and *Poder Popular* in Chávez's Venezuela

Michael M. McCarthy

Introduction

In Venezuela, the causal arrow between popular sector actors' mobilization and President Hugo Chávez's policies for organizing a state-led revolution runs in both directions. This is the synthesis to be drawn from literature that reignites a great debate over the top–down and bottom–up elements shaping radical populism. The more top–down accounts stress that Chávez is an autocratic populist bent on imposing socialism without regard for the low-level (or purely instrumental) nature of support this model enjoys among the population. Such interpretations view the high level of collective action through an Olsonian prism (Olson, 1971). The oil checkbook finances participatory initiatives with highly visible socioeconomic payoffs, which in turn attract strategic collective action from underprivileged actors (Hawkins and Hansen, 2006, Penfold, 2007, Corrales and Penfold, 2007, 2011, Hawkins, 2010a). Participation is not voluntary but fraudulent. Meanwhile, it provides a fertile environment for reinventing clientelistic linkages via state–citizen ties.

The more bottom–up account characterizes Chávez as a revolutionary concerned with redistributing political power. The Chávez government is developing Bolivarian democracy, a model that builds strong democracy through a state-in-society structure that relies heavily on what Michael Mann calls state infrastructural power (Mann, 1988). While participation is connected to the opportunity window created by Chávez's rise, under-privileged actors are active players in it, releasing pent-up social energy, expanding the scale of community activism, engaging institutions innovatively, and reimagining citizenship (Ellner, 2009a, 2009b, Ellner and Hellinger 2003, Smilde and Hellinger, 2011, Fernandes, 2010, Martinez et al., 2010, Cicerhelo-Maher, forthcoming).

Together, this literature makes three contributions: the high volume of participation is of intrinsic importance, promoting participation is a key policy of the Chávez government, and embedding microlevel politics in macrolevel processes is the sine qua non point of departure for comprehending popular sector participation in Venezuela today.[1] Yet, this debate is plagued by unresolvable points of disagreement such as contrasting perspectives on Chávez's rise, the conditions shaping his consolidation of power, and normative assumptions about what counts as meaningful participation.

This chapter attempts to move away from conflating empirical analysis of the scale of participatory input and the observed action output with normative approval of practices. To that end, I follow Fung and focus on one initiative of direct participation to carefully consider who participates, how participants communicate and make decisions, and what connections exist between participation and public action (Fung, 2006). This gives a better sense of "the range of proximate values that mechanisms of participation might advance and the problems they seek to address," in turn providing the empirical foundation for evaluating broader patterns (Fung, 2006, 66).

The Community Councils: Operationally Coproducing Organs

The focus of this chapter is on the primary example of state-promoted direct popular sector participation in Venezuela today, the population of 40,000 Community Councils. According to a recent review of the literature, authors construe the councils as either microlevel democracy at work or spaces highly subject to clientelism (Goldfrank, 2011, 42). Evidently, the conflating of empirical analysis with normative approval is alive and well. We need a definition of what councils do before hypothesizing what their operation reveals.

The councils are legally recognized, block-level communal governance organs constituted through public elections and operational through their embedding in the state governance matrix. Different councils use different collective action practices to manage their relationships with the state or other organizational forces. It is, therefore, exceedingly difficult to generalize about democratizing or undermining of democracy outcomes for the over 40,000 councils in the country. What is clear, however, is that the councils, in their operational mode, effectively become opportunities or cases for coproduction between state and society. By coproduction, I mean an active conjoining of state and society in which "inputs used to produce a good or service are contributed by individuals who are not 'in' the same organization" (Ostrom, 1996, 1073).

Thus, for purposes of examining the mechanisms of participation actually used and analyzing the observed effects, the councils may be classed as case studies in coproduction between, on the one hand, a communal governance organ that offers residents direct participation opportunities, and, on the other hand, agencies of the state enlisted to help communities address basic service problems. Moreover, the occasioning of coproduction and the highly flexible way bureaucrats and politicians administer this interactive process provides an opportunity to scale up. The councils can plausibly be construed as a programmatic example of how a macrolevel bargain over political incorporation is reproduced at the micro level. This bargain is structured by Chavismo, the political alliance associated with Chávez's rule. It is therefore shot through with dimensions of partisanship. We will need to describe the councils further to develop their connection to this bargain over incorporation and frame the puzzle.

Organizationally, a promotional team of self-motivated citizens and state-hired community promoters constitute a council. Then, the Assembly of Citizens, the forum in which the community population assembles, becomes the space through which the council is validated as a popularly or legitimately constituted organ. After acquiring a quorum of between 20 and 30 percent of the adult community, and then before the eyes of a state officiator, the assembly elects a committee of around 10–15 representatives whose two-year mandates can be revoked or renewed, and from which the executive leadership board is drawn. This constituent phase requires a great amount of community work and, it should be noted, depends on bureaucratic competence as to the community promoter's consistent application of the rules and filing of paperwork.

Functionally, a council serves as the community's authoritative board of governance, but, in terms of jurisprudence, there has not been a final word on whether a council is government per se. Suffice it to say, the council representatives mediate all activities in the community without formally governing over them. Spatially, the council's executive committee, which may operate in the street but have no permanent public office (i.e., may function out of someone's home), serves as the public gathering point of politics. It effectively becomes the "community seat" citizens visit to address a wide range of issues—from letters of residence to community service and conflict resolution—for between 150 and 400 families in urban areas, a minimum of 20 families in rural areas, and ten families in indigenous villages (*Ley de Consejos Comunales*, 2006, 2009). Councils operate throughout Venezuela as the center or seat of community politics, including in self-declared "independent republics" governed by the opposition.

Once councils are up and running, they have been registered with the state, and they effectively become the legitimate organ of *auto-gobierno* (self-government) a community uses for self-help. In their "community-centric" mode, councils perform governmental functions for the population they serve. Some representatives are paid out of council general funds for their labor while others are pro-bono volunteers. This raises an issue: where does the money for scaled-up self-help come from?

The councils' mandate for "state-centric" petitioning, coupled with their licensed status as fundable organizations with the capacity for financing community projects, is the jewel in their crowns. Their active role as functional project managers and doers that engage in commerce and source production make them highly valuable organs of community governance. It also speaks to the importance of their "state-centric" mode in which a council is dependent on the budgeting streams and the priorities of the formal state apparatus. The councils can raise funds through private sources. But since they lack fiscal powers and are embedded in a broader governance complex, they have weak self-help capacity. It should be apparent by now that state-based officials, working as community promoters, project liaisons, technical advisors, or donors, heavily mediate the constitutive and operational phases of the councils.[2]

According to government statistics, of the approximately 35,000 CCs that existed in the country in 2010, approximately one-third had in the past or were currently managing funds for community development projects, installing the stairs on a sloped walkway, paving a street, fixing inefficient water and sewage systems, repairing and/or modernizing houses, and building community centers (A. Moreno, director, Oficina de Atencion a las Organizaciones del Poder Popular, (Ministerio para las Comunas y la Proteccíon Social, personal communication, August 18, 2010). The number of projects is quite significant. However, their quality can be lacking, it is unclear if community management of project implementation is cost effective, and we do not have a good idea what the other councils do.[3]

Relatedly, the state's administration of the councils, which is headed by a central government ministry, exhibits serious shortcomings from the perspective of democratizing public administration. The ministry does not systematically process budget information pertaining to the councils—a census is reportedly in the pipeline of the ministry—or transparently explain the basis for funding community-solicited projects and providing different levels of technical support. Neither does the ministry sponsor a public deliberative process in which councils attend open assemblies and make presentations before state officials and neighbors about the viability and importance of their proposals (Machado, 2008).[4]

The councils, therefore, are not social movements, civil society associations, or neighborhood associations along the lines of Christian-based communities. Neither are they akin to participatory budgeting, a process described in Chapter 5 of this book and which can disclose spaces for political change on the scale of municipal accountability politics (Cornwall and Coehlo, 2007). Plain and simple, the councils are organs of community governance constituted through public elections and embedded in the state's governance matrix. They may, therefore, stimulate democratized collective decision-making, what some term "governance-driven democratization" (Warren, 2009), or they may be compelled from above in ways that undermine collective decision-making and produce cooptation (Selznick, 1984). The point to emphasize here is that outcomes will vary, case by case, on the context of state–society interaction. Recapping the problematic, then, we have a puzzle about the councils' practical function as mechanisms for coproduction, conceived as an active conjoining of state and society in which "inputs used to produce a good or service are contributed by individuals who are not 'in' the same organization," and the role of the bargain over political incorporation that works in the background animating this initiative (Ostrom, 1996, 1073).[5]

The Deal with the Councils

Centering on council activities pertaining to their state-centric mode, and viewing this mode of participation as taking place in an interstitial space between state and society, I address a practice-oriented question. Why has an organ of communal governance that, on the one hand, requires a great amount of citizen input to form and, on the other hand, possesses design problems for producing political change on the order of parish- or municipal-wide democratization, worked well enough to survive and expand its scope of operation as a valued form of participation? In other words, why, in spite of the significant work it takes to form a council and the flaws with the public administration of the initiative, do CCs advance values and acquire value?

My descriptive diagnosis of CC's constitutive and operational phases casts light on two general qualities of the councils: their practical problem-solving uses and the entry points they provide for actors to gain a sense of political recognition that involves making a public governance footprint and thus can be understood as resulting in political incorporation. These insights help us answer the puzzle of why the initiative has grown quantitatively—the council as a useful tool for self-help—and shed light on its qualitative appeal—the council as a vehicle for political recognition that results in a kind of political incorporation. But, there is an important connection between these two attributes, and therein lies the rub to the deal. The councils, through their interactions with other layers of government, do not reveal societal actors attaining equal access to the special dispensations offered to popular sector actors by the bargain over incorporation. True, actors opposed to Chávez can gain a sense of efficacy from their participation in a council, as they may take pleasure from contentious collective action in one or from appropriating a Chavista initiative for their own ends. But, their agency is much less likely to be recognized by Chavista officials at the center who, additionally, may see little reason to extend the deal's two special dispensations: discretion in the administration of funds and control over project management.

The argument presented in this chapter, that the councils are cases of state–society coproduction whose practice reveals a semiopen bargain of political incorporation, is a plausible generalization based on qualitative field work carried out in the capital city of Caracas, over three time periods, August, 2007, August 2008–December 2009, and August of 2010. Case studies of water projects executed by Community Councils, document analysis, semistructured interviews with council activists, formal interviews with government officials, and participant observations of different "community" and "state-centric" modes of activity by Community Councils in three different municipalities of Caracas constitute my data. Through my definition of the councils as cases of coproduction and reconstruction of how a bargain over political incorporation practically operates via the council experience, I suggest a practice-based rethinking of the categories regularly used to classify participation's meaning and score its value.

Objectives and Scheme of Analysis

In the first section I develop an analytic framework that situates my interpretation of the councils as communal governance organs offering opportunities for coproduction within the recent historical context. The second section sets the stage for a discussion of the councils' practical experiences by first analyzing how the transition to this model of community organization affected the organizational landscape. Then I offer a generic description of how a council comes into being and works as an organ for local governance coproducing with the state. The description gets thicker through examples of how a council can be converted into a problem-solving tool, how negotiations over project management can provide opportunities for political recognition and incorporation, and a rough sketching of coproduction's unintended consequence: governance networks between bureaucrats and citizens. I end the section by discussing the explicit and implicit ways in which partisanship affects council–state interaction and speculating on how this issue could manifest itself down the road.

Roots and Context of Popular Participation under Chávez

From between 1958 and 1973 Venezuela's "Punto Fijo" system was widely seen as a legitimate, consensus-based democracy (Martz, 1966, Levine, 1973). Then, in a shift exceeding the limits of this study, from 1974 to 1998 it became known as a "partyarchy," a government for the parties, by the parties, and of the parties (Coppedge, 1994). As to political action, participation was strictly representative (Molina, 2004) in that the system solicited indirect participation via the Social Democratic Acción Democrática, and the Christian Democratic (COPEI) Comité de Organización Política Electoral Independiente. Until 1989, for example, it was the parties that appointed mayors and governors. Moreover, the hierarchical internal structure of both of these political parties, and their ability to block contestation through the state, gave party elites significant discretion to determine the policy agenda (Coppedge, 1994, Crisp, 2000).

Simultaneously, the model of oil-based development began to fail. The plan to build *La Gran* Venezuela (The Great Venezuela) during the boom days of the 1970s oil shocks unraveled into a bust cycle, punctuated by the February 18, 1983, "Black Friday" currency devaluation and the Caracazo affair of rioting and looting over economic measures on February 27, 1989. Economic crisis dramatically changed the social landscape. By 1999 per capita gross domestic product (GDP) had fallen to 1962 levels, the purchasing power of an average salary was 33 percent of what it had been in 1978, and poverty was near 70 percent (Palma and Kelly, 2004). The expectation of social mobility that had attracted European immigration as recently as the 1960s and 1970s gave way to growing social resentment and class politicization (Ellner and Hellinger, 2003).

With a "throw the bums out" sentiment in the air Hugo Chávez's 1998 presidential campaign as an outsider candidate promising a *salve patria*—a revolutionary mission to rescue the homeland from neoliberalism—resonated widely. "Saving the patria" began with the creation of a popularly elected constituent assembly to rewrite the constitution. The new 1999 constitution created a stronger presidency as well as mechanisms for relocating debate over some policy issues to the local level, a trend that 1980s state reform had set in motion (López Maya and Gómez, 1990, Buxton, 2001). For example, the 1999 constitution's emphasis on "co-responsibility" between state and society stems from a conscious effort to prevent the reemergence of a sclerotic bureaucracy disconnected from ordinary people, as, critics argued then, was the case during the Punto Fijo system.

Toward this end, the constitution highlights the creation of linkages between the state and civil society as opportunities for societal groups to make bureaucracy responsive to public opinion (Article 326). As it is used in the constitution, "coresponsibility" invokes a particular notion of participatory democracy: it calls for society to play a "protagonist" role as a participant in public affairs ranging from elections, petitioning, recall referendum, and public consultations (Article 70) to the execution of welfare service projects at decentralized levels of government in which service delivery may be transferred to organized groups (*el pueblo organizado*) of society (Article 184). The councils, which first appeared in legislation as a potential future organizational form in a 2004 planning law (the Local Council for Planning and Participation Law, 2004) and were then created by statute in April of 2006 (Community Council Law, 2006), are now the legitimate form of *el pueblo organizado* sanctioned as the governance partner for coproducing welfare goods-bearing projects.

Interestingly, these new constitutional principles resonate with old patterns in state–society relations. Before parties became the vehicles for popular sector incorporation into the political system, the state welfare system served as the means for social incorporation. Coronil describes the Venezuelan state as a collective embodiment of the nation that, through incorporating citizens into the petroleum state's welfare system, doubles as a societal focal point for democratization (Coronil, 1997). Thus, the Venezuelan public sector, reported by Karl to be the largest in Latin America after Cuba (Karl, 1997), has always been a major point of reference for actors' demands while incorporation has in practice stood for democratization.

The historical structuring of civil society dependence on the state suggests two points. First, in the context of a departyfied organizational landscape, it was logical for Chávez to both encourage popular sector participation in public affairs and deploy the state to promote this initiative. In other words, parties, not the broader arrangement of political incorporation, through the state, a structural phenomenon rooted in the *rentier* culture associated with the country's petro-state (Karl, 1997), represented the problem with Punto Fijo democracy that could be changed.

Second, a "state in society" framework (Migdal, 1994) rejecting a rigid distinction between state and society is useful for gaining analytic purchase on the valuable qualities of the councils as organs of community governance. Such a framework alters our assumptions about what purposes participation serves. It helps us open the black box of state–society relations to see what operational dynamics take place between "public" and "private" actors embedded in interactive processes and model those dynamics as a factor intrinsic to the councils, but nonetheless, still independently influencing processes and outcomes. In this vein, the state-in-society framework does not turn resistance and domination into functionally useless or actually nonexistent options. It makes "voice" understandable in a variety of valuable forms, including voice as loyalty (Hirschman, 1970) and allows an emphasis on elements of participation that actually occur in practice, sometimes unintentionally, by dint of the collaborative state–societal governance taking place under the auspices of the council.

Simultaneously, the state-in-society framework encourages realistic thinking. The councils, through their mediations with higher levels of governance, form part of a state-in-society structure the Chávez government is trying to construct as part and parcel of its revolution. If microlevel participation inevitably engages a macrolevel process, then we need to carefully think through the implications of CCs' involvement in a governance regime they hardly control.[6] For example, a CC project can make an impact in a concrete way by improving the material conditions of local services and in a symbolic way by altering one's sense of self-esteem as a recognized political agent. Rejecting participation in a council, moreover, can be seen as an intentional effort to voice opposition to Chávez. Simply put, we cannot wish away the fact that the councils themselves are pregnant with political meaning.

Changing the Landscape: Transitioning to and Consolidating the Council Model

When the Chávez government initiated a massive effort to *organize* society in 2006 under the platform of *poder popular* (popular power), this broad mobilizing frame, billed as the fifth motor of the Bolivarian revolution, gained programmatic coherence through the simultaneous promotion of the Community Councils. Establishing coherence in the organizational landscape created costs and opportunities. The central government encouraged the integration of different thematic-oriented grassroots organizations—Water, Land, Health, Cultural Committee—under the councils' umbrella, and the transition to making the councils the structure for grassroots organization created varying levels of friction for different groups.

Sujatha Fernandes's 2010 study of long-standing urban social movements that express anarchist tendencies, but are also "Bolivarian" Chavistas, implicitly displays how partisan ties cushion the effects of programmatic disagreements. When displeased with government policy for not being sufficiently radical, these movements, instead of withdrawing their support for

Chávez, make a stink to call attention and gain leverage within *Chavismo*. Their radical militancy as Chavistas helps them receive state financial support and fend off efforts by the government to mediate or regulate their organizations. Moreover, because the CCs are territorially based organizations, a member of an "autonomous" Bolivarian social movement may also be an active participant in their council at no direct cost to their group (Fernandes, 2010, 248–249).

By contrast, the CC transition was of greater consequence to self-help grassroots groups that depend on the state for funds but have not cultivated political status within *Chavismo*. The near collapse of El Consorcio de Catuche and Proyecto Integral de Desarrollo Endogeno (Integral Project for Endogenous Development), Ojo de Agua, are illustrative examples.[7] Both based in the shanty towns of Caracas, these groups fulfilled the conditions for establishing collaborative relationships with the Chávez government, registering as civil society associations only to then learn they had to form councils to continue this relationship.[8] The government was not particularly flexible about the groups' decision to maintain their associations. For their part, leaders defended their position, reporting that reorganizing is not a chameleon-like process. Moreover, they pointed out, these organizations were specifically designed based on the nature and scope of a neighborhood-wide concern, which councils, because of their narrow territorial boundaries, may not be able to address as well.[9]

From a state power perspective, the main influence is inducing actors to participate in the councils as opposed to in other grassroots organization, such as a neighborhood association. The consolidation of the CCs as the legitimate model divides associational life into private nongovernmental associations, which face pressures from the government over their financing sources, and public state-sanctioned organs. This makes plausible the interpretation that, intentionally or not, organizational isomorphism is being structured (Dimaggio and Powell, 1983). In turn, the growth of these organizations legitimates the Chávez government's platform. However, when directly observing the interaction between street-level bureaucrats and CC leaders, one gets an impression different from that of the revolutionary rhetoric intimates.

Getting Organized and Operational

Getting a CC organized and operational is no day at the beach. With a bullhorn in hand a CC leader has to get the neighbors up and on their feet on weekends and has to follow detailed guidelines while completing a community inventory. Assembling an operational CC is a multistep organizational process that requires at least three skills: leadership, patience, and administrative diligence. It can easily take a full year to complete a community census and infrastructure map, hold successfully attended assemblies of citizens, schedule workshops to learn the rules, undertake elections, and carry out a diagnostic of community needs, not to mention the paper work for establishing the communal bank. The sustained commitment by residents, most importantly the promotional team that spearheads the effort, must be met on the state side by bureaucratic competence at the ministry and by way of a nondivisive but inspirational community promoter, the state's street-based employees who steer the residents through the logistics and rules of setting up a council process. More political personalities among community participation officers are likely to editorialize during workshops, noting, in no uncertain terms, which political leaders made this opportunity possible.

Once the executive and thematic committees are conformed, the council needs to be recognized by the state agency, FUNDACOMUNAL (La Fundacíon para la Comunidad y Promoccíon del Poder Communal), to become officially registered. FUNDACOMUNAL, the gatekeeper, is the only agency vested with the authority to recognize CCs.[10] Complaints that officials at FUNDACOMUNAL drag their feet in approving the paperwork of opposition or non-Chavista councils gain traction in the press because there is a perception, fed by the press, that state officials practice political discrimination. These reports are difficult to verify but the general opacity with which FUNDACOMUNAL functions and the obvious partisan affiliations of agency heads do not counter these suspicions.

After approval of eligibility and conferral of registered status from this agency, CCs cosign a notarized formal document with the state. Conformed and registered, CCs are given a seal to notarize paperwork (e.g., for completing letters of residence), which means they can designate council business as official. The next task is designing a project, getting its feasibility approved, and soliciting assistance from bureaucrats in completing the proposal. They are meant to submit to FUNDACOMUNAL but they can also submit project proposals to different public agencies, which, for different reasons, are interested in funding community development projects—some to show their commitment to Chávez's idea of *poder popular;* others to show that care for the community is not an exclusively Chavista idea. Hence, if the CCs complete the significant hurdle of FUNDACOMUNAL registration, then they enter into a polycentric governance system: if a project is rejected by the municipality, then its council designers can continue to lobby for the community by appealing to other elected (state governors) or unelected governmental centers (ministry's offices for community affairs) for funding.

Projects, which are sometimes channeled directly to an individual state agency and sometimes pass through an intermediary office that helps the CC design a project, are not always approved or rejected in a transparent manner. The criteria for approval and rejection are not very clear either, also a common complaint, while the state may shape the process according to disposable funds earmarked for specific projects. For example, a CC may be notified that a pot of money is available if the community has a shovel-ready project, that is, if the council submits a request for the project the government wants to fund. This can produce mixed reactions at the community level, where, depending on the level of need, the reaction may be "we need everything so, yes, we'll take it," or "we really need this, so why are you wasting my time about that!"

Getting to Work: Using Community Councils as Problem-Solving Tool

If a project is approved, the next step is getting the cash deposited in the CC "communal bank," a checking account opened in a state-owned bank.[11] With cash at its disposal, the CC can begin operating like a government office, issuing a call for project bids, choosing and contracting a company, and hiring labor to carry out the work. Within the overall scheme of the policy process, decisions over what company will do the work, who will be on the construction crew, and how materials are acquired (e.g., whether middle men are used or not) may appear very minor. However, it is important to remember that communities living in the shadows of the formal economy have probably not been involved in decision-making before and are accustomed to doing certain things (building their own houses, upgrading water systems, wiring their electricity, etc.,) their own way. Because in order to get by they have had to make do without the state, they are accustomed to being in control of doing projects, not the process of getting projects.

Once the process has reached this final stage of project execution and the CC is discharging orders on a daily basis, it is for all practical purposes operating like a government office. There may be state engineers that provide technical assistance but sometimes the community makes the calculations on its own and lives with the consequences. While the council is directly managing the process of project implementation, there is little the government can do in terms of regulatory supervision because so many little decisions are taken by the CC autonomously. While there is an accountability committee within the council structure, and councils that administer contracts within their financing guidelines, the incentives for graft are very high. In some contracts 50 percent of the budget is awarded up front and popular lore circulates of how cash was handed out during the first year of the initiative. By 2010, however, government liaisons to councils were spreading the rumor, also reported in the press, that the state will prosecute corrupt CCs (A. Moreno, personal communication, August 18, 2010).

Individual Chavista deputies have admitted concerns about the "probity" of certain CCs (*El Universal,* May 7, 2011), and according to press reports from both public and private media outlets there are 1,500 cases of corruption under investigation (*El Universal,* May 7, 2011, Aporrea.org, April, 27, 2011).[12] Still, even if through some miracle the cases were prosecuted swiftly and fairly, the amount of overlap between funding agencies and the flexible way money has been moved around may militate against efforts to seriously regulate the problem. The convoluted nature of the relationship between graft, CCs operations, and the government's capacity to control what has grown into a byzantine budgeting process is usefully illustrated by this conversation I had with a Community Council leader while shadowing him and a work crew trench a new pipeline for potable water in their community:

> "The people from SAFONAAC (a regulatory agency of the Venezuelan Ministerio para las Comunas y la Proteccíon Social—Ministry of the Communes and Social Protection) are coming up to visit the community today," said Asdrubal, reading his cell phone. "Why?" I asked. "They [the state] involuntarily gave our Community Council two different sums of money for the same project—laying a pipeline that will connect us to the city water system," he explained. Prying, I asked, "Will this be a problem?" Undisturbed, he continued, "No. We as a community have other needs; we want to build a police module, which in fact was our first priority according to the assembly of citizens. As long as we administer and execute the second project with our own hands in a way that benefits the community, everything will be fine. They will understand."
>
> *La Calle 8, Nuevo Leon, Caracas, September, 2009*

During the subsequent conversation between Asdrubal and the representatives from SAFONAAC (Servicio Autónomo Fondo Nacional de los Consejos Comunales)—who were wearing vests with the slogan *el pueblo rinde cuentas al pueblo* (the people hold the people accountable)—nothing approximating even a light slap on the wrist was mentioned. My three months of follow-up on the case suggested no attempt by the state to renegotiate and ask for the money back.

This is the essence of the bargain's special dispensation regarding the council as a problem-solving tool. CC leaders have the privilege to administer state funds with little oversight from the state. Because the state recognizes the importance of permitting local control, CC leaders are sometimes able to convert these organs for their own purposes, turning what appears to be the next great ideological tool for state power into a pragmatic problem-solving mechanism, reinforcing the point: it is in this last stage of project execution, wherein a CC is permitted to do pretty much as it pleases, that a community senses it has ownership of its own affairs and is perversely but truly exercising popular power.

Coproduction and Compliance: Recognition as Political Incorporation

A good criticism of coproduction as self-help is that it is a ruse of political incorporation. After all, if the state is the classic means for political incorporation in Venezuela, then how does self-help qualify? The hazard of policymakers enacting coproduction in a way that passes responsibilities onto an undercapacitated citizenry is real, as evidenced by the inadequate quality of some public works projects undertaken by councils. But the difference lies in the details of how coproduction is translated through the platform of *poder popular* and interpreted by CCs from marginal zones.

The government has melded the elements of state-promoted community mobilization and an understanding of popular sovereignty as self-government to argue that exercising popular power requires that "the people" assume some of the important rights and responsibilities of rulers. In turn, coproduction is intentionally managed to give state-society relations the feel of a collaborative enterprise sensitive to local norms of community development. The fashioning of coproduction as the deploying of state offices to link government with community organization, but then letting participants drive the execution process, is a special dispensation of the bargain over incorporation meant to increase popular power's appeal.

In Santa Lucia, a *barrio* (neighborhood) nestled in the valleys of Baruta, a largely middle-class municipality of Caracas, a Water Committee that has since become a Community Council, asked the public utility if it could be in charge of procurement and hiring of the work crew. Their complaint was that state employees have side-deals with particular contractors who inflate costs and hire workers that are rude to the community residents. Moreover, if the work crew consisted of hands from Santa Lucia, it would work harder than privately hired labor, ask for a lower wage (no transportation costs), and inspire a positive spirit in the community—usually someone on the block makes lunch and coffee, and the entire crew eats and breaks there together. Council participants wanted to engage in "home grown" community service funded by the state.[13] Of course, the state has an interest in feeding this perception since in this image its hands appear helpful, not meddlesome.

The main point underneath the economic efficiency argument is that it is not easy for the central state to enter into communities that the political system has neglected and announce it would like to now lend a hand. This particular community had a contentious history with the water company that took years to work out. It had protested at the public utility's headquarters many times before it formed a water committee and willingly accepted help for its problems. At this level, where the actors' engagement with the political system is primarily through exclusion, communities first have to allow the state to lend a hand. That is, after years of perceiving exclusion, residents may not accept the state's assistance since they may not trust the seller.[14]

To extend this argument further, in shanty town areas the Venezuelan central state's steering capacity over the stage of policy implementation is dependent on bureaucrats' coordination of networks of informally organized groups of "public and private actors who interact in order to define common goals and ways to realize them" (Sorensen and Torfing, 2003, 610). Governance networks provide a crucial intervening variable: the wherewithal for state and society to solve each other's problems. They mobilize capacities (including important intangibles like community compliance) for approved policy to become implemented projects (Keck and Abers, 2006: 7, 2009). Moreover, they create momentum for actors to rehearse different roles in order to solve the problem at hand.

Rehearsing these alternate roles may leave an important imprint on a community's perception of the council and the state agency that employs the networking bureaucrats. Along these lines, the promotion of the CCs as a process of coproduction that funds the work that residents already do out of their own pockets can subtly transform a normally antagonistic process into one of cultivating community will to participate. In this sense, the model of popular power can be enacted to softly elicit the mobilization that an organization needs. Similarly, it can provide a deft enough touch for actors to feel recognized for the efforts on their own terms and be incorporated by dint of their community-level contributions to public governance.

Discussion: The Layering of Partisan Politics

State-society collaborations that are synergistic in this way may represent the minority experience. What about examples in which, instead of state-society collaboration, there is state-society conflict? According to complaints from groups that organized councils but then faced great difficulty in gaining state registration from FUNDACOMUNAL, having the will and means to participate actively while following the rules of organizing a CC is not necessarily enough to guarantee effective political action in Chávez's Venezuela (*El Nacional*, January 22, 2012; personal communication, Miguel Gonzalez Marregot, vice-president, Consejo Local de Planificación Publica, Baruta). This raises a question: is the background role of partisanship as a justification for actors to participate becoming a foreground tool bureaucrats use to recruit and sponsor certain participants' organizations over others?

The mixing of partisan and programmatic elements has reached a level beyond the threshold of a party or politician forcefully defending their policy record as an exclusive reflection of their efforts. This not only refers to the Community Councils Law reform in 2010 and passing of laws regulating *poder popular,* which incorporated language about participatory organs as representing and promoting socialistic values and sparked concern that CCs not deemed "socialist" could have their mandates invalidated. More directly relevant is the fact that Chávez and his ministers apply partisanship bluntly, dividing the people into revolutionary and antirevolutionary segments, and claim state policies are Chavista policies as when the Minister of Participation—now the president's chief of staff—appealed for all Community Councils and grassroots groups promoted by the government to join Chávez's campaign for the elimination of term limits on elected office in January, 2009. Policy conferences with councils sponsored by bureaucratic offices have introduced electoral politics dimensions by inviting Chavista politicians on the campaign trail to address the audience (Personal field research).

These changes coincide with the construction of the Partido Socialista Unida de Venezuela (PSUV), which began in 2006, immediately generating skepticism about the connections between the party and the councils. There have been numerous reports of partisan meddling in the affairs of the CCs (Garcia-Guadilla, 2007). Defining meddling, though, can be tricky. A CC leader may also be a local representative of the PSUV, and a council may meet on Saturday while the party sessions on Sunday. The party's presence at the grassroots certainly represents a change in how politics is organized within society. Up until 2008, when the PSUV made its electoral debut in regional elections for mayors and governors, *Chavismo* had governed without a well-organized party structure while grassroots organizations have been a fixture of the landscape throughout and before Chávez's tenure.[15] Aware that making politics too organized could be at cross purposes with its vision of democracy as popular sovereignty and could evoke bad memories of the Punto Fijo system, Chávez moved carefully to promote the party and foster the CCs. In the first three years of their coexistence, 2007–2009, the judgment that the two organizational forms could coevolve, mediating each other without one disrupting the other's order, seemed correct.

On the one hand, there continues to be converting from below, by which I mean that members of the CCs appropriate the meaning of their organizations in line with their own understandings of how they should function. The flexible way government has gone about implementing the initiative of promoting the CCs and the lax attitude it has shown in enforcing the rules of the CC Law, including the reforms to the law, are in a sense concessions to community activists that they may engage in conversion. As suggested, the tolerance or noncontestation of conversion from below is a way of paying respect to the bargain about incorporation.

On other hand, with a base to build on, layering from above has begun. This layering refers to bureaucrats or local party brokers who keep a watchful eye over the affairs of the CC through the *Gobierno Parroquial* (Parish Government) arms of the mayor's office or the PSUV-run *Sala de Batalla* (the Rooms for Ideological Battle), which has gained salience as a Chavista-rallying space in the opposition-governed Caracas municipality of Caracas. Interviews, personal observations, other reports, and media analysis suggest that there is favoritism, but that (unlike what occurred under the PRI in Mexico, for example) membership in the PSUV is not a widely applied prerequisite for participating in or forming a council or for a constituted council to generate effective participation in its relationship with the state. Nevertheless, the pervasive influence of informal rules and practices suggests a different structural hypothesis: central government bureaucrats are less likely to expend energies forming the relational ties with councils that are not on the "correct" side of the pro/con Chávez debate.

The opposition does have the capacity to form its own networks. But because most of the agenda-setting elements (control of eligibility and registration, project approval and financing) of the CC process are centralized in FUNDACOMUNAL and the other agencies of the Ministry of the Communes and Social Protection, the Bolivarian networks of *Chavismo* possess higher likelihood of producing coproduction. Such effective participation with the state contributes to *pareto* efficient outcomes. It increases the lot of some without directly reducing the lot of others, thus producing inequalities that may not strike us as having resulted from an intentional plan to skew the distribution of goods. Thus, the broader Chavista political project, which rejects pluralistic cooperation with the opposition, curtails the openness of the CC process and limits the possibilities for some citizens' direct action to be translated into public action, creating a zero-sum game of inclusion and de facto exclusion.

A potential intervening factor is opposition support for the CCs, which is growing but still a bit lukewarm. Nevertheless, competition between Chavista and opposition parties over who is more "popular" and a better ally of "the people" is not likely to overcome polarization on either side, even if there are examples of councils where different viewpoints successfully cohabitate. Many anti-Chávez actors instinctively perceive initiatives promoted by the government to be Chavista policies. To them, not participating in them is akin to expressing opposition to the government. The reverse is true for many pro-Chávez actors. A process of self-selection in which pro-Chávez actors see CCs as avenues for supporting the president may well explain why they are more likely to participate in state-promoted processes (Hawkins, 2010b). According to Venezuelan anthropologist Fernando Coronil, "During his [Chávez's] rule, "the people" (*el pueblo*) have become widely recognized as the sovereign (*el soberano*). Even if much would have to happen to turn this principle into reality, in my view this is a formidable accomplishment. Now it is impossible to participate in politics in Venezuela without recognizing the centrality of common people" (Coronil, 2008). If this discursive shift really makes a difference by placing popular politics front and center and prompting a learning cycle that may either burn out (Levine, 2006) or leave reservoirs of social energy (Hirschman, 1984), then the setbacks for pluralism need underscoring, too. The argument that intense politicization of all policies, which Chavistas justify as part of their freedom to express political viewpoints as citizens, inevitably generates the dissolution of borders between party and state on the one hand, and party and public on the other hand needs serious consideration in order for common people to have effective voice (Gómez, 2009).[16]

Certainly, some actors will never feel welcome speaking in publics, let alone partisan publics, which, if trends continue, could grow into an inherent trait of council experience. Yet partisan and public are not necessarily mortal enemies. Put differently, there is no public without politics. This is not to say that all-out polarization is the form of political contestation preferred to pluralism. If partisan and popular politics become imbricated to the point of yielding non-Habermasian partisan publics, then this would be a marked improvement over the fate of the Committees for the Defense of the Revolution in Cuba that went from instruments for cultural transformation to vigilante groups of an authoritarian state (Fagen, 1969). But it will also be a far cry from the most successful cases of participatory budgeting in which transition from one administration to the next did not spell the demise of the policy (Abers, 2000, Gómez, 2007).

Conclusion

This chapter has shown that analysis of the Community Councils in Venezuela can focus on the variety of values and purposes this governance mechanism can advance as it is used from above and below in what I have termed cases of coproduction. This approach may be useful since we typically assume that the service provider stands above and outside the context of its users, contacting them at the moment of service delivery and then subsequently withdrawing. I have used coproduction to describe the councils because it refers to a process in which the operational dynamics of service delivery consist of mutually impinging activities by individuals from state and society. Thus, there is no passive dimension to the relationship, complicating any neat fit between the case and the conventional notions of citizenship and clientelism.

The emphasis on the councils' practical function has hopefully not conflated the empirical questions of scale of input and scope of output with normative concerns of whether these outcomes are produced the right way. This is not to say attention has been diverted away from whether the problem-solving methods councils rely on are proper. The fact that actors can gain a sense of political recognition, and we can plausibly understand them to have been politically incorporated through perverse means such as graft or irregularly handling state funds, raises provocative questions about what it means to be a political player or, shall we say, entrepreneurial activist, in Venezuelan politics.

Since the decadent 1970s at least, this is not a terribly new phenomenon in Venezuelan politics. Coronil's and Karl's studies of how the petroleum state created a spoils system that ran throughout political relations, creating divisions and alliances in its wake, certainly ring true (Coronil, 1997, Karl, 1997). That this spoils system is being reinvented in more pointed form with acerbic language of polarization doing the legwork of establishing strict terms of conflict for being cut in to the bargain or not is a pity.

But a reimagination of what it means to be politically included has also taken place as a result of the councils, and the flexible way they have been managed. Whether actors are expressing their voices through the seemingly minor issue of community control over project execution or demanding they be given the right of first refusal, that is, the option to accept or reject state assistance, the councils have fruitfully changed the terms of political dialogue and action for those operating from the margins. Meanwhile, as an initiative with a widening level of acceptance across the political spectrum, the councils' relative success story has increased appreciation in society of what those who felt excluded want to do for government and for government to do for them. This success story helps explain why people would pour their time and energy into projects of significant scope and how the combined actions of state and societal actors make that sort of participation possible, effective, and widely valued.

Acknowledgment

I gratefully acknowledge Fulbright-IIE, the Inter-American Foundation Grassroots Development Fellowship, and the Ford Foundation for their financial support in carrying out this research's fieldwork. I would like to thank the editors of the book for their comments that helped improve the coherence of this chapter, as well as Sam Handlin and Manuel Antonio Garretón, discussants at workshops for this book, whose feedback aided my thinking about the subject matter greatly. Any errors, of course, are my own. The names of the actors interviewed and the places where the author observed their participation have been changed

Notes

1. Popular sector participation refers to a particular arena and method of political action. In Venezuela, the arena is the grassroots level such as the local school house, community center, or even the street count. The phrase *los sectores populares* before conjured images of lower-class and lower-middle-class workers engaging in functional-based political action, primarily through labor unions. Today, according to Collier and Handlin (2009), it refers to the same category of actors but it increasingly refers to direct participation aimed at discrete problem solving. I use popular sector participation in this sense—referring primarily to the mechanisms used for community self-help processes.
2. The distinction between community and state-centric modes of participation is inspired by Houtzager and Acharya (2011).
3. Rumors of the CCs replacing the municipal system have proven to be unfounded so far, though the elimination of parish-level representative boards, the Junta Parroquial, does not really allay fears.
4. Some municipalities do, however, sponsor such open air assemblies through the public planning meetings guided by the Consejo Local de Planificación y Participación (CLPP) law that was first passed in 2002, then drifted into a trivially significant mechanism, and was recently updated in 2010 during the passage of a new package of popular power laws.
5. For Ostrom, the main factor differentiating organizations is their places within the broader category of state and society. Thus, it is a bit unclear if she would consider the collaboration of two separate civil society organizations, for instance, a church charity and a grassroots neighborhood association, to be coproduction. Yet, her general point remains valid (Ostrom, 1996, 1073).
6. This approach has a strong affinity with a practice-grounded methodology of analyzing political socialization as it takes place through state–society encounters. For a splendid use of this approach to explain Peronist politics, see "From the Client's Point(s) of View. How Do Poor People Perceive and Evaluate Political Clientelism," Auyero (1999).
7. On the case of Catuche, see Barreto (2009). Information regarding the PIDE organization was compiled through participant observation and interviews by the author.
8. This trend correlates with *Chavismo*'s record of trying to mediate secondary associations from corporate and union sectors. If that intervention fails to convert how the organization operates, they promote parallel organizations that are more aligned with its platform, both in form and content (Salamanca, 2004).

9. The term "civil society" has mostly disappeared from Venezuelan political discourse. After the opposition appropriated the term "civil society" to frame its opposition to the Chávez government as a democratic society's struggle against an authoritarian regime, it became a highly charged term that was understood as code for private opposition to the government.

10. Popularly elected administrations and governmental offices of the civil service employ community participation promoters who are knowledgeable about the process of forming CC. Thus, a community promotion officer may aid a community in the process of forming a CC, though their specific mandate may not be to promote CCs. The only offices specifically dedicated to forming and registering CCs are those housed within the Ministerio para las Comunas y la Protección Social, formerly—as of 2008—known as the Ministerio de Partcipación y la Protección Social.

11. The 2010 reform to the Community Councils Law eliminated the Banco Comunal in an effort to change perceptions of the council's financing function, which is now formally known as la Unidad Administrativa y Financiera.

12. One case of corruption has been publicly prosecuted—by the attorney general's office in Merida state. After being published on the attorney general website on March 22, 2012, http://www.ministeriopublico.gob.ve/web/guest/principal?p_p_id=101_INSTANCE_CZf9&p_p_lifecycle=0&p_p_state=maximized&p_p_mode=view&p_p_col_id=column-3&p_p_col_pos=1&p_p_col_count=2&_101_INSTANCE_CZf9_struts_action=%2Fasset_publisher%2Fview_content&_101_INSTANCE_CZf9_urlTitle=condena-para-representante-de-consejo-comunal-por-corrupcion&_101_INSTANCE_CZf9_type=content&redirect=%2Fweb%2Fguest%2Fprincipal, accessed March 22, 2012. Online tracking of the story revealed that it primarily circulated in the private media and was not republished by the official news agency of the state, the *Agencia Venezolano de Noticias*, or newspapers supportive of the government. Corruption can be easily and effectively polarized in the Venezuelan public sphere, and the government is keenly aware of this fact.

13. In a survey of popular sector actors' perceptions of the councils, 61 percent of those surveyed argued that more responsibilities should be transferred from local government to the councils. About this insight, the survey's main investigator, Jesus Machado, said, "The people perceive there to be a better relationship with the Council than with the Central Government. People are looking for democracy without intermediate links or institutions" (Centro Gumilla, 2010; *El Universal,* March 14, 2010).

14. For example, *Hidrocapital,* the public water company for the Caracas region that plays a very large role in the lives of marginal communities, used to be derided as *Hidrocriminal.* The credibility that the company has earned among some sectors stems from its dedicated community affairs team that, since 1999, has been holding public meetings called the *Consejo Comunitario de Agua* (the Water Community Council) in neighborhoods with low-quality service.

15. Chavismo's previous party form, the *Movimiento de Quinta Republica,* was never employed in an effort to organize society.
16. From within Chavismo, long-term members of "la lucha popular" who spoke out against party cooptation of labor unions and peasant federations during Punto Fijo have voiced serious concerns about the intolerant posture of the PSUV toward autonomous organizing. See, for example, Lander (2011), Arconada (2009, 2011), López (2011).

References

Books and Articles

Abers, Rebecca, 2000. *Inventing Local Democracy: Grassroots Politics in Brazil.* Boulder, CO: Lynne Rienner Publishers.

Arconada, Santiago, 2009. "La Conciencia: Carta abierta a Presidente Chávez," Accessed January 16, 2009 http://www.aporrea.org/poderpopular/a70514.html.

Arconada, Santiago, 2011. "Carta abierta al Presidente Hugo Chávez Frías: El otro diálogo," Aporrea.org, 02/02/11, Accessed March 16, 2011 http://www.aporrea.org/ideologia/a116888.html

Auyero, Javier, 1999. "From the Client's Point(s) of View: How Do Poor People Perceive and Evaluate Political Clientelism," *Theory and Society,* Vol. 28, pp. 297–334.

Buxton, Julia. 2001. *The Failure of Political Reform in Venezuela.* London: Ashgate.

Cicerhelo-Maher, George, forthcoming. "We Created Him: A People's History of the Bolivarian Revolution," Unpublished Manuscript.

Collier, Ruth Berins and Samuel Handlin, eds., 2009. *Reorganizing Popular Politics: Participation and the New Interest Regime in Latin America.* University Park: Pennsylvania State University Press.

Coppedge, Michael. 1994. *Strong Parties and Lame Ducks: Presidential Partyarchy and Factionalism in Venezuela.* Stanford: Stanford University Press.

Crisp, Brian, 2000. *Democratic Institutional Design: The Power and Incentives of Venezuelan Politicians and Interest Groups.* Stanford: Stanford University Press.

Cornwall, Andrea and Verta Shattan Coelho, eds., 2007. Spaces for Change? The Politics of Citizen Participation in New Democratic Arenas. London: Zed Books.

Coronil, Fernando, 1997. *The Magical State: Nature, Money, and Modernity in Venezuela.* Chicago: University of Chicago Press.

—— 2008. "Chávez's Venezuela: A New Magical State?" *ReVista: Harvard Review of Latin American Studies,* Vol. 8, No. 1, pp. 3–4.

Corrales, Javier and Michael Penfold, 2007. "Venezuela: Crowding Out the Opposition," *Journal of Democracy,* Vol. 18, No. 2, pp. 99–113.

—— 2011. *Devil in the Tropics: Hugo Chávez and the Political Economy of Revolution.* Washington: Brookings Institute Press.

Dimaggio, Paul and Walter Powell, 1983. "The Iron Cage Revisited: Institutional isomorphism and collective rationality in organizational fields," *American Sociological Review,* Vol. 48, No. 2, pp. 147–160.

Ellner, Steve, 2009a. "A New Model With Rough Edges: Venezuela's Community Councils," *NACLA*, May/June.

—— 2009b. *Rethinking Venezuelan Politics: Class, Politics, and the Chávez Phenomenon*, Boulder, CO: Lynne Rienner Publishers.

Ellner, Steve and Dan Hellinger, eds., 2003. *Venezuelan Politics in the Chávez Era: Class, Polarization, and Conflict*. Boulder, CO: Lynne Reiner Publishers.

Fagen, Richard F., 1969. *The Transformation of Political Culture in Cuba*. Stanford: Stanford University Press.

Fernandes, Sujatha, 2010. *Who Can Stop the Drums? Urban Social Movements in Chávez's Venezuela*. Durham: Duke University Press.

Fung, Archon, 2006. "Varieties of Participation in Complex Governance," *Public Administration Review*. December, pp. 66–75.

Garcia-Guadilla, María Pilar, 2007. "El poder popular y la democracia participativa en Venezuela: Los Consejos Comunales." Paper presented at the 2007 Meeting of the Latin American Studies Association (LASA), Montreal.

Goldfrank, Benjamin, 2011. "Los Consejos Comunales: Avance o retroceso para la democracia venezolana?" Iconos n. 40, FLACO-Ecuador.

Gómez Calcaño, Luis, 2007. "The Politics of Deepening Local Democracy: Decentralization, Party Institutionalization, and Participation," *Comparative Politics*, 39:2 (January).

—— 2009. La dissolucion de las fronteras: sociedad civil, representación, y política en Venezuela. Caracas: CENDES-UCV.

Hawkins, Kirk, 2010a. *Venezuela's Chavismo and Populism in Comparative Perspective*. Cambridge: Cambridge University Press.

—— 2010b. "Who Mobilizes? Participatory Democracy in Chávez's Bolivarian Revolution," *Latin American Politics and Society*, Vol. 52, No. 3, pp. 31–66.

Hawkins, Kirk and Hansen, Jason. 2006. "Dependent Civil Society: The Circulos Bolivarions in Veneuzela," *Latin American Research Review*, Vol. 41, No. 1, pp. 102–132.

Hirschman, Albert O. 1970. *Exit, Voice and Loyalty: Responses to Decline in Firms, Organizations and States*. Cambridge: Cambridge University Press.

—— 1984. *Getting Ahead Collectively: Grassroots Experiences in Latin America*. New York: Pergamon Press.

Houtzager, Peter and Acharya, Arnab, 2011. "Associations, Active Citizenship, and the Quality of Democracy in Brazil and Mexico," *Theory and Society*, Vol. 40, No. 1, pp. 1–36.

Karl, Terry Lynn, 1997. *The Paradox of Plenty: Oil Booms and Petro-States*. Berkeley: University of California Press.

Keck, Margaret and Abers, Rebecca, 2005–06. "Civil Society and State-Building in Latin America," *LASA Forum*, Winter.

—— 2009. "Mobilizing the State: The Erratic Partner in Brazil's Participatory Water Policy," *Politics and Society*, Vol. 37, No. 2, pp. 289–314.

Lander, Edgardo, 2011. "Venezuela: ¿Radicalizar el proceso? ¿Más estatismo verticalista y personalista o más democracia y más participación?" in *Cal y Arena* número 1, Caracas, enero.

Levine, Daniel, 2006. "Civil Society and Political Decay in Venezuela," in Richard Feinberg, Carlos Waisman and Leon Zamosc, eds., *Civil Society and Democracy in Latin America*, New York: Palgrave Macmillan/St Martins Press, pp. 169–192.

Levine, Daniel, 1973. *Conflict and Political Change in Venezuela*. Princeton: Princeton University Press.

López, Reinaldo, 2011. "La invisibilización de la crítica produjo mucho daño a la revolución," Correodel Orinoco, February 6. Accessed on March 8 at http:// saberypoder.blogspot.com/2011/02/la-invisibilizacion-de-la-critica.html

López Maya, Margarita and Gómez Calcaño, Luis, 1990. El tejido de peneolope: La reforma del estado en Venezuela (1984–1988). Caracas: CENDES-UCV.

Machado, Jesus, 2008. "Estudio de los Consejos Comunales en Venezuela." Caracas: Centro Gumilla.

——— 2009. "Estudio cuantitativo de opinión sobre los Consejos Comunales." Caracas: Centro Gumilla.

Mann, Michael. 1988. *States, Wars, and Capitalism: Studies in Political Sociology*. Oxford: Blackwell.

Martz, John, 1966. Accion Democratica: The Evolution of a Modern Democratic Party. Princeton: Princeton University Press.

Martinez, Carlos, Michael Fox, and Jojo Farrell, 2010. *Venezuela Speaks!:Voices from the Grassroots*. Oakland, CA: PM Press.

Migdal, Joel, 1994. "The State in Society: An Approach to Struggles for Domination," in Migdal. et al., *State Power and Social Forces: Domination and Transformation in the Third World*. Cambridge: Cambridge University Press, pp. 7–34.

Molina, Jose Enrique, 2004. "The Unraveling of Venezuela's Party System: From Party Rule to Personalistic Politics and Deinstitutionalization," in McCoy and Myers, eds., *The Unraveling of Representative Democracy in Venezuela*. Baltimore: Johns Hopkins University Press, pp. 152–180.

Olson, Mancur, 1971. *The Logic of Collective Action: Public Goods and the Theory of Groups*. Vol. 124. Cambridge, Mass: Harvard University Press.

Ostrom, Elinor, 1996. "Crossing the Great Divide: Coproduction, Synergy and Development," *World Development*, Vol. 24, No. 6, pp. 1073–1087.

Palma, Pedro and Kelly, Janet, 2004. "The Syndrome of Economic Decline and the Quest for Change," in McCoy and Myers, eds., *The Unraveling of Representative Democracy in Venezuela*. Baltimore: Johns Hopkins University Press, pp. 202–230.

Penfold-Becera, Michael, 2007. "Clientelism and Social Funds: Evidence from Chávez's Social Missions," *Latin American Politics and Society*, Vol. 49, No. 4, pp. 63–84.

Salamanca, Luis, 2004. "Civil Society: Late Bloomers," in Jennifer McCoy and David Myers, eds., *The Unraveling of Representative Democracy in Venezuela*, Baltimore: Johns Hopkins University Press.

Selznick, Philip, 1984. *TVA and the Grass Roots: A Study of Politics and Organization*. Berkeley: University of California Press.

Smilde, David and Daniel Hellinger, eds., 2011. Venezuela's Bolivarian Democracy: Participation, Politics, and Culture under Chávez, Durham: Duke University Press.

Sorensen, Eva and Torfing, Jacob, 2003. "Network Politics, Political Capital, and Democracy," *International Journal of Public Administration*, Vol. 26, No. 6, pp. 609–634.

Warren, Mark E., 2009. "Governance-driven democratization," *Critical Policy Studies*, Vol. 3, No. 1, April 2009, pp. 3–13.

Official Documents

Asamblea Nacional Constituyente, 1999. *Constitución de la República Bolivariana de Venezuela*, Caracas: Venezuela.

Asamblea Nacional, 2006. *Ley Orgánica de los ConsejosComunales*, Gaceta Oficial No. 5. 806, 6 de April, 2006.

Asamblea Nacional, 2009, *Ley Orgánica de los Consejos Comunales*, Gaceta Oficial No. 39.335, 28 de Diciembre, 2009.

Asamblea Nacional, 2002, *Ley Orgánica del Consejo Local de Planificación Pública*, la Gaceta Oficial Ordinaria N° 37.463, 12 de junio de 2002.

Media

El Universal
El Nacional
Aporrea.org

CHAPTER 7

Direct Democracy in Uruguay and Venezuela: New Voices, Old Practices

Alicia Lissidini

Most Latin American countries incorporated or expanded mechanisms for direct or participatory democracy as part of significant constitutional reforms during the 1990s. Many of these reforms were institutional responses to the democratic processes of countries that had experienced authoritarian regimes (such as the Brazilian constitution of 1988 and the Paraguayan of 1992); others sought to establish pacts around presidential succession (such as Argentina's 1994 constitution) or strengthen the power of the executive (Peru in 1993); still others promoted participation and sought to overcome problems with representation, such as the Colombian constitution of 1991 and the Bolivian constitution of 2009. Recently, Hugo Chávez (2007) unsuccessfully tried to pass another reform of the Venezuelan constitution to advance his project for "21st century socialism," while in Bolivia (2009) a constitutional reform through referendum introduced important changes in indigenous people's representation, autonomy and territorial organization, and land tenure and the balance among branches of the government, and also established "communitarian democracy" alongside representative and direct democracy.

This chapter analyzes direct democracy in two countries: Uruguay and Venezuela. The Uruguayan case was chosen because it is the country with the longest tradition of direct democracy in Latin America (between 1917 and 2009 citizens voted in 24 popular consultations). However, Uruguayan direct democracy changed with redemocratization, becoming more reactive and more eliciting of "voice" in the Hirschman sense. Because of this, and because of the rise of direct democracy in Latin America beginning in the 1990s, Uruguay is no longer exceptional, and therefore the comparison with another case is useful for analyzing popular consultations and the impact of direct citizen participation on democracy. Three countries have had the greatest number of national consultations in Latin America since the 1990s: Bolivia (4), Ecuador (7), and Venezuela (6). Comparing Uruguay and Venezuela is useful because both have expansive direct democracy legislation. Both countries require that all constitutional reforms be submitted to popular consultation, and citizens of both countries have the power to propose constitutional reforms and laws to the legislature as well as to repeal laws through popular consultation. Moreover, both countries experienced a long period of democratic stability, although in the Uruguayan case with an interregnum between 1973 and 1984 because of a coup d'etat. There are some differences in the legal structures: Venezuelans can initiate a referendum to recall the president and all elected officials and the president has the authority to call for a popular consultation. The Uruguayan constitution does not include either of these mechanisms. Table 7.1 summarizes the mechanisms established in each constitution.

Table 7.1   Direct democracy in Venezuela and Uruguay

Direct Democracy Mechanisms	Venezuelan Constitution[1]	Uruguayan Constitution[2]
Obligatory Popular Consultation	Articles 16, 171 and 172: In cases of modification to national or municipal territorial boundaries or affecting national sovereignty. Article 120: To indigenous peoples over natural resources. Article 279: In cases of legislation proposed to congress by the citizenry failing to receive a vote in the stipulated time frame, must be submitted to referendum. Article 205: If the National Assembly is unable to agree on the election to the office of Citizen Authority, a popular consultation must be held.	Article 331: For constitutional reform

		Article 340–346: To change or amend the constitution	
Optional Binding Referendum	Executive Initiative	Article 73	Does not exist
	Legislative Initiative	Article 73	
	Popular Initiative	Article 73	
Non-Binding Consultative Referendum	Executive Initiative	Article 71	Does not exist
	Legislative Initiative	Article 71	
	Popular Initiative	Article 71	
Abrogative Referendum	Citizen Initiative	Article 74	Art. 79 and Law No. 17,244
	President's Initiative	Article 74	Does not exist
Recall of Elected Officials		Article 72 (Art. 233)	Does not exist
Citizen Initiative	Legislative	Articles 204 and 205	Article 79
	Constitutional Reform	Articles 341 and 342	Article 331
Other Mechanisms for Direct Participation		Articles 348 and 347 National Constituent Assembly, Open Town Hall, and Citizens Assemblies	Do not exist

Source: Prepared by author.
Note: 1. Constitución de la República Bolivariana de Venezuela (1999).
2. Constitution of 1967 (with plebiscite modifications on October 31, 2004).
Law 16017: Reform of the Law for elections (April 6, 1989).
Law No. 17244: Recourse to referendum to repeal laws (July 6, 2000).

Through a comparative analysis of direct democracy in two countries, this chapter hypothesizes that in each case the characteristics of direct democracy are determined by the legal structure, the characteristics of the actors involved, and, especially, the social and political context and preexisting political dynamic. While in Uruguay popular consultations have generally tended to reinforce democracy by energizing the political system and promoting public debate and citizen participation, in the Venezuelan case most consultations have increased political delegation and social polarization. In the two cases, direct democracy reveals contrasts in the role of political parties and their capacity for representation: in Uruguay political parties were central, whereas in Venezuela citizens mostly did not believe they were represented by the political parties.

Political Party Centrality and Direct Democracy
in Uruguay: Voice Without Exit

As mentioned above, Uruguay has held the most popular consultations (plebiscites and referendums) of any country in Latin America. Graph 7.1 shows that exercises in direct democracy have taken place throughout Uruguayan history. In contrast to the Venezuelan case, the recourse to direct democracy occurred in the context of expansion and consolidation of democracy rather than a crisis of representation.[1] Under the government of José Batlle y Ordóñez, which promoted these mechanisms, liberalism, republicanism, and state centrality were combined in a democratic discourse of social reform. The democratic character that *batllismo* imprinted on the political system was original in the Latin American context and fundamentally defined Uruguay's politics. Political parties, artifices of this democracy, operated in a pluralist system and had a high degree of organization, social penetration, and historical continuity. Although the figure of Batlle was fundamental, his power arose and grew with the Colorado Party rather than outside of it. The party did not depend on Batlle as a caudillo (chief of state) to carry out social and political transformations (unlike Perón in Argentina or Cárdenas in Mexico). Understood in terms put forth by Albert Hirschman (1977) and reviewed by the editors in Chapter 1 of this book, the inclusion of consultation and popular initiatives secured an effective use of "voice," thus preventing

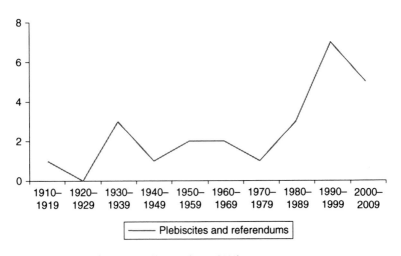

Graph 7.1   Direct democracy in Uruguay (1917–2009)

Source: http://www.corteelectoral.gub.uy/gxpsites/hgxpp001.aspx Last accessed: July 27, 2012. Prepared by author.

"exit," and reinforcing "loyalty" toward political parties and decisions made by them.

There were three stages in the history of direct democracy in Uruguay. In the first, direct democracy was a proactive tool used by political parties to reform the constitution. During the second stage the authoritarian military government used it to try to institutionalize its continuity in power. Finally, beginning in 1989, direct democracy took a reactive form: social organizations used it to curb or reject decisions of parliament.

Political Initiatives in a Bipartisan Order: Proactive Direct Democracy and Loyalty That Preempts Exit (1917–1971)

Until 1971 these initiatives were framed by bipartisan competition, and although most of the proposals were consistent with the prevailing legal order, some were designed principally to displace one or another political faction from electoral representation. During this period, political parties sought agreements between competing political factions. All of the referendums came from the political parties; there were no "independent" initiatives sponsored by citizens or social organizations outside the parties. Legislative rather than popular initiatives were the source of referendums, although this mechanism was also used by political parties. Thus, incorporation of direct democracy provisions in the constitution and their use in practice in this first period did not stem from a crisis of representation and did not at any time question the representative character of Uruguayan democracy.

Constitutional reforms (the proposals and their success) became useful indicators for analyzing the political and party systems: they reflected the weight of each party and of each sector within the parties, as well as their consensus-building capacity. This last point was crucial to the extent that no proposition with single-party support received sufficient votes to pass, so that the success or failure of the propositions depended on prior agreements reached among political factions of different parties. Moreover, the consensus forged among party factions rested on a high level of party discipline among the citizenry—a strong degree of loyalty, since the decisions made by the party leadership were accepted by a citizenry strongly identified with the parties (Blancos and Colorados). Plebiscites granted legitimacy to the parties' actions through the direct validation of the citizenry. Governments, even nondemocratic ones, sought the people's ratification to enact constitutional reforms. As Hirschman (1977) observes, loyalty discourages exit and activates voice, and in the Uruguayan case, proposals for constitutional reforms and the popular consultations that approved them contributed to reinforcing identification with traditional parties. In other words, (high) electoral participation in popular consultations (as well as in national elections) was another way of reaffirming and strengthening political incorporation (Pizzorno, 1989).

Finally, these mechanisms were established and used to resolve the differences between the Colorado and National parties and their factions. The possibility that a third party or independent social sectors could promote direct democracy against its "creators" did not enter the political calculus of the traditional actors. During this period, direct democracy was an effective mechanism for avoiding exit, in that it prevented dissatisfaction that might result in a withdrawal of the electorate from traditional political parties. However, in 1958 and 1966 groups on the left edged in with their own constitutional reform proposals. These initiatives can be considered antecedents to the "plebiscites of contestation" that began in 1989: voices that emerge outside of traditional parties appealing to nonparty support. In 1952 Christian Democratic Party jointly with other leftist political groups advanced an "anticolegialista" reform. And it received 10.9 percent of the votes, a proportion roughly similar to the one those same groups got in 1958.

Thus, in a context of strong politicization, some members abandoned the traditional parties due to perceived lack of response to their interests (which would be a change in loyalty in the Hirschman sense or of identification following Pizzorno) and founded new political organizations outside traditional parties. Some voices opted for an exit within representative government and others chose a more radical exit (such as armed political organizations). In 1967, the left used the popular initiative tool to present its own reform proposal, the "Popular Reform," supported by some unions and backed by a coalition of leftist parties known as FIDEL—Frente Inzquierda de Liberación (Leftist Liberty Front).[2] This project was considered by the citizenry together with another three, but given the possibility that none of the projects would get the required votes, an interparty agreement was reached between the Blancos and Colorados that led to the "orange reform" (Constitution of 1967).[3] To ensure that the project was finally approved, the parties agreed to use a procedure established by Article 331, paragraph B, which allows the General Assembly in bicameral session to formulate legislation instead of a popular referendum.

Direct democracy began to become a mechanism for voice for those who sought to exit from traditional parties. However, the 1973 coup eliminated the strength of "vertical voice," in the sense articulated by Guillermo O'Donnell (1987), that is, the possibility of pressuring the government without fear of sanctions.

The Authoritarian Plebiscite in a Nondemocratic Government: Oblique Voices Confronting Silence (1980s)

In addition to repressing the citizenry, the military government (1973–1984) attempted to justify and even formalize authoritarian intervention. It tried to reform and control traditional parties and restrict their share of power outside the dictatorship. To this end the regime imposed a plebiscite,[4] which, had it passed, would have installed a "tutelary democracy" that excluded sectors of the political left and controlled the branches of government, the citizenry, and the traditional parties. This military plebiscite originated in excessive confidence in the power of fear. The economically favorable moment and falling unemployment rate—mostly caused by migration to Argentina—contributed to the military leadership's sense of security. Additionally, there was pressure to counter Uruguay's progressively deteriorating international image, as reflected, for example, in the Carter administration's complaints about the military government's systematic violation of human rights.

Unlike other authoritarian regimes in the region, almost no group from the traditional political elite actively supported the process. Nor did the regime succeed in building loyalty. The decisive factor in the citizens' rejection of the reform (56 percent voted against) was the presence of a political culture based on negotiation and peaceful coexistence. Uruguayans voted against repression and persecution, against an imposed style that departed from their traditions, and in favor of redemocratization. "Horizontal voices," especially the "oblique" ones, were decisive despite the silence enforced by the military government: "although the oblique voice is practiced in a context of apparent depoliticization, it is intrinsically linked to a public commitment. This capacity to link the most personal with the most public, not only with the oblique voice but all types of horizontal voice, is what makes it so politically important" (O'Donnell, 1987: 41).

The most immediate consequences were the delegitimation of the military and the formation of a common front opposing the regime. The outcome of the plebiscite brought on the crisis of the military regime and opened the way for a transition to democracy, forcing the military's exit.

Reactive Direct Democracy: Voices That Challenge the Parties (1989–2009)

In 1989, a third period began that marked the end of bipartisanism and the growth of the left coalition Broad Front-Progressive Encounter (Frente Amplio-Encuentro Progresista) Unlike the first period (1917–1971) in which the central actors were the "traditional" political parties (Colorado Party and

National Party), after 1989 it was the social and political organizations with capacity for voice that initiated mechanisms for direct participation. Direct democracy was used as a reactive mechanism to oppose parliamentary and government resolutions and served as a challenge to the entire spectrum of political parties. The success of proposals depended on the capacity of social groups to impose an issue and bring it to the direct consideration of the citizenry, but generally, the results tended to prevent exit and reinforce party loyalties. Table 7.2 summarizes the popular consultations in this period, their sponsors, and the political support they received.

We can categorize exercises in direct democracy in Uruguay during the 1989–2009 period into four types:

(A) Direct democracy as a tool for justice.

The 1989 referendum sought, unsuccessfully, to repeal the law granting amnesty to the military for human rights violations under the military government.[5] Subsequently, the 2009 plebiscite did not garner the support necessary to reform the constitution to annul some of the articles of that law.[6] In both cases, human rights organizations were the key actors. In the 1989 referendum, the Frente Amplio and some sectors of the National and Colorado parties were central to achieving the required signatures and votes, whereas in the second instance (2009) most of the Frente Amplio's members were reluctant to promote the initiative and then only gave it timid support. In both cases, support for repeal or annulment was similar (44 and 48 percent respectively), which was insufficient for the reform to pass. The decision made by the Parliament was therefore validated. Nevertheless, in mid-2011, to address impunity, Frente Amplio legislators approved a law revoking the statute of limitations on homicides committed by the military regime, although this measure was limited to cases that were tried in the courts. Thus, voices were heard and the exit of citizens loyal to the governing party (Frente Amplio) was averted through a legal solution.

(B) Direct democracy to stop privatizations.

Like other Latin American countries, Uruguay has had a strong central state combined with extensive legislation requiring the executive to seek parliamentary agreements (e.g., unlike in Argentina the executive could not decree structural adjustment). In a multiparty context with high party factionalization, direct democracy had an important impact on limiting the role of the state. In 1992, the privatization law passed by the Parliament was partially repealed through referendum. That law gave the executive the power to privatize or break up

Table 7.2 Direct democracy in Uruguay (1989–2009)

Popular Consultations	Convening and Supporting Organizations	Percentage Votes in Favor	Percentage Abstention
April 16, 1989 Referendum prohibiting statute of limitations for State crimes.	Organization of Mothers and Relatives of the Detained-Disappeared Frente Amplio and left sectors in the traditional parties. Union Confederation (PIT-CNT)	43.9 (Failed to pass.)	15.28
November 26, 1989 Plebiscite for pension adjustment according to the Average Salary Index	Coordinator of Retirees of the Social Welfare Bank Frente Amplio (except the MPP). Colorado Party (except Jorge Batlle's group). National Party, with the exception of the governing sectors (Lacalle-Aguirre)	81.78 (Approved)	10.89
December 13, 1992 Referendum against the Public Enterprises Law	Union Confederation PIT-CNT, especially the telephone company workers union. Frente Amplio and some sectors of the Colorado Party (especially the Batllista Forum, led by Julio María Sanguinetti). Some groups and leaders from the National Party (like the Encuentro Wilsonista, led by Alberto Zumarán) and from the Nuevo Espacio	72 (Partial repeal of the law approved)	17.20
August 18, 1994 Plebiscite on "minimal" constitutional reform (enabling split-ticket voting, salary set for councilors, and reduced their number)	Colorado Party (except the rightist sectors) Support from the National Party and some sectors and leaders from Frente Amplio	31.3 (proposition failed)	14.59

Table 7.2 (Continued)

Popular Consultations	Convening and Supporting Organizations	Percentage Votes in Favor	Percentage Abstention
November 27, 1994 Plebiscite to repeal reforms to social security and to prohibit institutional changes introduced through the Budget process.	Social Security Workers Association, National Organization of Retirees and the Union Confederation (PIT-CNT) Frente Amplio; Colorado Party (except Jorge Batlle) and the Alberto Volonté sector of the National Party	69.8 (Reform approved) Beginning with this consultation, the Electoral Court decided that the vote would only be for "yes"	13.76
November 27, 1994 Plebiscite to establish constitutional obligation to allocate 27 percent of the National Budget to Public Education	Education unions (especially teachers and administrators) Frente Amplio	32 (reform failed)	*
December 8, 1996 Constitutional reform plebiscite. Important reforms are introduced: Single presidential and vice-presidential candidacies from each party (preceded by internal elections in all the parties); distinct timing of national and departmental elections and the introduction of the second round or run-off voting	Proposition sponsored by the Colorado Party and the National Party and supported by a sector of Frente Amplio (led by Danilo Astori) and Nuevo Espacio.	50.45 (reform passed)	13.83
October 31, 1999 Plebiscite to prohibit directors of Autonomous Entities from running for elected office	Nuevo Espacio (sponsor), theoretically all the political parties supported the measure, although in practice very few campaigned for it.	37.7 (proposition rejected)	*

Date and description	Supporters	Result	
October 31, 1999 Plebiscite to enable the judiciary's financial autonomy	Judicial Officials Association, Actuaries Association, Public Defenders Association, Bar Association, Notaries Association and Social Workers Association Supported by sectors of the Frente Amplio and the National Party	42.3 (not approved)	*
December 7, 2003 Referendum to repeal the "ANCAP law" that allowed deregulation of the company's monopoly on importing, exporting, and refining crude oil and its derivatives	Committee for the Defense of ANCAP; PIT-CNT (unions) and the Encuentro Progresista- Frente Amplio (some sectors, such as those led by Astori and Rubio, were opposed to repealing the law).	62.2 (the law was successfully repealed)	16.75
October 31, 2004 Plebiscite that proposed two constitutional articles on the administration and use of water—prohibiting their privatization.	Committee in Defense of Water and Life. Federation of OSE Workers (public water company) Frente Amplio and sectors of the National Party (especially National Alliance)	63 (reform approved)	*
October 25, 2009 Plebiscite to decide whether Uruguayans abroad can vote (beginning in 2014).	Encuentro Progresista-Frente Amplio	37.42 (Not approved)	*
October 25, 2009 Plebiscite to annul Articles 1, 2, 3, and 4 of Law No. 15848, December 22, 1986. Law exempted members of the military from criminal liability for human rights abuses.	National Coordinator to Annul the Statute of Limitations Law. Sponsored by the political sector of Frente Amplio, the Party for the People's Victory, and the PIT-CNT. Formally had the support of the entire Frente Amplio	47.96% (Not approved)	*

Source: Prepared by author.

*In these cases, voters could only vote in favor of the reform; voting against or abstaining was not allowed.

monopolies of any kind of state enterprise or service without regard to the Parliament's position. Public sector unions were the central actors promoting the initiative; they were the voices that put the issue on the political agenda and mobilized citizens, although they enjoyed the support of all of the Frente Amplio and important sectors of the Colorado party, and some in the National Party as well. Similarly, in 2003 a referendum was initiated against the law deregulating the monopoly that the state-owned oil company (Administración Nacional de Combustibles, Alcoholes y Portland (ANCAP)) had on the import, export, and refining of crude oil and its derivatives. Again the union was key along with political party support. In 2004, neighborhood and environmental organizations together with the state water company union promoted a plebiscite to prevent the privatization of water service and declare that "access to potable water and access to sanitation are fundamental human rights"; they won with 63 percent of the vote. All of the antiprivatization initiatives that reached the voting stage passed, although some propositions did not make it to the ballot, such as the one sponsored by the gas company union. In all of these cases there was an effective use of "voice" in the Hirschmanian sense of the term.

(C) Direct democracy as a tool for defending sectoral or corporatist interests.

The plebiscite that gave origin to this type of initiative took place in 1989, when retiree organizations successfully mobilized for pensions to be adjusted in accordance with the Average Wage Index.[7] In 1994 these same actors proposed another successful plebiscite to repeal the Lacalle administration's social security reforms and to prohibit any change in the retirement system through the Budget Report.[8] Also included in this category is the 1994 plebiscite sponsored by the teachers unions that sought to allocate 27 percent of the national budget to public education, and the 1999 plebiscite sponsored by professional organizations gave the judiciary financial autonomy (the proposition banned executive influence on budgeting for the judicial branch and removed its veto power over the budget proposal presented by the Supreme Court). None of these constitutional reforms passed, but they were supported by a substantial number of votes, roughly equivalent to votes for the Broad Front in that period.

(D) Direct democracy to change the electoral system.

This was the classic use of the plebiscite in Uruguay, and it reappeared during this period. In 1994 the Colorado Party, with the support of sectors from the National Party and the Frente Amplio, presented a proposition that allowed, among other things, voting for candidates from different parties in national and local (departmental) elections; the proposition failed.[9] In 1996 another attempt at reform revived some of the earlier proposals and introduced the second ballot or run-off election. This reform passed and had the support of the National and Colorado parties and important sectors of the Frente Amplio. In 1999 the party New Space (Nuevo Espacio) proposed a reform that prohibited directors of the autonomous entities from being candidates in the national elections. This initiative did not pass since only the party that sponsored the initiative—Nuevo Espacio—campaigned for it. Finally, in 2009 along with the national elections and the plebiscite on the statute of limitations law, voting by Uruguayans living abroad was proposed. That initiative, which was hardly debated and was very imprecise, was sponsored by the Frente Amplio but was not supported by the Frente's voters.

Venezuela: Voice, Exit, and Recognition

The Venezuelan constitution of 1999 considerably expanded the mechanisms of direct democracy with the explicit objective of promoting greater citizen participation in public affairs.[10] Within Latin America, Venezuela is one of the countries that most extensively embraces citizen initiatives, popular consultations, and referendums. Similar to the practices in Bolivia and Ecuador, Venezuelans also can recall the president and the president has the power to call for popular consultation. The participatory spirit was enshrined in Article 70 of the constitution:

> Mechanisms for the people's participation and leadership in exercising their political sovereignty are: elections for public offices, referendum, popular consultation, recall, legislative, constitutional and constituent initiatives, open town halls and citizen assemblies, the decisions of which are binding, among others, co-administration, all forms of cooperatives including credit unions, savings banks, community businesses and other associative forms guided by the values of mutual cooperation and solidarity.

This reform can be understood in the context of the social and political environment in which it was made: the commitment to direct participation in the Venezuelan case is related to the decline of political parties and the deinstitutionalization of politics. It is also linked to the tension between authoritarianism and democracy that preexisted Chávez's assumption of the presidency (Gómez Calcaño, 2011).[11] Until the mid-1980s, Venezuela was politically stable and enjoyed sustained growth and low inflation. The state had a central role: it implemented a strong redistributive and social welfare policy that supported social mobility and mass education. Not only were the majority political parties allied with one another; they also sustained alliances with the unions, the oil sector, and the Catholic Church. The armed forces were subordinate to civilian command and social demands were channeled through political parties. The party system was organized around the spirit founded by the Punto Fijo pact: conflicts were resolved consensually among the actors involved, but others were excluded in an authoritarian way. The high rents from oil exports financed politics, mostly through corruption and clientelism. During oil bonanza periods, large public expenditures supported the redistribution of resources, preventing significant conflicts from arising. As Fernando Errandonea (2006) observed,

> There is no strong voice or available exits because there is no incentive for either of those mechanisms. And there are no incentives because the systemic corruption reached all strata, even to the level of the family; because beneficiaries of the system experienced short-term increases in income, status or power, and were unaware that this development model was not sustainable over the long-term; because democratic legitimacy was obtained through distribution of public goods on a universal as well as private level, and although the payout was stratified, it went to a large portion of the population (retributive legitimacy); and also because no one had deconstructed the model or proposed any serious or viable alternative. In effect, there are no actors to exercise voice or to exit.

The fall in the price of oil (especially at the end of the 1980s) left the political parties with little room for response in an economy dependent on petroleum rents. In some sense, Chávez was able to reproduce the preexisting clientelistic logic (especially that of the Acción Democrática [AD] governments), although with different "political families."

The 1989 crisis was marked by a chain of events, some of which were symptoms of the collapse of a type of democracy while others fed the fall, in effect fueling the Hirschmanian exit. The first indicator of the economic crisis was the collapse of the currency on February 18, 1983 (known as "black Friday"). In that decade poverty and social inequality increased at the same time that the first economic adjustment measures were applied. Those measures subsequently contributed to poverty and social inequality, as well as to unemployment and growing informal sector employment.

The Caracas riots (known in Spanish as the *caracazo*), which occurred on February 27, 1989, made clear that the social and political pacts were also in crisis and that the parties and unions had lost their representative capacity and ability to channel social discontent. It was a spontaneous, loosely organized citizen response to the first concrete "orthodox" economic adjustment measure (price increases in public transportation), announced on February 16 by

Carlos Andrés Pérez's government (negating a campaign promise).[12] The first electoral symptom of the crisis in the parties was growing electoral abstention beginning in 1978 (another indicator of exit), at a time when party identification with AD and the Christian democrats (Comité de Organización Política Electoral Independiente, or COPEI)progressively declined, mostly due to strong internal disputes.[13] The two attempted coups in 1992 were the clearest manifestations of party decadence and political crisis, and augured the emergence of Hugo Chávez as a political leader who was "the voice" that channeled exit. Although the attempts at "exit" through coups failed, the retreat of the military wound up as a collapse of the parties and the end of the pact. Exit was manifestly the choice of an outsider (Chávez) and the punishment of the party systems.

Criticism of the "partyocracy" and the need for institutional reform to produce a radical change was the central focus of the Movimiento Quinta Republica's (Chávez's Fifth Republic Movement, MVR) campaign. Chávez promised to elect a Constituent Assembly that would terminate the Punto Fijo pact and redesign the Venezuelan political system. The commitment to indigenous rights added issues of race and poverty to the dispute, which had generally been absent from the discourses of the governing elite (made up for the most part by light-skinned people). Chávez's appearance in Venezuelan politics was a deep break with the vision of social progress open to all sectors prevalent in the four decades after World War II. He became "the general of the poor," arguing that the "Bolivarian Revolution" not only meant to put an end to the "corrupt partyocracy" but also intended to produce a profound social transformation, bringing to the fore sectors that had been invisible in the past (Gómez Calcaño, 2002, 2011).

Shortly after taking power, Hugo Chávez called a constituent assembly in which social organizations could participate in drafting a new constitution. The resulting document, despite some questionable components, did establish a very broad set of human rights (environmental rights, women's and indigenous peoples' rights) and expanded the mechanisms for citizen participation at the electoral level as well as in local public administration and in the design of public policies.

The Venezuelan constitution incorporated extensive mechanisms for direct democracy (see Table 7.1). Throughout Chávez's terms, other forms of formal and informal participation were added, like "missions," technical committees for water, energy, and telecommunications, communal councils, and more recently, socialist communes. Although most of these mechanisms promote direct citizen participation, they are designed (and in some cases controlled) by the executive. The following section, depicted in Table 7.3, provides a description of direct democracy in Venezuela.

Table 7.3 Direct democracy in Venezuela (1999–2009)

Popular Consultation	Initiative and Support	Result	Abstention
April 25, 1999 Referendum with two questions, the formation of a National Constituent Assembly to draft a new constitution, and its powers—basically the requirement that it must approve a new constitution in 6 months to submit to popular consultation	Government with the support of social organizations and political parties affiliated with Hugo Chávez	Question 1 Passed Yes: 87.75 No: 7.26 Question 2 Passed Yes: 81.74 No: 12.75	62.1%
December 15, 1999 Constitutional reform: Inclusion of human rights, mechanisms for direct and participatory democracy, greater power to the executive	Government with the support of various political and social organizations	Passed Yes: 71% No: 28%	54.74%
December 2, 2000 Referendum requiring selection of union leadership through secret vote	Chávez's government (did not have the support of the Union Confederation)	Passed Yes: 62.50% No: 27.34	75.5%
August 15, 2004 Recall of Chávez's presidency	Democratic Coordinator (CD), made up of business groups (Fedecámaras), political parties (AD, COPEI, Primero Justicia and other anti-government groups), CVT, and social organizations	Rejected Yes: 40.63% No: 59.09%	30.08%
December 2, 2007 Constitutional reform that proposed, among other things: no presidential term limits, increase in presidential term from 5 to 6 years, reduction of the workday to 6 hours, dependence of the Central Bank on the executive, responsibility for citizen security and domestic order given to the armed forces, increased power to the president	President Hugo Chávez's proposition. Block A Proposition from the Constitutional Assembly (Pro- Chávez groups). Block B	Rejected Yes: 49.29% No: 51.05% Rejected Yes: 48.94% No: 51.05%	44.1%
February 15, 2009 Constitutional reform to abolish term limits for all elected offices.	Chávez government	Approved Yes: 54.85% No: 45.14%	29.67%

Source: Prepared by author (data from the CNE).

Popular Consultation for a Constituent Assembly: Voices Seeking Recognition

The first consultation promoted by Chávez once in government was the call for a Constituent Assembly (April 1999). The opposition challenged the convention, and especially one of the questions that arguably infringed on the legislature's powers by granting the executive discretionary power to define the means for convening and conducting the Constituent Assembly. The Supreme Court found in favor of some of the suits brought against the presidential decree and challenged the second question for failing to meet the requirements of a consultative referendum, granting the National Electoral Commission (Comisión Nacional Electoral—CNE) the authority to draft the referendum.[14] The consultation took place on April 25th after a short campaign run almost exclusively by the government. Although part of the opposition called for abstention, intending to subsequently denounce the popular consultation as plebiscitary, most did not get actively involved because of the perceived strong consensus around the need for change. The opposition was trapped between resistance to the process and late, ineffective engagement to try to remain in the political game. The two questions passed, although abstention was very high (see Table 7.4). Given the favorable response to the second question, two central issues were defined for Chávez's project: the number of members in the assembly who would be elected by each federal entity and the way in which the candidates would be nominated (on an individual basis, through gathering a percentage of signatures proportional to the number of votes in each entity). This blocked the parties from proposing closed lists and forced them to seek support for each candidate to the assembly.

Table 7.4 Presidential elections, electoral support, and abstention in Venezuela (1958–2006)

Presidential Elections	Party	Votes	Abstention
1958 – Rómulo Betancourt	AD	49.2	7.85%
1963 – Raúl Leoni	AD	32.8	9.22%
1968 – Rafael Caldera	COPEI	29.1	5.64%
1973 – Carlos Andrés Pérez	AD	48.7	3.48%
1978 – Herrera Campins	COPEI	46.6	12.44%
1983 – Jaime Lusinchi	AD	56.7	12.25%
1988 – Carlos Andrés Pérez	AD	52.8	18.08%
1993 – Rafael Caldera	Convergencia/ MAS and others	30.5	39.84%
1998 – Hugo Chávez	MVR/ MAS and others	56.20	36.54%
2000 – Hugo Chávez	MVR/MAS and others	59.8	43.69%
2006 – Hugo Chávez	MVR/MAS and others		25.3%

Source: Prepared by author based on data from the CNE.

In the campaign to elect representatives to the Constituent Assembly candidates declared their positions on the criteria to be included in the new constitution. During this period, social organizations that focused on improving quality of life through efficient economic development and respect for civil rights were growing in importance. The nominal system worked in practice as a party list for the Chavistas. As a result, while the opposition votes were dispersed among multiple candidates, those in favor of Chávez were concentrated on the official candidates. The high level of electoral abstention (60 percent) raised doubts about the legitimacy of the winners and demonstrated the degree of alienation from political parties.

Direct Democracy and Constitutional Reform

The Constituent Assembly's proposed constitutional reform was submitted to popular consultation in December 1999. There are divergent evaluations on the process and the result of the constitutional reform. For some, the active participation of social organizations and movements was a positive. For example, Carrasqueño, Maingon and Welsch (2001) state that "the Constituent Assembly invited citizens and organized groups to present proposals, opened an office for popular assistance and set up a Web page; it received numerous inputs from the organized public and in general, and hotly debated ideas and opinions" (70). Social organizations managed to develop highly successful innovative strategies, like connecting in networks and making the most effective use of the media and national and international electronic networks. Of the 624 proposals drafted by the working groups of the Association of Civil Society Organizations (Sinergia), more than 50 percent were included in the constitution, in the text itself or in style changes. The Constituent Assembly strengthened the popular sectors' identification with Chávez, especially the social organizations led by him.

The campaign against constitutional reform was weakly organized by the traditional parties, who especially challenged the concentration of powers in the executive (increase in term length to six years and the possibility of a single reelection) and the institutionalization of a new relationship with the armed forces, which weakened military subordination to civilian command, delegated military command appointments to the armed forces themselves (except the highest grades, in which the president could intervene), and restored their right to vote. Positive aspects of the reform included those referring to state obligations, human rights, and guarantees. In these areas, the Venezuelan reform followed the approach of recent Latin American constitutional reforms by recognizing and extending new rights, such as those of indigenous people and the environment. Other positive aspects include substantive advances for the judiciary and in mechanisms for political oversight.

The greater power of the "people" through direct democracy is an especially innovative element that is highly relevant given that the constitution represents part of a project of participatory democracy. As Álvarez (2003) notes, its purpose is to: (1) subject governing officials to popular recall and (2) foster people's self-government through direct participation in legislative processes, consultative referendums, repeals and approvals, constitutional and constituent initiatives through consultation, and citizen assemblies. The government's confidence in citizen participation led it to support and promote a wide range of original organizational forms, including "missions," the technical committees for water, energy, and communications, communal councils, and more recently, socialist communes.

However, the debate did not focus on the merits of the constitutional proposal; rather, it revolved around acceptance or rejection of Chávez, becoming a kind of plebiscite without much debate of the proposition's content. The referendum renewed Chávez's legitimacy (71 percent in favor, 28 percent against), although again there was very high abstention (62 percent). The process, which began in April 1999, culminated in July 2000 with the "mega-elections" that renewed the mandates of elective offices and gave the Partido Popular the majority. Participation at that time increased considerably (apparently reverting the tendency back to the norm).

Referendum on New Union Leadership: The Limits of Power?

"End union dictatorship in Venezuela!" was the clearest expression of Chávez's objective with the referendum he brought for citizen consideration on December 5, 2000. Relations between the union movement and Chávez were tense from the start, which is largely explained by the type of corporatist unions created by the Punto Fijo pact that had close relationships with Venezuela's traditional political parties. The leadership of the Venezuelan Workers Confederation (Confederación de Trabajadores de Venezuela—CTV) was at that time another actor linked to the past that Chávez sought to remove. Thus, he reduced government subsidies to the unions to a minimum and threatened to dissolve the existing union structure.

Ellner (2003) observes that government pressure brought about a deep democratization of union structure that has few equivalents on a global scale. In effect, the CTV reacted by calling its Fourth Extraordinary Congress (April 1999) in which new bylaws were approved with measures for direct election by the membership of the Executive Committee, automatic affiliation of all unions legalized by the Ministry of Labor, as well as retiree organizations and professional associations, referendums for workers to approve collective bargaining agreements and to remove leaders, and elimination of party control over the electoral commission of the confederation. They also declared themselves ready to consider CNE supervision of union elections.

Despite these reforms, Chávez held a popular consultation that proposed suspending the existing union leadership for 180 days to allow the rank and file to elect new leaders.[15] The initiative was challenged as a violation of the autonomy of the workers' movement. The Inter-American Commission on Human Rights (IACHR) found that "allowing the general population to participate in this referendum, i.e., including people other than workers belonging to the Confederation, was a violation of the right to organize and of the right of workers to elect their own leaders." The International Labor Organization (ILO) also challenged the legality of the referendum, as did foreign and domestic labor and human rights organizations. With this referendum, levels of abstention reached 75 percent (several labor organizations promoted abstention). Although the referendum passed (62.5 percent in favor and 27.3 percent against), it did not result in government control of the unions. After the vote, the CTV organized "leadership committees," pending new elections. Most of the leaders with close ties to the traditional parties (AD and COPEI), who were accused of corrupt practices, were excluded, and members of several parties and groups on the left (such as Bandera Roja and The Radical Cause (La Causa Radical (LCR))), which until then had refused to participate in the confederation leadership, were now included.

Although the consultation turned out as the government planned (the temporary removal of union leadership), the union elections themselves illustrated the limits of Chávez's power, since he could not control the process or destroy the CTV. Indeed, the union organization was reactivated. However, the CTV followed the course of the Latin American union movement in that it steadily lost the capacity to represent and mobilize society. In the 2002 coup, which led to a brief defeat of Chávez, it demonstrated very little leadership capacity and an authoritarian attitude. Chávez's attack on the unions continued to have effect.

Recall Referendum and a Chávez Who Will Not Leave

The oil workers' strike and business boycott, as well as the 2002 coup, contributed to a general climate of instability and polarization that the government used to discredit the opposition, radicalize political discourse, and pass laws and decrees, some through the use of extraordinary powers, such as the enabling acts.[16] The spiral of confrontation began with the first mass action: the "civil strike" on December 10, 2001. Chávez threatened to shut down the National Assembly and make a law limiting the media; he challenged the opposition: "Now we will see who is stronger, you—the oligarchy—or the Venezuelan people" (Hugo Chávez, November 28, 2001). In February of 2002 the conflict escalated with the dispute between the government and the PDVSA—Petróleos de Venezuela, S. A. (Venezuelan Petroleum Corporation) leadership over the appointment of a new board of directors. The CTV supported the PDVSA by calling for a general strike, which culminated in the ephemeral coup of April 12. Throughout 2002 there were massive opposition and government marches and countermarches, often violent. On the 11th of every month—the date of the coup—the Coordinator for Democratic Action (Coordinadora Democrática—CD) held a march and on the 13th the government responded with a countermarch. The fourth "civil strike" paralyzed the PDVSA from December 2002 to February 2003 and caused a disastrous economic crisis (López Maya, 2004). The coup represented the exit of Chávez's most radicalized opposition; an unexpected consequence was the politicization of Venezuelan society, which reinforced loyalty to Chávez and further alienated the citizenry from the traditional political parties. The long journey that led to consultation was characterized by conflict and mutual distrust between the opposition and government supporters, and by the often contradictory and poorly reasoned decisions of the CNE, which reflected the internal tensions within the commission.[17] On one side of this conflict was the opposition grouped under the umbrella organization CD, which included the business sector (Fedecámaras), political parties (AD or Primero Justicia), and later on, the CVT and social organizations. Private media companies played an important and constant role in supporting the opposition. At first they pursued a civil disobedience strategy and later decided to sponsor a recall election.

The organizations that supported Chávez ranged from the "Tactical Command for the Revolution" to "Maisanta Command," and were made up of weakly institutionalized parties: the Fifth Republic Movement (Movimiento Quinta República—MVR), Patria (Fatherland) for All (Patria Para Todos—PPT), the Venezuelan Communist Party (Partido Comunista de Venezuela—PCV), and "Podemos" ("We Can"), a detachment from the MAS. The alliance was also made up of social organizations like the Bolivarian Circles, urban land committees, and cooperative and union organizations, among others. The government as well as the opposition made intensive use of the media, and the government relied heavily on the executive's official website (López Maya, 2004).

The 2004 recall election challenging Chávez's continuity in office ratified his presidency with nearly 60 percent of the vote, but the political climate did not improve, since the opposition insisted that he won through fraud, even though international organizations such as the Carter Center and the OAS—Organization of American States certified the final results; Chávez did not call for dialogue.

The referendum did little more than confirm the political polarization that had existed in Venezuela since 1998: while the poorest social sectors supported Chávez, the middle and upper classes rejected him (López Maya, 2004). Aside from the questions raised about the process itself (which included abuse of power, irregularities, and accusation of fraud), undeniably Hugo Chávez had gained the support of nearly 60 percent of the electorate. The president's legitimacy is partly explained by a favorable economy in which he initiated a number of social policies, especially the "missions." The missions were crafted to improve citizens' quality of life and alleviate poverty. They were most active from 2003 to 2006 and they covered sensitive social areas, especially education, health, and food, through the installation of service centers in the most impoverished areas. According to the Family Expenditures and Budget survey in 2007, 48.3 percent of the population benefited from at least one mission (that figure reaches 60.7 percent for the first decile of the income distribution pyramid, 64.2 percent for the second decile, and 65.4 percent for the third decile). One of the objectives was to reach the population directly, bypassing the state bureaucracy, which to a large extent was achieved by creating a parallel administration. *Mision Barrio Adentro*, which placed Cuban doctors in neighborhoods to provide primary care, was one of the most widespread missions. The Mercal missions provided low-cost access to food through local networks in communities, and the Robinson missions worked to eliminate illiteracy and provide instruction up to the sixth-grade level for adults with low literacy. The missions were one of the government's most successful strategies and largely explain the support for Chávez in the 2004 recall referendum. This support not only stemmed from the missions' concrete impact on the population but also fostered popular mobilization, strengthened loyalty to the president, and left a positive impression on the poorest sectors, who saw Chávez as "one of us."

No to the 2007 Reform but Yes to Chávez in 2009

The agreement with Cuba, which involved selling 53,000 barrels of oil in exchange for services and technology, radicalized Chávez's discourse. This transformation became clearer with the legitimacy gained through the 2004 recall referendum and the 2005 elections.[18] Thus, the so-called new phase was launched (promoted by Marta Harnecker, among others) in which participatory democracy became popular power, endogenous development became expropriation, and anti-neoliberalism became socialism for the twenty-first century. After Chávez was reelected in 2006 (with 62.9 percent of the vote), he called for building the United Socialist Party of Venezuela (Partido Socialista Unido de Venezuela—PSUV) in "service to the revolution" and presented his first socialist plan for economic and social development, which proposed refounding the nation and constructing the "new man for the twenty-first century."

As part of this project, and as one of the five motors of socialism, a constitutional reform was proposed. On August 15, 2007, Chávez presented the reform proposal, which modified 33 of the 350 articles of the constitution that had been approved in 1999. Unlike that reform, other political and social actors did not participate in the drafting and public debate was very limited. On November 2 the National Assembly approved the president's proposals and added other changes, for a total of 69 articles proposed for modification. The proposition eliminated presidential term limits and extended the term from six to seven years, created new types of cooperative and community property, converted the armed forces into Bolivarian militias, universalized social security, expanded the right to vote to 16-year-olds, reduced the workday from eight to six hours, and eliminated the rights to information and due process during states of emergency. Additionally, the reform prohibited monopolies and *latifundios* (large landed estates) and shifted control of monetary policy to the government, thus undermining the Central Bank's autonomy.

For the first time since he took office, Chávez was rejected by the electorate, although by a slim margin, when the constitutional reform was defeated on December 2, 2007. The proposition was divided into two blocks. Block A, the reforms proposed by Chávez, received 49.36 percent of the vote in favor (50.7 percent against), and block B, the National Assembly's proposals, received 48.94 percent versus 51.05 percent (CNE data). Like other exercises in direct democracy in Venezuela, this consultation served as a plebiscite on Chávez and his political project. Student organizations emerged as key actors in the opposition to Chávez's proposed reforms. In 2007 these organizations gained considerable influence, first for opposing the closing of Radio Caracas Televisión Venezolana (RCTV) and then their stand against the constitutional reform. This outcome was not so much a win for the opposition but appeared to be Chavistas themselves punishing Chávez for proposing a reform without consultation that was also long and confusing. The references to socialism, especially in a consumerist country that defends private property, are not supported, or even understood, by the majority of the population.[19] Although the PSUV succeeded in unifying most of the parties and groups that supported Chávez in 2006, the word "socialism" does not have a single meaning, since for Chávez's opposition it is synonymous with communism, for Chavistas socialism is Chávez, and most of them reject the Cuban model, and therefore rejected Chávez's proposition.

The outcome was a serious reversal for Chávez, who accepted the defeat even as he discredited the victory, and he made no effort to generate a climate of dialogue. To the contrary, on November 30, 2008, Chávez ordered his followers to initiate an amendment process that would allow him to run for a third six-year term in the 2012 presidential elections, and additional terms beyond that, "if God and the people so desire." A referendum on February 15, 2009, with a 54.86 percent majority (against 45.1 percent) approved a reform abolishing term limits for all popularly elected offices, including the presidency. This outcome not only enabled Chávez to run in the next presidential elections (October 2012) but also signaled a vote of confirmation in the high degree of identification that he still maintains with an important percentage of the population.

New Voices, Old Political Practices

The rise of direct democracy is usually associated with a crisis of representation (Lissidini 2011). However, this is not true in the case of Uruguay, the Latin American country with the most experience of direct democracy. Throughout Uruguay's history of popular consultations, political parties retain centrality, even in the "contestation" phase, when the citizens have greater autonomy from the parties. All the propositions that reached a popular vote (referendums or plebiscites) had the support of at least one political group. The initiatives that did not have considerable political backing did not make it to the ballot. Additionally, the electoral rise and growth of the Frente Amplio was central to the type of direct democracy practiced after 1989.

Although political parties remained key, they have undergone a significant transformation in recent years. For the first time in history, they were constrained by corporatist organizations (such as retiree groups[20] and teachers unions[21]) in taking certain political positions that were at times at odds with the ideological stance of the party. Moreover, the simultaneity of plebiscites and national elections strengthened the partisanship of the consultations and influenced electoral outcomes. And for the first time, the parties were not always supported by their followers in consultations, such as in the electoral propositions of 1994 and 2009 (which would have enabled voting by citizens abroad). On the other hand, the referendums and plebiscites generated interparty alliances and led to new electoral alignments and parliamentary coalitions. As a result, the citizenry could eventually feel better represented. Thus, direct democracy in Uruguay did not lead to exit from the system of political party representation; rather, it contributed to the strengthening and generation of new party identities.

In contrast, in the Venezuelan case a crisis of representation explains Chávez's ascendancy and the difficulties the opposition had in impeding the reforms he promoted and implemented. Unlike the Uruguayan case, citizens' rejection of political parties (including the party structures proposed by Chávez himself) explains why direct democracy in Venezuela was basically a plebiscite for supporting or rejecting Chávez. The results should be read as something more than a strategic calculation by those who supported him: the "circle of recognition" that Pizzorno (1989) alludes to, that is, the networks of relationships that allow me to recognize myself and be recognized, makes for stronger loyalty than simple adhesion to an ideological project. High rates of electoral abstention are partly a reflection of the majority of Venezuelans' lack of political identity and are a legacy of the crisis and decomposition of the party system. This representational vacuum was not filled by social organizations; even though they do exist and have been relevant in specific instances (like the *Coordinadora Democrática*, which brought together most of the opposition, especially in 2002, and organizations like *Súmate*, which was important in collecting signatures to enable the recall referendum of 2004), they continue to be relatively marginal and have little connection to the most impoverished sectors. When social organizations gained some relevance, as was the case with the university students in 2007, they enriched the political debate; they were the voice that obligated the government to reverse some of its decisions. At the same time, although elections (with the exception of 2007) have benefited Chávez, he has not been able to construct a political structure capable of representing citizens and giving them continuity and institutionality for their political project beyond the figure of Chávez himself.

More Consultations, More Democracy?

The supposedly democratizing character of popular consultations and citizens initiatives requires some parsing. In Uruguay, plebiscites and referendums tend to polarize and stigmatize opponents: *neoliberals* versus *statists*, *modernizers* versus *conservatives*, and so on.[22] In some cases, proponents mobilized for a particular interest (raising pensions, maintaining public employment, increasing salaries for public school teachers), without considering the economic, technical, and political consequences. Popular consultations made the use of opinion research more relevant, influencing the attitudes of politicians as well as citizens, and strengthening the "plebiscitarian model" of adopting policy decisions based on opinion surveys.[23]

The positive repercussions of this mechanism in the Uruguayan case include some instances in which direct democracy was the ideal mechanism for resolving deep societal differences, for halting unpopular policies like privatizations, and especially for channeling protest (voice) and preventing exit.

Moreover, none of the issues that were debated and directly decided by the citizenry were minor questions: human rights, social welfare, management of public administration, and education, among others. The referendums and plebiscites obligated the parties to generate responses and proposals that had the greatest social and political support. Even more than deepening the political debate, the processes awakened citizen interest and stimulated public involvement. In the Uruguayan case, direct democracy, despite all the fears and prejudices, generated greater politicization of society, although notably, "sovereign" decisions were not always accepted by the "losers": as was the case with consultations on human rights policy with respect to the military abuses during the authoritarian government.

Unlike the Uruguayan case, direct democracy in Venezuela tended to strengthen the power of the president at the cost of other mechanisms for representation, such as political parties and autonomous social organizations. However, the formal mechanisms were not responsible for fostering delegation; this was Hugo Chávez's policy, for which the opposition had no effective response. In effect, the legal constraints of ratification of constitutional reforms via popular consultation forced Hugo Chávez to convene the citizenry in 1999, 2007, and 2009. Contrary to the view of some analysts, citizens had the opportunity to support or reject the reforms, thanks to the legal design of direct democracy in Venezuela. Thus, the rejection of the 2007 proposition not only meant a defeat for Chávez; it also put a stop to a constitutional reform that would have increased presidential power even more. Moreover, the popular consultations helped politicize Venezuelans, many of whom had been at the margin of political debates and abstained from participating in elections during the 1990s and part of the early twenty-first century (see Table 7.3). Finally, the electoral results from the consultations were very similar to the election votes, reflecting the popular support enjoyed by Chávez and the difficulties the opposition has in proposing alternative policies that represent the citizenry.

Indeed, these exercises in direct democracy (as well as participatory democracy) are reflections of the ambiguities inherent in Venezuelan democracy made problematic by a leader who fosters citizen participation but with a significant dose of authoritarianism, and who recreates old clientelistic practices with historic roots in Venezuela. Venezuelan "politics" in all its manifestations is permeated by weak institutions and limited civil society autonomy in a country with significant economic and social differences further polarized by Chávez's leadership.

Venezuela's legal framework allows the president to propose constitutional reforms and convene consultations, unlike in Uruguay, where the executive does not have these powers. To a certain extent, this explains the consultations and reforms sponsored by President Chávez. However, the differences in the use of direct democracy in the two cases are rooted in the political trajectories of the countries, in their political dynamics, and the characteristics of the respective political actors. While in Uruguay the party system and the political culture obligate actors to seek consensus, and voice is used to avoid exit, in Venezuela a much more clientelistic and less democratic logic prevails.

Acknowledgment

I am grateful to Eric Hershberg, Maxwell Cameron, Fernando Errandonea, Marcelo Cavarozzi, and to the anonymous evaluators' comments on previous versions of this chapter. To analyze the Venezuelan case, a series of interviews were carried out that are listed at the end of this chapter.

Notes

1. See Alicia Lissidini (1998) for an analysis of the origin of direct democracy in Uruguay.
2. Beginning in 1966, parties on the left steadily increased their participation in the Parliament: in 1966 the group FIDEL (the Frente Izquierda de Liberación, or Leftist Liberation Front, a coalition of several leftist parties) won five seats in the House of Representatives and one in the Senate; in 1971 under a broader coalition, called Frente Amplio (Broad Front), they had 18 representatives and 5 senators.
3. Significantly, prior to development of this interparty project, the electoral court had ruled that voters could not vote "yes" for more than one project, which meant that if more than one proposition is on the ballot it would be difficult for any single one to get the necessary majority to pass.
4. The constitutional reform project eliminated the prohibition on night raids and gave the executive the authority to regulate the right to strike. The armed forces took jurisdiction over all aspects of "national security" and the executive was strengthened at the expense of the legislature. For political parties, the simultaneous double vote was eliminated in favor of a single candidate for each party. Comprehensive proportional representation was modified and limits were placed on the operations and formation of political parties.
5. The amnesty law was passed in the parliament as a result of the "governability pact" between the majoritarian sector of the National Party (under Wilson Ferreira) and the ruling party, the Colorado Party. The then president of Uruguay, Julio María Sanguinetti, proposed a group of laws as part of the so-called pacification policies. These measures included: (a) amnesty for political prisoners (March 8, 1985), which freed all prisoners incarcerated for political reasons or connected to political activity; (b) reparations to destitute public officials

(November 25, 1985); (c) repatriation of people in exile (April 11, 1985); and, (d) the Statute of Limitations for criminal prosecutions (December 22, 1986) that granted amnesty to members of the military who had committed human rights crimes during the period of the "fight against subversion" and during the military government.

6. The referendum was in fact a popular consultation, since citizens voted "yes" or "no," but in the plebiscite, citizens were only allowed to endorse the proposition, so that there was no explicit "no" vote.

7. *Sign here and we will raise your pension* was the slogan of the social organizations that gathered signatures for the plebiscite.

8. The Budget Report is the annual report that the executive is required to present to the legislature. In this report, the executive can propose changes that it deems indispensable to the total amount of expenditures, investments, and salaries or resources, and create, suppress, and modify programs for duly justified reasons. The legislature must approve it so that it can be executed.

9. On the reasons for this rejection, see Lissidini (1999).

10. Article 181 of the Organic Law for Suffrage and Participation of 1998 was a precursor to the consultative referendum. Source: http://www.analitica.com/Bitblio/congreso_venezuela/sufragio.asp.

11. As Luis Gómez Calcaño observes, this authoritarian tendency in Venezuelan political culture can be seen in former president Caldera's decision to go against his party in 1992, as well as in the popular support for Chávez's 1993 coup against democracy, and later (2002) in the call for a strike (personal interview, Caracas, February 2011).

12. Among other measures, Pérez eliminated bank regulations, lifted most price controls, privatized the national telephone company (CANTV), the port system, and the airline VIASA, and opened up the oil and other strategic industries to private capital. See Ellner, Steve (2003).

13. AD's decadence was evident in the 1997 elections when it declared Luis Alfaro Ucero (member of the founding generation) candidate "by acclamation," without consulting the base, but the desertions and expulsions began with Carlos Andrés Pérez's presidency in 1988. COPEI split in 1993, creating the group CONVERGENCIA (Convergence). La Causa Radical (the Radical Cause) also suffered from divisions because of leadership conflicts, and the group Patria Para Todos—PPT (Patria for All) split off and allied with Chávez.

14. The rulings and declarations of the old Supreme Court are indicative of the level of dispute between Chávez and that institution, which was subsequently substituted by the Supreme Tribunal of Justice. They also show the vacillations around the popular consultation. Finally, the following was posed in the consultation:

First question. Will you call for a National Constituent Assembly with the purpose of transforming the state and creating a New Legal Order to promote the effective functioning of Social and Participatory Democracy? Second question. Do you agree with the Executive's proposals for the framework of the National Constituent Assembly, which were examined and partially modified by the National Electoral Council in its March 24, 1999 session, and published in their entirety in the Official Gazette of the Republic of Venezuela Number 36,669, March 25, 1999?

15. The question asked was this: "Do you agree with a change of union leadership after a period of 180 days, following the electoral statute in accordance with the principles of alternability, direct and secret universal election established in article 95 of the Constitution, and that the powers of the directors of the unions, their federations and peak organizations be suspended?"

16. Enabling laws are those sanctioned by three-fifths of the National Assembly to establish the guidelines, purposes, and framework for the subjects that are delegated to the president of the Republic with the status and force of law. See the list of laws at: http://www.asambleanacional.gov.ve/ns2/leyes-habilitante/ LISTADO%20HABILITANTES.asp.

17. A detailed analysis of this journey can be found in Lissidini (2008) http://www. unsam.edu.ar/escuelas/politica/documentos/32.pdf.

18. In the parliamentary elections of 2005, the opposition committed one of its worst errors by withdrawing from the electoral contest. As a result, the ruling party won all the seats in parliament.

19. As Javier Biardeau observes, "*no se le ve el queso a la tostada* [there was no meat in the sandwich]: the discourse was so flat, so doctrinaire, that only the hardest sector of chavismo could identify with it (. . .) it left out the whole base that was more identified with the anti-neoliberal process, popular mobilization and a promise of social as well as political democratization that wasn't happening and that concentrated decision-making in the executive" (personal interview, February 2011, Caracas).

20. Although undoubtedly, social security was a means of obtaining clientelistic advantages since the 1950s and there was always pressure on the political parties, the coercion had never been so transparent. A comment from Elías Yafalián, member of the board of directors for the National Organization of Retirees and Pensioners of Uruguay (ONAJPU), was illustrative: "Today we retirees are the cabaret stars for the political parties, so we are going to give the candidates our demands so that they go on the record before October 31" (*El Observador* n° 2462, October 3, 1999).

21. In the 2004 plebiscite sponsored by the education unions, Frente Amplio had to support the constitutional reform, even though several party leaders were against the proposition. Something similar happened in 2009 with the plebiscite promoted by the human rights organization.

22. This stigma occurred even in the case of the amnesty for the military, in which the principal reason for voting either to retain or repeal the law was paradoxically the same: the consolidation of democracy.

23. Further research is needed on failed efforts to initiate referendums, as well as the impact of threats to repeal laws via referendum. For example, in 2002, signatures were collected for a referendum to repeal a law regulating the cellular telephone service (ANCEL); facing the possibility of a referendum, Congress decided to repeal Articles 612 and 613 of Law No 17,296. In that case, just the threat of referendum had an immediate political effect.

Bibliography

Álvarez, Ángel (2003) "La reforma del Estado antes y después de Chávez", in Ellner and Hellinger (eds.), *La política venezolana en la época de Chávez. Clases, polarización y conflicto*, Caracas, Nueva Sociedad.

Biardeau, Javier (2009) "Del árbol de tres raíces al socialismo bolivariano del siglo XXI," *Revista Venezolana de Economía y Ciencias Sociales*, Vol. 15, No. 1 (January-April) 57–114.

Carrasqueño, José Vicente; Thais Maingon and Friedrich Welsch (eds.) (2001) Venezuela en transición: elecciones y democracia 1998–2000. RedPol CENDES-IEDP-LUZ-IEP-UCV-IESA-USB/ CDB publicaciones. Caracas.

D'Elía, Yolanda and Thais Maingón (2009) La política social en el modelo Estado/Gobierno venezolano. Documento de trabajo, ILDIS-CONVITE.

Ellner, Steve (2003) "El sindicalismo frente al desafío del chavismo," in Ellner and Hellinger (eds.), *La política venezolana en la época de Chávez. Clases, polarización y conflicto*, Caracas, Nueva Sociedad.

Ellner, Steve (2006) "Las estrategias desde arriba y desde abajo del movimiento de Hugo Chávez," *Cuadernos del Cendes*, May-August, Vol. 23, Caracas, 73–93.

Errandonea, Fernando (2007) "Salida, voz y lealtad en Venezuela" (1958–2002). Unpublished paper. Mexico City: Colegio de Mexico.

Harnecker, Marta (2002) *Hugo Chávez Frías. Un hombre, un pueblo*. Interview by Marta Harnecker. Available at Biblioteca Virtual de CLACSO. http://bibliotecavirtual.clacso.org.ar/ar/libros/cuba/mepla/venezu/lib2.pdf.

Hirschman, Albert O. (1977) *Salida, voy y lealtad*. Fondo de Cultura Económica, México.

Hirschman, Albert O. (1986) *Interés privado y acción pública*. Fondo de Cultura Económica, México.

Lissidini, Alicia (1998) Los plebiscitos uruguayos durante el siglo XX: ni tan autoritarios ni tan democráticos," *Cuadernos del Claeh 81–82*. Revista Uruguaya de Ciencias Sociales. Edited by CLAEH, 2nd series, year 23, 1998/1–2 (195–217).

Lissidini, Alicia (1999) "El 31 de octubre también se ejerce la democracia directa. Dos plebiscitos, dos lógicas". *Revista tres* No. 193 (October) 28–29.

Lissidini, Alicia (2000) "A dos décadas del rechazo explícito a los militares. Plebiscito autoritario con resultados democratizadores," *Revista Posdata* No. 321, December 1, Montevideo (59–64).

Lissidini, Alicia (2008) "Democracia directa latinoamericana: riesgos y oportunidades," in Alicia Lissidini, Yanina Welp and Daniel Zovatto (eds.), *Democracia directa en América Latina*. Buenos Aires: Editorial Prometeo, pp. 13–62.

Lissidini, Alicia (2011) *Democracia directa en América Latina: entre la delegación y la participación*. Buenos Aires: Consejo Latinoamericano de Ciencias Sociales.

López Maya, Margarita (2004) "Venezuela 2001–2004: actores y estrategias," in Cuadernos del Cendes, Vol. 21, No. 56 (May-August) 109–132.

López Maya, Margarita (2008) "Venezuela: Hugo Chávez y el bolivarianismo," *Revista Venezolana de Economía y Ciencias Sociales*, Vol. 14, No. 3 (September-December) 55–82.

Maingon, Thais, Carmen Pérez Baralt and Heinz R. Sonntag (2001) "Reconstitución del orden políticos: el proceso constituyente de 1999,"in Carrasqueño, José Vicente, Thais Maingon and Friedrich Welsch (eds.), *Venezuela en transición: elecciones y democracia 1998–2000.* CDB Publicaciones- REdPol, Caracas.

O'Donnell, Guillermo (1987) "Retirada, voz y lealtad. Sobre las fructíferas convergencias de las obras de Hirschman . . . " *Revista de Ciencia Política* 1/1987, Instituto de Ciencia Política, Facultad de Ciencias Sociales, Universidad de la República (22–45).

Pizzorno, Alessandro (1988) "Los intereses y los partidos en el pluralismo," in Suzanne Berger (comp) *La organización de los grupos de interés en Europa Occidental.* Centro de Publicaciones Ministerio de Trabajo y Seguridad Social, Madrid.

Pizzorno, Alessandro (1989), "Algún otro tipo de alteridad: Una crítica a las teorías de la elección racional", Sistema 88, Florencia (27–42).

Interviews (February 2011)

Yolanda D'Elia (Convite, Acción Solidaria, Provea, Sinergia and Civilis).
Thais Maingon (CENDES)
Tito Lacruz (Universidad Católica Andrés Bello)
Luis Salamanca (Universidad Católica de Venezuela)
Javier Biardeau (Universidad Central de Venezuela)
Luis Fuenmayor Toro (Former Rector of the Universidad Central de Venezuela)
Miguel Lacabana (Universidad de Quilmes)
Luis Gomez Calcaño (CENDES—Universidad Central de Venezuela.)
Teodoro Petkoff (newspaper *Tal Cual*)
Margarita López Maya (CENDES—Universidad Central de Venezuela.)
Valentina Maninat (Unión Radio)
Heinz Sonntag (CENDES)

CHAPTER 8

Participation and Representation in Oaxaca, Mexico's Customary Law Elections: Normative Debates and Lessons for Latin American Multiculturalism

Todd A. Eisenstadt and Jennifer Yelle

The trade-off between participation and representation has been frequently problematized in political theory, but not so often in empirical studies. If we hold the concept of participation to be direct involvement of citizens in the decision-making process and allow for the historical debate among meanings of representation, we may insert ourselves into a debate that has lasted for hundreds of years. Indeed, the anti-Federalists prior to the founding of the United States argued, famously, for elected representatives who retained a strict responsibility to their constituents. As characterized by Herbert Storing, to anti-Federalists like Thomas Jefferson, "responsibility is ensured by the absence of much differentiation between the people and their government . . . Effective and thoroughgoing responsibility is to be found only in a likeness between the representative body and the citizens at large" (Storing, 1981:17). By contrast, elitist notions of representation such as Edmund Burke's held that "the more a theorist sees the representative as a member of a superior elite of wisdom and reason, as Burke did, the less it makes sense for him to require the representative to consult the opinions or even the wishes of those for whom he acts" (Pitkin, 1967: 211). The anti-Federalists clearly preferred greater direct participation (and representation based on the views conveyed by citizens), whereas the

Federalists and Burkeans championed diminished roles for citizens, both as purveyors of a popular will through participation via elections, and also in the translation of that will into policy.

Throughout the Americas, indigenous people have been arguing—with international validation—that they required representation in local, national, and international fora. In southern Mexico, calls for greater indigenous representation and participation in governance came forcefully in the 1990s at the time of the Zapatista indigenous uprising in Chiapas state and in neighboring Oaxaca. Adelfo Regino Montes, an Oaxacan Mixe intellectual and collaborator in the Zapatistas' framing of their message, stated, "It is important to recall that before the arrival of the Spanish the collectivities present in these lands were peoples, with their own culture and social, political, economic, and judicial institutions.... They believed, as some continue to affirm today, that these categories and concepts should impose themselves on the essence of things" (Regino Montes, 1996). His argument to the Foro Indígena Nacional (National Indigenous Forum), based on this strong concept of collective rights, was that "the recognition of our collective rights is necessary so that we can truly enjoy our individual rights" (Regino Montes "Taller 2—Libre Determinación de los Pueblos Indígenas" n.d.).

What was the result of these claims for indigenous representation at the national level and for local indigenous participation via new forms of elections and governance? The more radical Zapatista movement in Chiapas has largely passed (although many citizens took from the rebellion renewed indigenous identities, symbolic membership in an ongoing "imaginary Zapatista" movement did have concrete results—see Eisenstadt, 2011: 129–156). But in more gradualist Oaxaca, where indigenous community autonomy was already de facto recognized, new forms of indigenous electoral participation and ideas of representation emerged. This chapter addresses the trade-offs inherent in these new forms of citizen involvement. Although Oaxaca's form of governance provides citizens with new and unique institutional channels in which to exercise voice in the community, these institutional channels also diminish the voice of dissenters and other excluded individuals.

Valuing participation by all (or at least all in the enfranchised groups) and recognizing no role for Burkean elite expertise whatsoever, customary law recognition in Oaxaca—and in other areas where it exists—has restored the institutions of native peoples' to Regino's "essence of things." However, with regard to participation they have created barriers to individuals and minority groups whom they exclude. And with regard to representation, they have implemented a philosophical position favoring loyalty and seniority at the expense of merit and technical expertise. This chapter discusses these choices and their implications, but first we consider what is meant by customary law and how these practices came about in the Mexican context.

Customary law-observing communities use a mix of Western and traditional electoral means: citizens elect federal and state authorities according to standard liberal electoral processes of secret ballot and universal suffrage, and they elect municipal authorities via indigenous customs (known in Spanish as *usos y costumbres* or UC). The definition of *usos y costumbres* practices is often debated. In Oaxaca, UC can refer to a range of practices for selecting leaders—from forming communitywide assemblies to appointing a council of elders to make decisions, from raising hands to support a candidate to drawing hash marks beneath a candidate's name. In general, voting under UC is done publicly and there is no guarantee of universal suffrage. Rather than rigidly define UC practices and establish a legal baseline for them at the moment of recognition, Mexican state authorities allowed Oaxacan legislators to designate UC municipalities and grant local citizens the right to elect leaders via the system of their choice.

Throughout indigenous Latin America, new forms of representation are being adopted as several nations conduct constitutional assemblies and others adopt new forms of indigenous representation or finally accept old ones. This trend is in part fueled by the 1989 creation of the International Labor Organization's Proposition 169, which binds countries to international standards for recognizing indigenous rights, and in part by the 1992 quincentenary celebration of Columbus's voyage to the Western Hemisphere. Indigenous rights movements emerged across the continent including Mexico's Zapatista Rebellion in 1994, the Pachakutik movement/party's success in Ecuador in 1999, and most recently, the victory in 2005 of Evo Morales's Movement Toward Socialism (MAS) in Bolivia. These movements have expressed themselves across a range of institutions of representation, from comprehensive recognition of local autonomy in Bolivia to judicial support for indigenous groups in Colombia to partial recognition, at least of electoral practices, in parts of Mexico.

Hale (2002) has argued that multicultural rights recognition, even by some of Latin America's more conservative governments, has been accorded because rights recognition (without any implementing laws or commitment of resources) costs nothing, and offers a gesture of solidarity to large blocks of indigenous voters. He argues that rights recognition "menaces" indigenous rights movements by driving them to complacently desist from further demands even though what they tend to receive from the states granting these rights is really nothing.

In Mexico, the inherent ambiguities and gray areas surrounding UC practices have led victims of unfavorable *usos y costumbres* judgments to argue that customary law is so loosely defined that traditional-style chieftains are empowered to exercise arbitrary rule under the guise of communitarian decision-making. Moreover, UC elections have created a tension between individual and communitarian rights. A study of traditional leader selection practices in the original 412 UC municipalities (Ríos, 2006:36) revealed that 18 percent do not allow participation by women and 21 percent forbid the participation of citizens living outside of the *cabecera*, or municipal seat, where most decisions are made. Unofficial reports suggest that women are not permitted to vote in 70 percent of Oaxaca's now 570 UC assemblies (Tapia, 2010). Our 2008 survey of Oaxaca, Mexico, Customary Law Municipalities (summarized on Table 8.1), showed that discrimination was even more pervasive after the 1995 state legal reforms legalizing UC, which had been practiced for centuries without legal validation.

This chapter seeks to better understand the implications for participation and representation of the emergence of indigenous customary law practices in Oaxaca, Mexico. We consider how customary law, which was perceived as a great threat to the Mexican state in the early 1990s, was nonetheless tolerated by the country's traditional political elites by the mid-1990s. We describe the variant types of UC practices and we explore the strengths and weaknesses of participation and representation under customary law. We consider the normative benefits and liabilities these practices carry with regard to theories of democratic representation. We contrast this to the actual practice of customary law and survey the number of conflicts related to these issues of representation. In conclusion, we relate the participation/representation debate to the quest for autonomy, as it is often framed in Latin America, and

Table 8.1 Participation in UC municipality customary governance institutions as measured in 2008

Different Groups	Men in Population "Seat" (%)	Women in Population "Seat"	Men in Agencia Hamlets	Women in Agencia Hamlets	Non-Catholics	Migrants
Direct Participation by Vote in Elections	94.20	75.50%	44.10%	38.20%	76.30%	No data
Tequio	95.50	60.9	30.2	20.5	88.3	22.5
Fiesta Organizer	95.8	86.1	32.4	28.7	47.8	31.2
Posts in Civil Govt.	96.80	42.8	31.7	13.4	89.2	29.4

Source: 2008 Survey of Oaxaca, Mexico Customary Law Municipalities. Directed by Moisés Jaime Bailón Corres, Michael S. Danielson, Todd A. Eisenstadt, and Carlos Sorroza and sponsored by Higher Education in Development (HED), the United States Agency for International Development (USAID) and the Benito Juárez Autonomous University of Oaxaca (UABJO). The total N was 404 of Oaxaca's 418 UC-governed municipalities. The questionnaire was administered to town mayors by local representatives of the state government's adult literacy agency, which also asked questions for which it sought responses.

draw implications from the Mexican debate about indigenous autonomy to questions of representation in indigenous Southern Mexico.

Historical and Contemporary Dilemmas of Oaxaca's Customary Law Elections

During the Spanish conquest, with the exception of a few short rebellions, Oaxaca's indigenous communities surrendered quickly and were then mostly ignored by the Spanish. According to Bailón Corres, "The Zapotecs, Mixtecs and other Oaxacan indigenous groups had developed forms of political, cultural, and ethnic organization which gave them consistency and passive resistance against colonial dominance; this permitted them to conserve their lands and even initiate old agrarian disputes with neighboring communities and peoples" (Bailón Corres, 1999:21). In other words, Oaxacan indigenous communities were still exploited via an extraction of tribute, but were not subjected to the direct servitude imposed in other parts of Mexico. The Oaxacans retained the integrity of their lands and communities during colonial rule.

By the mid-1800s, several decades after Mexico won its independence, Oaxaca was divided into administrative units (municipalities) of 200 residents or more and then subunits (known as hamlets or *agencias*) of fewer than 200 residents. The autonomy that the municipalities possessed served both the municipal seats and the outlying communities. This changed when the power to allocate federal funds was passed to the municipalities in the 1980s and the amount of allocations increased in the 1990s. Since the rise of financially empowered municipal seats, these municipalities experienced internal conflict between the outlying communities and the municipal seat over the outlying communities' lack of rights in political participation.

After the federal government's negotiations with the Zapatista insurgency in neighboring Chiapas stalemated in the late 1990s, subnational multicultural policies became a favored strategy for the government to defuse ethnic tensions before they reached a boiling point. While Oaxaca had historically possessed autonomous indigenous communities, authorities figured it might be time to recognize this autonomy legally as a means of stealing the agenda of radical proethnic rights activists like the Zapatistas. Political elites across Mexico had been surprised by the success of the Zapatistas in disseminating their agenda of multicultural rights. Oaxaca's state officials, particularly members of the diminished Party of the Institutional Revolution (PRI, which ruled hegemonically in Mexico from 1929 to 2000), thought that perhaps recognition of UC could diminish any threat of contagion from the neighboring Chiapas Zapatista uprising of 1994. The weakening PRI also believed that a UC system would keep the other rising political parties from continuing to make inroads in rural Oaxaca (Anaya Muñoz, 2002; Recondo, 2007). The 1995 Oaxaca law and 1998 amendments were presented as legitimizing traditional cultural practices and representing a crucial first step toward giving Oaxacans authority over the land they had occupied for centuries. In short, the measure may have been politically motivated, but it was a real concession by the state to indigenous group rights.

For decades, Oaxacans received the de facto autonomy—as seen by the variation in UC systems, *tequio* systems, and *cargo* systems—coveted by their neighbors in Chiapas (where local elites brutally repressed local indigenous peasants for centuries). But after this laissez-faire autonomy (operationalized as self-determination) was legalized in 1995, Oaxacans became easy prey for outsiders, as certainty no longer existed about who was to defend their individual rights. Customary law ensured ethnic autonomy and representation but at the cost of representing other identities such as those formed by gender, occupation, and religion.

Efforts to legislate recognition of customary law in Oaxaca in 1992 were resoundingly vetoed by Mexico's powerful national government. Juan Manuel Cruz Acevedo, a PRI dissident reformer and protagonist of the 1995 Oaxaca reforms, said that he approached the subsecretary of the Interior Arturo Nunez about legalizing *usos y costumbres* in 1992, but that the executive branch representative accused him of promoting a "state of exception" (Cruz Acevedo interview). Indeed, the timing was not ripe for such reforms until 1995, when a couple of important factors converged. Politicians of the era (e.g., Bailón Corres, Cruz Acevedo, López) openly acknowledged that *usos y costumbres* was legalized to prevent what they imagined might occur if Zapatista-led indigenous uprisings spread to Oaxaca (Bailón Corres, Cruz Acevedo, López 2010 interviews and presentations). Scholarly analysts have suggested that it was a way for the PRI to perpetuate its monopolistic hold over Oaxaca's rural areas in the face of the party's national decline in the late 1980s. For instance, Anaya-Muñoz (2002) and Recondo (2006) have made a cogent argument that even though a consensus existed among Oaxacan state officials and PRI partisans that something had to be done about the Zapatista rebellion, the immediate cause of *usos y costumbres* electoral reform was that in August 1995 the PRI in Oaxaca experienced the most precipitous decline ever in their winning margin in state legislative elections.

Implications of UC for Participation and Representation

Oaxacan UC-based systems constitute, inter alia, a range of practices for selecting leaders, from local assemblies where participants raise their hands to support a candidate (such as San Miguel Chimalapa) to drawing hash marks beneath their candidate's name (such as in Coatecas Altas) to lining up behind their candidate (such as in San Pedro Yolóx). Rather than rigidly defining these practices and establishing legal baselines for them, Mexican state authorities allowed Oaxacan legislators to differentiate UC municipalities from those with political parties and secret ballots, and presumably granted local citizens the autonomy to decide how to implement these practices. So participation clearly favors accountability to the group in the form of citizens' public expression of votes, at the expense of Western-style individual rights to convey one's views at the ballot box. As with the early US regime of electoral institutions, UC was heavily deliberated and implemented after a consensus by those enfranchised to participate. However, for the large minorities excluded in Mexico (and the majority in the United States—non-landowner men, women, African Americans), it could be a nightmare.

The actual electoral rules span a wide range of practices, from leaders selected via communitywide assemblies to leaders selected by five old men in a Council of Elders meeting. In addition to custom-designed elections, UC municipalities also often involve *tequio*. *Tequio* is short-term volunteer work to complete a specific goal such as paving a road or building a school. The precise form these traditions take varies from community to community (similar to the electoral system). In general, the practices are used in public goods-providing communal endeavors that benefit the entire community and succeed only when all citizens are culturally (not legally) compelled to contribute. While UC elections refer to participation in electoral practices, *tequio* reflects ongoing participation in governance. Another indigenous institution, the *cargo* system (or "ladder of community volunteer and elected positions") reflects more the Oaxacan variant of inclusive representation (also characterized by the anti-Federalists referred to in the opening of this chapter).

Under the system of *cargos*, public service is an obligation. All citizens (or, as is often the case, all men, or all Catholic men, or all men residing in county seats rather than outlying communities) must offer service on a rotating basis,[1] every several years, and with increasing responsibilities as they get older. Roles include serving as *topil* (village security agent), errand runner, church caretaker, *mayordomo* (sponsor of patron saint feast days), and mayor. Many communities have separate *cargo* hierarchies for civilian and religious governance. Under the civilian governance system (the one of concern here), the community knows its mayor intimately and the mayor knows all the basic institutions and their functions. *Usos y costumbres* reinforces *cargos* because it recognizes the experience of men who have given a lifetime of public service, and values this lifetime history of loyalty ahead of any other criteria (such as popularity, platform, or skills) for selecting leaders. *Tequio* likewise offers an enormous community benefit, if it is properly supported. This system of voluntarism has been essential to providing community enhancements in poor areas where local governments can contribute, for example, the cement and basketball hoops, but not the labor to build courts.

Cleavages in UC Community Participation and Representation

The introduction of *usos y costumbres* ensured indigenous representation at the municipal level. It did not ensure representation for migrants, women, and people in outlying regions (known as *agencias*). In other words, people gained representation for their ethnic identity but not for their gender, religion, merits, or geographic location. This resulted in conflict. The most prevalent cause of conflict is from discrimination against people in the outlying communities.[2] After this, discrimination against migrants and women are the two most common sources of conflict.

A survey of Oaxaca's municipalities found that conflicts are endemic in the state.[3] Some 52 of the 409 UC-based municipalities surveyed experienced conflicts in the 2007 local elections alone. Twenty of these municipalities fought explicitly over issues related to internal municipal conflicts between groups in the *cabecera* (municipal seat) and groups in the *agencia* (outlying region) or explicitly over the distribution of resources in the municipality.

When asked to provide concrete reasons for the conflicts, survey respondents often stated that the conflicts were caused by issues of participation and representation in the municipal government. The municipality of Santiago Miltepec had a conflict over voting participation. San Juan Lajarcia had a conflict over a female candidate, Olivia Ortíz Ruíz. Teococuilco de Marcos Peréz had a conflict because of migrant participation. Animas Trujano and San Agustin de las Juntas both had problems over the participation of community outsiders (*avecindados*) in the elections. In case after case, the "minority majority" (indigenous groups who gained UC recognition on the claim they were discriminated against by the broader community) was accused of discriminating against "new minorities" within their midst.

As these cases show, in many versions of the UC system, there is a lack of respect for nonethnically derived individual rights, such as those due to citizens regardless of their gender or religion. For example, as per Table 8.1, only 76.3 percent of non-Catholics are allowed to vote, and even women in the county seat are denied the vote 75.5 percent of the time. Indeed, gender discrimination is a problem (Danielson and Eisenstadt, 2009), and postelectoral conflicts are thought to be the tip of the iceberg of broader social grievances, such as resource maldistribution, corruption, agrarian conflicts, and territorial disputes over municipal lines (Eisenstadt, 2004:132–161). The secret ballot exists only in some 12 percent of UC elections, and in some 21 percent, the PRI is actively involved in officially nonpartisan elections as either the office where candidates registered or as an interest group that vetted candidates, or as an arbiter of the electoral rules (Eisenstadt, 2007:62). The greatest source of disenfranchisement, by far, was that of citizens residing in village hamlets outside the county seat who were routinely and summarily denied the right to vote.

Ironically, UC recognition may have defused tensions relating to ethnic representation, but it exacerbated the existing tensions between center and peripheral communities. Since the 1990s, residents of outlying communities have increasingly protested their inability to participate in elections or share in the allocation of federal transfers. In 2003 alone, residents of Oaxaca's 731 outlying communities (all located within the state's 570 municipalities) filed more than 200 complaints alleging they did not receive fair portions of the federal resource distribution (Hernández-Díaz and Juan Martínez, 2007:180). To Hernández-Díaz and Juan Martínez, "These contradictions between communities within a municipality have found articulation in the electoral process which they use to pressure to have their demands attended to or if they are customary law communities, they demand participation in the process whereby their municipal authorities are elected" (2007: 162).

It is also worth noting that even where the seat-hamlet cleavage is not decisive, it is still prominently felt. For example, in San Miguel Tlacotepec, the conflict over proper election procedures between two longtime political clans after the 2007 UC election only mattered in the municipal seat; elections were not even held in the outlying communities. "They are just forced to sign the results," said Orlando Molina Maldonado (interview 2009), the losing candidate. In Santa Catarina Minas, despite the fact that women were denied the right to vote, groups of women voted in the 2001 town assembly elections anyway and demonstrably changed the outcome of the election. Feminist Graciela Ángeles Carreño, who encouraged the women to vote, said that the response to their movement varied widely between *agencia* and the municipal seat, and even within different neighborhoods with their own UC traditions. She said the debate over whose procedures to follow became so heated one time that a brawl broke out on the village basketball court between teams from different geographic areas of the community (interview 2009). While bigger philosophical questions, like those relating to multicultural rights were also in play, they were often subordinated to much more mundane and localized concerns, like who got how much of the federally directed budget for a given municipality.

Clientelism in Participation and Representation, Despite Efforts to Remove Parties

Indigenous rights movements, such as that in Oaxaca, are palliatives to the hardships of being heard in the countryside where old corporatist forms of interest articulation have been dismantled without being replaced by any new means of aggregating or expressing citizen voices. Some had argued that UC recognition would break the patronage stranglehold the PRI had over rural Mexico where votes were routinely traded for a few sheets of roof laminate or cans of food. Before legalization of *usos y costumbres,* votes would be harvested by local *caciques,* or chieftains, who were affiliated with the PRI and rewarded accordingly for loyal service. Prior to the economic crisis of the mid-1980s, the PRI had actually established a patronage supply network to respond to the thousands of requests from local affiliate groups. Nationally, the PRI's patronage supply network included 778 union stores, 155 butcher shops, thirty-five consumer cooperatives, fifteen bakeries, fifteen supply depots, and one pharmacy (González Compeán, and Lomeli, 2000:533).

This grip was increasingly important to the PRI as it started facing real electoral competition in local races in the late 1980s. Oaxaca was known as a bastion of PRI support and provided a strategic reserve of votes, so-called green votes, which could be easily mobilized (or falsified) in Mexico's rural hinterlands. Turnout in Oaxaca was often dubiously high and suspiciously one-sided. This was the case in the heavily contested 1988 federal elections. (It is possible that that election was actually won by Party of the Democratic Revolution (PRD) founder Cuauhtémoc Cárdenas, although the PRI's Carlos Salinas was ultimately inaugurated.) In that contest, 87 Oaxaca electoral precincts granted 100 percent of their 40,664 votes to the PRI (Aziz Nassif and Molinar Horcasitas, 1990:166). This was a particularly unlikely event given that it was a tight, three-way election. Official returns granted Salinas a 20-point margin of victory (51 percent Salinas to 31 percent Cárdenas) and credible allegations of fraud were widespread. While savvy and organized opponents, particularly PAN lawyers (dubbed "parachutists" because they were dropped in from Mexico City [Eisenstadt, 2004:181 fn 17]), contested PRI fraud in critical races, Mexico's small, rural communities were largely ignored. It was possible for the PRI to maintain hegemony in these areas and claim to have received all municipal votes cast.[4]

Direct recognition of UC in 1995 has weakened the PRI's hold in that rural communities can now undertake local elections and make decisions without direct state intervention. But, UC could not completely dismantle the strong corporatist ties that have permeated Oaxaca's peasant associations[5] or the end practice of local *caciques* buying votes for the PRI in state races with fertilizer, school supplies, or canned food. The PRI can still channel desperately needed resources to indigenous communities in order to coopt votes or repress dissent.[6] And political parties still control nearly all discretionary spending because local taxation authority is minimal.

UC recognition has not completely loosened the PRI's monopoly in Oaxaca. Stories abound of local partisans appropriating party ticket colors for their supposedly nonpartisan leader selection processes or of PRI operatives recruiting voters in local elections (Recondo, 2006). In the 2008 survey, we found that parties were often cited as one of the disputing groups in conflicts in UC communities. There are six instances of PRI leaders disputing electoral results in UC communities, two instances with PRD leaders, and three with PAN leaders. And although parties need to continue to operate if UC municipalities are to influence state and national races where customary law does not apply, UC systems at the local level may be dampening indigenous participation in these federal and state non-UC elections. A recent study by Goodman and Hiskey (2008) shows that turnout in national elections is lower among voters from UC municipalities, which, like most of Oaxaca's municipalities, seem to also be growing independent of the PRI.

Perhaps even more important has been the inability or unwillingness of Oaxaca state courts to judicially intercede in UC controversies. In the absence of judicial challenges, Oaxaca's unicameral state legislature (in partnership with the governor) has been able to manipulate UC election outcomes. The state legislature has dissolved hundreds of Oaxaca's 570 municipal governments over the last five years on grounds of "ungovernability."[7] However, unlike during the PRI's heyday, when the legislature (often at the governor's bequest) allowed at least some opposition participation on appointed interim city councils (albeit in secondary roles), the increasingly beleaguered party, which narrowly defeated a left-right coalition of the PRD and PAN in the 2004 gubernatorial race and finally lost the governorship in 2010, increasingly used the state legislature to dissolve local governments and substitute nonelected administrators directly responsible to the governor during the administration of Murat (1998–2004). More recently—and offering a partial explanation for the PRI's 2010 defeat—Governor Ulises Ruíz (2004–2010) did not even bother. According to several informants (Arnaud Viñas, Fernández, Hernández Fernández, Juan Martínez interviews), Ruíz imposed his will without even pursuing legalistic cover, leading the governor to intractable difficulties in relations with interest groups and political factions, which led to the 2006 Oaxaca teachers' strike and civil society social movement, and the state's subsequent political paralysis.

By seizing the opportunity disorder presented to send armies of administrators into dozens of UC municipalities, especially between 2001 and 2004 (see Blas López, 2007:89–119), the PRI was able to consolidate support in key areas prior to the closely contested gubernatorial race in 2004. That same strategy fell short in 2010, however, as Governor Ruíz's authoritarianism led Oaxacans to elect a non-PRI governor for the first time since before World War II. More shocking, perhaps, have been the PRI's efforts to directly intervene in customary elections. In more than one-third of the allegedly pure UC municipalities, the PRI participated in deciding how customary elections would transpire, candidate selection and registration, and/or election organization and certification, according to the 1997 catalogue of elections in Oaxaca's 418 UC municipalities (Aquino Centeno and Velásquez Cepeda, 1997). Indeed, analysts are watching closely to see how quickly change at the gubernatorial level trickles down to Oaxaca's localities. Even if internal norms had developed consistent with individual rights guaranteed in Mexico's constitution, the aggressive intervention by Oaxaca's governor in UC local affairs, with or without the PRI, greatly limited the effectiveness of UC representation and in some cases, at least, made indigenous communities vulnerable to the authoritarian governor, as they tilted at the windmills of *usos y costumbres*.

Internal autonomy says nothing about resources of the state destined to autonomous regions. Nor does it speak to broader relations, in terms of representation, between state authorities (governors, state legislators, national congressional members), all beholden to their political parties, and the local administrations, elected via UC. And in Oaxaca, particularly, unlike nations with national-level indigenous rights movements—like Bolivia—the bond between UC local administrations and party-elected state and national representatives is tenuous.

Broader Implications of UC Recognition in Oaxaca

UC recognition has helped ignite a fierce normative debate over whether to legally recognize existing cultural differences and strengthen group identities, emphasizing forms of representation based on kinship loyalty, or to view culture as basically conditional and incorporate the rights of individuals to maximize their potential (i.e., Burkean elitist representation based on merit). The Mexican constitution includes impressive language about individual and group rights, although until the 1990s this language went largely untested. At that time, individual rights started to gain importance through a gradual strengthening of the human rights ombudsmen, electoral institutions, and then the judiciary. Also, while labor law in Mexico had traditionally been strong, in that it protected the PRI-state's corporatist pillars, a preliminary debate over multiculturalism arose as perhaps the first vital group rights discussion in democratizing Mexico apart from labor law.[8] Nothing very substantive came of it, but this new debate about multicultural rights laid the groundwork for what was to come: the Zapatista uprising. Their multicultural, progroup rights, antiglobalization, and antigovernment rhetoric generated tremendous debate in Mexico and around the world about the meaning of multiculturalism in a liberal democracy.

Before describing the set of municipalities where UC recognition increased conflicts, it bears mention that in some cases, those where UC is practiced by consensus in a harmonious manner, the reforms seem to have decreased municipal unrest, increased respect for longstanding traditional practices, and even reduced partisan involvement in the electoral process. Although the PRI did stay involved in communities where it had gained footholds, as described later in this chapter, many municipalities remained relatively free from partisan influence with regard to local elections.[9] So when we speak of increasing conflict in UC communities we are addressing a sizable minority of Oaxaca's 418 UC-governed municipalities.

At Odds with Theory, Customary Law in Practice

Before UC was formally recognized, elections in Oaxaca were haphazard and undemocratic affairs. Local authorities would select leaders via UC and then have to legitimize those selections by registering the winners as unchallenged PRI candidates (Recondo, 2001: 94; Velásquez, 2000: 96–98). But political representation by this local candidate was not guaranteed because the unicameral state legislature routinely dismissed duly elected mayors and replaced them with gubernatorial appointees from a pool of politically acceptable local PRI loyalists. Starting in the 1970s and 1980s, opposition party candidates, frustrated by election rigging and corrupt vote tallying, protested their losses and demanded the creation of multiparty municipal councils as an alternative to the appointment of interim mayors. Under this system, at least they were assured of holding some position. By the early 1990s, conflicts occurred in more than 15 percent of local elections (Eisenstadt, 2007:58).[10] UC was intended to diminish the frequency and intensity of these conflicts and, thereby, cut back on the state's involvement in naming interim governments and municipal councils. This practice had begun to take up an inordinate amount of the state legislature's time and attention. In 1992, 48 percent of the 116 decrees issued by the Oaxaca state legislature addressed the composition of new municipal governments (Oaxaca State Legislature Decree Book, 1993). UC recognition seemed like a means of improving local representation without much of a cost to the grassroots groups that had been short-changed by the authoritarian political boss system.

UC advocates like Jaime Martínez Luna, a long-time Oaxacan activist, for example, claim that governance through UC community assemblies, *comunalicracia,* as he calls it, increases accountability because all decisions and positions have to be defended publicly. According to the advocates, electoral assemblies (which are held instead of secret ballot elections) are an effective means of vetting candidates, even though they may not draw out the specific platforms of incoming governments in the traditional sense. And while some 70 percent of mayors surveyed said that preelectoral assemblies in their towns do address the selection of candidate slates, only about 21 percent tend to offer any evaluation of the prior administration, and about 15 percent consider policy priorities for the incoming administration (Eisenstadt, 2011:109). In other words, communal assembly participants did usually have a role in deciding who would govern them, even if community priorities for the incoming administration were less frequently considered. *Comunalicracia,* to varying degrees, can be representative and democratic, although it does emphasize loyalty and service, and "being known in the community," as advocates call it, over individual merits and political platforms.

The success of UC in promoting harmonious local governance may also be overly romanticized. Those seeking to end legal recognition of UC argue that, in addition to discriminating against minorities, the system allows local communities to emphasize hierarchy at the expense of meritocracy. Young people with university educations rarely return to their UC villages, say detractors like López López (interview 1998), because they will have to spend up to one-third of their time serving in generalist *cargo* positions rather than using their professional training. In extreme cases, young accountants and lawyers serve as errand runners for semiliterate or illiterate mayors who are unable to fill out municipal expenditure spreadsheets or interpret local ordinances but who spent decades scaling the *cargos* hierarchy. The traditional view of community service as voluntary also may be impractical. Authorities in some communities are beginning to receive payment for service; otherwise, they are forced to migrate to seasonal fruit-picking jobs in Sinaloa and Baja, California. They can better support their families as undocumented workers in US agriculture, construction, or service sectors than they can through subsistence farming and volunteer public service in Oaxaca.[11]

The idea that UC will diminish postelectoral conflict is also not borne out by empirical evidence. Between 1995 and 2007, the number of postelectoral conflicts (contestation of the results by losers through protests and mobilizations) in Oaxaca's UC communities actually doubled overall. Nationally, the percentage of contested elections diminished over the same electoral cycles. In Oaxaca, postelectoral conflict in municipalities with party-based elections fell from a rate of 33 percent in 1995 to 17 percent in 2007. In UC communities, that rate started at 5 percent in 1995 and doubled to 10 percent in 2003 and 2007. Oaxaca's postelectoral conflicts, while not as numerous as those in neighboring Chiapas, for example, which had an average conflict rate of 24 percent over the last five electoral cycles, were much more severe, resulting in dozens of deaths (Eisenstadt, 2004).[12] In Oaxaca, some 39 people died in postelectoral conflicts between 1989 and 2003, and while the intensity of conflicts has diminished since then, their frequency has continued to climb in UC municipalities while dropping everywhere else. In contrast to Oaxaca, there were 18 postelectoral conflict fatalities in Chiapas over those 15 years and 196 nationwide. The overall intensity of conflicts in UC municipalities was 2.3 on a scale of zero to three (zero meaning no conflict and three meaning conflict with mortalities), which is about the same as for Oaxaca's party-based municipalities.[13] However, more than 11 percent of Oaxaca's conflicts (counting UC and party-based elections) reached severity level three, whereas fewer than 8 percent of conflicts nationwide were that severe.

It is important to consider the procedural reality of legal norms within UC electoral systems to better understand the relationship between civil unrest and lack of participatory rights in UC communities. Process tracing of conflict resolutions shows that the lack of formal jurisdiction of electoral courts and institutes over UC elections does contribute to the degeneration of contested elections into power plays. Loud demonstrations of strength are more decisive than carefully constructed legal arguments. Political activists (Moreno Alcántara interview, 1998; Cruz López interview, 2004) and election authorities (Jiménez Pacheco interview, 1998) acknowledge that the ability to mobilize supporters carries more weight than formal legal procedures under current UC legislation. Whereas electoral courts have jurisdiction over party-based elections, conflicts over UC elections have been mediated on an ad hoc basis. In other words, as stated by Ángeles Carreño (interview) in reference to Santa Catarina Minas's turbulent 2001 election: "The electoral institute lawyers and director of *usos y costumbres* came in the middle of a heated conflict to tell us that UC was whatever we wanted it to be." This lack of legal structure encourages losers to wage their battles in the streets because they know a strong legal case is not worth the paper upon which it is written. This is perhaps why most conflicts in the previous election ended without a legal agreement (19 municipalities of the 52 total). Of the 52 conflicts in the previous election, only Santa María La Asunción ended with a legal agreement. That means that 51 yielded no official legal resolution, but instead relied on informal settlements and mediations (and 12 municipalities did not reach any resolution at all).

Mass mobilization and political finesse, however, can lead to bargaining table victories. The lack of clear mechanisms to resolve postelectoral disputes under UC only encourages groups to ratchet up their level of civil disobedience. In the words of one former Oaxaca government mediator, "Winning and losing elections used to be absolute; now it's relative" (López interview).

Recall Hale's warning that discrimination against individuals could presumably trigger federal government intervention in defense of citizens' constitutional rights. However, state and national officials have been ineffective in their efforts to protect individual rights. Individual rights violations caused by the UC system have thus far not been remedied by state or federal electoral authorities. The federal government is the final arbiter of elections; local decisions are nonbinding.[14] However, rather than establishing a policy of seeking to maximize state and local autonomy, the federal government seemingly has just not bothered to enforce its dictates. In other words, rather than implementing a policy of neoliberal rights as Hale warned (which would undermine indigenous communal rights), Mexico's national government seemingly has just not really taken a position, at least not explicitly (such as in the enforcement of constitutional norms in precedent cases).

In the few cases where the federal electoral court (Tribunal Electoral del Poder Judicial de la Federación (TEPJF) or the Electoral Tribunal of the Federal Judicial Power) has demonstrated that it will favor the constitutional rights of citizens over local traditions, thereby limiting indigenous autonomy (Morales Canales, 2008), there has been no effort by judicial authorities to actually enforce these verdicts. In 2000 Asunción Tlacolulita, for example, the TEPJF overturned the state legislature's routine annulment of a controversial election when two individuals argued that their rights had been violated by the annulment. The TEPJF ordered the Oaxaca Electoral Institute to do "whatever was necessary" to reconcile the factions in the political dispute, including holding of a special election to solve the crisis (Electoral Tribunal, 2001:xix). The special election was never held, however, and subsequent UC elections, although more peaceful, continued to exclude "women, some young people, neighbors from the hamlet *agencia* of San Juan Alotepec, and local citizens who lived outside the community" (Services for an Alternative Education, 2002: 20; 2005: 14–20).

Minority Participation in Customary Law Communities

Asunción Tlacolulita is an example of a larger trend. Conflict over elections continues throughout the state, a throwback to regional and national politics in the last quarter of the twentieth century, when opposition parties tried to win on the streets and at the postelectoral bargaining tables what they lost at the ballot boxes. In Oaxaca's 2007 local election cycle, conflicts emerged due to a multitude of factors, many of which are rooted in barriers to participation. The most commonly cited cause of conflict was the administration and distribution of resources (12 municipalities cite this as a cause of conflict in the previous election) and the tension between the *cabecera* and *agencias* (eight cite this tension between "municipal seat" and outlying hamlet communities as a cause of conflict in the 2007 cycle). Indeed these two categories often capture the same phenomenon because the tension between *cabecera* and *agencia* is usually caused by the *agencia's* lack of ability to participate in the elections and have a say in the distribution of resources.

Discrimination by the municipal seat against the outlying hamlets is pervasive (see Table 8.1) and is a factor in every municipality with *agencias* (most of Oaxaca's municipalities). The scores of conflicts over municipal cleavages basically revolve around a demand that *all* residents be permitted to participate in elections for officeholders (i.e., the mayor and municipal government) who determine how municipal funds are spent.

The scope of the problem in *agencia-cabecera* relations is exemplified by the remote Zapotec town of Santiago Yaveo, where residents from the 11 outlying hamlet communities demanded their right to vote in the communal assemblies prior to the 2001 election. Based on claims that 80 percent of the population was not receiving its share of federal government funds and appeals to universal human rights norms, the county seat guaranteed that two of the six city council positions would be held by hamlet residents to be decided among the hamlet villagers (Gottwald and Morales 2003, 48). The hamlets rejected the offer, however, wanting an even more equitable distribution of seats, and held their own separate elections for all six seats. The state's administrative electoral institute invalidated the hamlet election and named the victor of the county seat elections mayor, even though only 496 of 3,347 residents of the municipality had been allowed to vote. The state legislature overturned that ruling and sent a town administrator to run Santiago Yaveo until a special election could be held in 2002 (Gottwald and Morales, 2003:48).

In the meantime, the hamlets organized protests to keep pressure on the municipal seat. They blocked roads, temporarily kidnapped uncooperative state government representatives, and organized meetings to establish a consensus and define new strategies. A lawyer was hired to take the case of *agencia* disenfranchisement to the federal electoral court, but some hamlets sought to informally resolve the conflict by negotiating through political parties and elected representatives. When negotiations failed, the governor named a permanent administrator to run the municipality, who initiated public works projects with *agencias* that would "work with" him (Gottwald and Morales, 2003:50). Conflict reemerged when that administrator failed to finish public works, opting instead to start new projects in other politically beneficial locations, which exacerbated longstanding disagreements between the ranchers and farmers over property rights. After months of deliberation, the federal court ordered a special election in 2002. That election was never held because the Oaxaca Electoral Institute argued that conditions were not suitable to guarantee free and fair elections (Hernández-Díaz and Juan Martínez, 2007:188; Gottwald and Morales, 2003:51–53). Santiago Yaveo did not hold elections again until 2007.

Such was the case—to one degree or another—across Oaxaca. Hernández-Díaz and Juan Martínez (2007) documented a dozen other cases where similar postelectoral conflicts stemmed from this center-periphery cleavage. Among the most notorious were conflicts in Zapotitlán del Río, San Miguel Mixtepec, and Santiago Matatlán. In each of these cases, the authors write, "The demand by the hamlets to re-establish elections by parties is directly linked to assignment of financial resources.... Their preference for partisan elections is strictly instrumental: they want to guarantee the *agencias*... a more favorable position in distributing municipal budgets" (Hernández-Díaz and Juan Martínez, 2007:191).

In addition to participatory barriers to those in the outlying communities, UC communities exhibit other forms of barriers to groups within the *cabecera* (municipal seat). Most notably, women have been discouraged in large and small ways from participating in political life in UC communities. In 2009, Betriz Leyva Beltran, a teacher and PRD activist, was killed after challenging the decisions of municipal authorities in San Pedro Jicayan in Oaxaca's Mixe region.[15] However, the most heinous cases may be those of de facto discrimination, without even claims to de jure legitimacy, as in the aforementioned cases, where the men at least argued they sought to discriminate on the basis of existing norms or rules. In Capulalpam de Mendez, Municipal Treasurer Olga Toro described the reaction by men to the increased participation of women in communal assemblies: "To suppress their active participation, anytime a woman attempted to speak, the men would make disruptive noise by vigorously shaking a cup or a can filled with pebbles (Danielson and Eisenstadt, 2009:171)." While this practice has ceased over the last couple of years, Toro cited the antagonism it brought as perhaps part of the reason why, as of 2007, she remained the only woman who participated regularly in municipal community assemblies.

Lastly, migrants have a similar story of participation barriers. The lack of representation is most visible in the municipality of Santa Ana del Valle in Oaxaca where they exclude the migrants who constitute over half of the community's economically active population from voting in UC elections. The community has one of the highest migration rates of all Mexico. More than 1,000 of the town's 3,000 residents live abroad (including two-thirds of the male population between 19 and 60 years old).[16] Even though they are excluded from voting, they are still expected to contribute to Santa Ana's communal well-being. This double standard is a constant source of friction, as citizens' lands are expropriated when migrants fail to return to serve in volunteer *cargo* positions. The tensions are leading in Santa Ana, and elsewhere in Oaxaca, to innovative new *usos y costumbres*. For example, community leaders sought technological solutions to barriers to participation by holding separate assemblies in Santa Ana, and for expatriates, in Los Angeles. While the procedural mechanisms are still being fine-tuned, FAX machines, the Internet, and Skype long-distance phone conferencing may help the community reach middle-ground accommodations, which grant migrants representation back in Santa Ana while they are working in the United States and sending home remittances.

The Trade-off Between Ethnic Autonomy and Democratic Participation

Would experiments in self-governance by southern Mexico's indigenous citizens have fared better if they had included more expansive autonomy rights such as those sought by Chiapas' Zapatistas (a form of geographical autonomy granting self-governance to indigenous communities)? Critics, like the former director of the Oaxaca electoral institute, Cipriano Flores Cruz, say greater autonomy would have prompted the state to abandon autonomous areas. He argues that the more extreme groups who have sought indigenous autonomy in Mexico (i.e., the Zapatistas) do not actually wish to govern and "will not define, nor execute, nor evaluate" policies (interview 2005). Ultimately, this would leave the region's interests totally unrepresented at the national level, where the overwhelming amount of Mexico's public resources is doled out. Flores Cruz argues that better representation of indigenous positions within existing government and partisan structures is what's needed. In their ideological migration from revolutionary Marxists to ethnic warriors to social democrats, the Zapatistas seem to have implicitly acknowledged this.

The broader point is that autonomy must be coupled with strong representation and local governance in order to deliver communities the independence they seek from the state. Autonomy coupled with weak representation and poor quality local governance will be manipulated and disenfranchise the very groups it is intended to empower. To Burguete (2009), autonomy has four preconditions: (1) some sort of territorial definition, (2) internal self-government, (3) set jurisdiction over territory and internal governance, and (4) "specific, constitutionally-established competences and powers" (2009:13). What the Zapatistas in neighboring Chiapas and Oaxaca's

UC advocates showed was that recognition without a share of state resources or competent governance is of limited use. Autonomy is only beneficial to communities that have the resources and capacity to effectively call their own shots. Furthermore, and with regard to the questions of participation and representation, autonomy is always relative. The granting of autonomy to one central group can deny it to minorities within the same zone of territorial autonomy. This point could not be more obvious in Oaxaca.

The fact that collective rather than individual rights claims of participation and representation have dominated southern Mexico's conversation—often in the form of debates over autonomy—during a decade when neoliberal globalization, deregulation, and open markets continued to bear down on rural Latin Americans had real costs. Despite these large-scale economic transformations, indigenous rights advocates kept their focus dogmatically trained on indigenous autonomy rather than on the broader issue of rural sustainable development that encompasses indigenous autonomy. Liberalization of corn commodities markets in 2005 hit Mexican rural dwellers especially hard. As stated by Otero (2007:76) in a salient critique of Yashar (2005), this narrow "ethnic politics" focus "misses important class-structural aspects behind the fight for autonomy, such as control over land and territory," and furthermore equates corporatism only to ethnic-based organization (i.e., that which is not indigenous) rather than as a system of interest articulation that can occur around class or economic interests.

President Felipe Calderón (2006–2012) of the right-leaning National Action Party (PAN) did not further Mexico's prospects for rural development when he abolished the secretariat for agrarian reform in the summer of 2009, markedly weakening the future of communal lands that had been granted starting after the Mexican Revolution's constitution of 1917 as state-supported group-held lands. While the effort to survey and title all these lands during the Fox and Calderón administrations did not succeed in rural southern Mexico to the same extent as it did in the more privatized North, most observers assume that Mexico's interest in using land reform as a redistributive mechanism to help bolster livelihood in the countryside has ended. Rural dwellers, without state supports for agricultural products, have increasingly had to sell their land and move to Mexico's cities or to the United States.

For those who have stayed behind in Oaxaca, UC continues to repress individuals and minorities in indigenous communities, including Protestants and other non-Catholic groups, residents of outlying hamlet communities not connected to municipal seats, and women. Oaxaca human rights activists like Méndez (interview 2005) still believe that individual and communal rights can be reconciled: "We understand that the community has to reproduce itself, but on the other hand, we want authorities to consider the position of individuals and it is time for rights to be recognized from inside communities as well as just from the outside." Assuming that the Oaxacans can articulate a coherent vision for reform of UC with enfranchisement and participation for all, despite the indigenous movement's history of disunity there (compared to Chiapas), Oaxaca could ultimately offer the most useful model of partially autonomous institutions for places like Bolivia and other burgeoning Latin American rights movements.

Notes

1. In some communities, migrants tapped by the municipal religious and/or civil authorities (often called the Council of Elders) must return to serve or be banished. Increasingly, however, migrants to the United States are allowed to "buy" the services of someone local to fulfill their *cargo*. This trend is accelerating the decline of this custom and increasingly allowing women to offer *cargos* as "acting" heads of household (Alcántara Guzmán interview, 2004).

2. A causal analysis by Eisenstadt and Rios (2011) found that the decisive cause of scores of conflicts after local elections in Oaxaca was tensions between municipal "seats," which receive federal and state funding and must then dole out resources to outlying areas, and outlying *agencias*, which often claim (with justification) that they have not received their share of transfers.

3. This survey was conducted also with Moisés Jaime Bailón Corres, Michael S. Danielson, Cipriano Flores Cruz, and Carlos Sorroza, as part of a collaboration between American University and the Benito Juárez Autonomous University of Oaxaca (UABJO). The total N was 404 of Oaxaca's 418 UC-governed municipalities. The questionnaire was administered to town mayors by local representatives of the state government's adult literacy agency, which also asked questions for which it sought responses.

4. This circumstance did not hold in 2010, as allegations of authoritarianism, an apparent unwillingness to distribute patronage, and the left-right coalition against his centrist platform overwhelmed Governor Ruíz and his party. While the PRI's political machine is still powerful in Oaxaca, Governor Gabino Cue may start to actively dismantle the PRI's generations-long hold on local politics.

5. The National Peasant Confederation (CNC), headed until recently by Senator Heladio Ramírez López, a former PRI Oaxaca governor, is still more powerful in Oaxaca than elsewhere. As one Oaxaca PRI leader said matter-of-factly, "Whenever an uncontrolled mobilization happens, I call the head of the peasant confederation (Cortés López interview)."

6. The PRI infiltrated dozens of UC municipalities over decades. Three municipalities openly accepted that the means of selecting new leaders was designed by the PRI, and more than 40 acknowledged that the PRI openly participated in certifying the winner. More than 160 admitted that even before UC was legalized, the custom was routinely practiced as a sort of definitive primary. The

leader was selected by assembly, a Council of Elders, or via another customary method. The winner registered with the PRI (and/or other parties starting in the 1990s) to be formally "elected" via the party ticket, even though she or he was the sole candidate and the outcome of the election was a foregone conclusion (Aquino Centeno and Velásquez Cepeda, 1997).

7. Governor José Murat (1998–2004) suspended 140 municipal governments, as many as 30 at a time (Del Collado, 2003), ensuring PRI dominance. He also punished mayors in even the poorest communities who could not find sizable enough campaign contributions to support the PRI in their paltry budgets.

8. The effects of *indigenismo* in the Mexican countryside around the middle of the twentieth century are aptly characterized by Rus: "The Cárdenistas and their successors reached inside the native communities, not only changing leaders but rearranging the governments, creating new offices to deal with labor and agrarian matters at the same time they were granting vast new powers to the officials charged with maintaining relations with the party and state.... To some extent, the result of this process—the centralization of political and economic power within communities and the tying of that power to the state—resembles the *caciquismo*, or 'bossism,' that characterizes Mexican rural society in general" (Rus 1994: 267). More broadly, this was part of the corporatist tradition by which the ruling Party of the Institutional Revolution (PRI) organized the National Peasant Confederation (CNC in Spanish) as one of its three "pillars" by which massive organizations of government supporters were mobilized (the other two "pillars" were the urban workers and the "popular sector," which included millions of teachers and government employees).

9. Overall, 92 percent of municipal authority members surveyed said that it was "never" necessary to be proposed by a political party to be elected as a member of the municipal government. Also, when asked, 70 percent of mayors said they were not members of a political party. The community of Guelatao de Juárez was cited as one where no parties had strongholds in local races. However, even in such municipalities, parties did try to mobilize for state and national elections, and hence could not be excluded entirely.

10. While still rife with conflict, preliminary data from 2008 local elections in Oaxaca indicate that postelectoral conflicts have diminished slightly from previous cycles.

11. Nationwide, remittances from migrants to the United States served as the primary income source for over 1.6 million households (Sarabia and Galán) by 2005. The 2000 census estimated that 2.6 percent of Oaxaca's men over 18 had migrated to the United States, but this estimate is thought to severely underreport the true number.

12. According to former governor José Murat (as quoted by Flores Cruz interview, 2005), "Postelectoral conflicts in Oaxaca are measured by the number of cadavers they produce."

13. These averages fall between severity level two (multiple-event mobilizations lasting less than one month) and three (conflicts producing serious injuries and/or building occupations or other manifestations lasting longer than one month).

As per Eisenstadt (2004, 135–140), with conflation of the four categories into three, postelectoral conflict intensity was coded as follows: Three for conflicts resulting in deaths, two for conflicts producing serious injuries and/or building occupations (or other manifestations) lasting longer than one event, and one for single-iteration (one-day) mobilizations.

14. Reforms to Oaxaca's state law were approved by the state legislature in 2008, allowing the possibility—for the first time—that UC elections might also involve electoral court complaints, but there was, as of 2010, still no implementing legislation or rules to bring electoral court mediation/regulation of UC into effect (Oaxaca Electoral Institute 2009, 169–173).

15. Mexico's attorney general in June 2009 instructed Oaxacan authorities to investigate Leyva's death and the National Human Rights Commission issued a similar proclamation that an investigation was needed to see if there had been any political "cover up" of Leyva's politicized death (Zafra, 2009).

16. According to the National Population Council (Conapo), Santa Ana del Valle has the highest "index of migration intensity" of any municipality nationwide. Population data are from 2000 census, although the count of 360 males between 19 and 60 present in town, with 608 absent, was taken in 2003 (Molina Ramirez, 2006).

References

Alcántara Guzmán, Armando, Oaxaca delegate of the Commission of Indigenous Rights (CDI), Oaxaca City, Oaxaca, July 17, 2004.

Anaya-Muñoz, Alejandro. 2002. "Governability and Legitimacy in Mexico: The Legalisation of Indigenous Electoral Institutions in Oaxaca." Department of Government, University of Essex, Ph.D. thesis.

Ángeles Carreño, Graciela, former secretary of Santa Catarina Minas and poll worker during 2001 postelectoral conflict, interview in Santa Catarina Minas, Oaxaca, June 22, 2009.

Aquino Centeno, Salvador and María Cristina Velásquez Cepeda. 1997. *Usos y costumbres para la renovación de los ayuntamientos de Oaxaca.* Oaxaca City: Centro de Investigaciones y Estudios Superiores de Antropología Social/Instituto Estatal Electoral de Oaxaca.

Arnaud Viñas, Enrique, former finance director for Oaxaca governor Diodoro Carrasco, interview in Oaxaca City, Oaxaca, June 29, 2009.

Aziz Nassif, Alberto and Juan Molinar Horcasitas. 1990. "Los Resultados Electorales" in González Casanova, Pablo, ed. *Segundo Informe la Democrácia: México el 6 de Julio de 1988.* Mexico City: Siglo Veintiuno Editores, 138–171.

Bailón Corres, Moisés Jaime. 1999. *Pueblos Indios, Élites y Territorio—Sistemas de Dominio Regional en el Sur de México—Una historia política de Oaxaca.* Mexico City: El Colegio de México.

Bailón Corres, Moisés Jaime, presentation at annual conference of the National Association of Political Science and Public Administration Students, "Recapitulating

Usos y Costumbres 15 Years Later (Recapitulando los Usos y Costumbres 15 Años Después)," Oaxaca City, Oaxaca, November 10, 2010.

Blas López, Cuauhtémoc. 2007. *Oaxaca, Insula de Rezagos—Crítica a sus gobiernos de razón y de costumbre.* Oaxaca City: Editorial Siembra.

Burguete Cal y Mayor, Araceli. 2009. "Constitutional Multiculturalism in Chiapas: Hollow Reforms to Nullify Autonomy Rights," paper presented at the conference "Reconciling Liberal Pluralism and Group Rights: Oaxaca, Mexico's Multiculturalism Experiment in Comparative Perspective," February 20, American University, Washington, D.C.

Cortés López, Elías, Oaxaca PRI sub-secretary of elections, interview in Oaxaca City, Oaxaca, November 26, 1998.

Cruz Acevedo, Juan Manuel, interview in Oaxaca City, Oaxaca, November 10, 2010.

Cruz López, Oscar, PRD state legislator, interview in Oaxaca, Oaxaca, July 20, 2004.

Danielson, Michael S. and Todd A. Eisenstadt. 2009. "Walking Together, but in Which Direction? Gender Discrimination and Multicultural Practices in Oaxaca, Mexico," *Politics & Gender* 5: 153–184.

Del Collado, Fernando. 2003. "Murat, Retrato de un Cacique: Entrevista con José Murat," in *Enfoque* insert to *Reforma* (October 19), 13–18.

Electoral Tribunal of the Judicial Power of the Federation. 2001. Colección Sentencias Relevantes No. 4: Elección de Concejales al Ayuntamiento del Municipio de Asunción Tlacolulita, Estado de Oaxaca, por Usos y Costumbres (Caso Oaxaca). Mexico City: Tribunal Electoral del Poder Judicial de la Federación.

Eisenstadt, Todd A. 2004. *Courting Democracy in Mexico: Party Strategies and Electoral Institutions.* New York: Cambridge University Press.

Eisenstadt, Todd A. 2007. *"Usos y Costumbres* and Post-Electoral Conflicts in Oaxaca, Mexico, 1995–2004: An Empirical and Normative Assessment," *Latin American Research Review* 42.1: 52–77.

Eisenstadt, Todd A. 2011. *Politics, Identity, and Southern Mexico's Indigenous Rights Movements.* New York: Cambridge University Press.

Eisenstadt, Todd A. and Viridiana Rios. 2011. "Multiculturalism and Political Conflict in Indigenous Latin America: Mexico in Comparative Perspective." Typescript.

Fernández, Tania, leader of "Cinco Señores" barricade during 2007 Oaxaca APPO movement and UABJO graduate student in sociology, interview in Oaxaca City, Oaxaca, June 29, 2009.

Flores Cruz, Cipriano, advisor to the PRI and ex-director of the Oaxaca State Electoral Institute, interview in Oaxaca City, Oaxaca, July 22, 2004 and May 17, 2005.

González Compeán, Miguel and Leonardo Lomeli. 2000. *El Partido de la Revolución: Institución y Conflicto (1928–1999).* Mexico City: Fondo de Cultura Económica.

Goodman, Gary L. and Jonathan T. Hiskey. 2008. "Exit Without Leaving: Political Disengagement in High Migration Municipalities in Mexico," *Comparative Politics* 40.2, 169–188.

Gottwald, Dorothee and Lourdes Morales. 2003. "Espacio político y jurisdicción electoral: el caso de Santiago Yaveo," *América Indígena* LIX (2), April-June, 43–58.

Guerra Pulido, Maira Melisa. 2000. "Usos y costumbres o partidos políticos: una decisión de los municipios oaxaqueños." Undergraduate thesis in political science, Centro de Investigación y Docencia Económicas (CIDE), Mexico City. Typescript.

Hale, Charles R. 2002. "Does Multiculturalism Menace? Governance, Cultural Rights and the Politics of Identity in Guatemala," *Journal of Latin American Studies* 34.3: 485–524.

Hernández Fernández, Sylvia, teacher in Section 22 and leader of Popular Revolutionary Front (Frente Popular Revolucionario—a component of the Popular Assemblies of the People of Oaxaca, or Asambleas Populares del los Pueblos de Oaxaca APPO component group), Oaxaca City, Oaxaca, June 28, 2009.

Hernández- Díaz, Jorge and Victor Leonel Juan Martínez. 2007. *Dilemas de la Institución Municipal—Una Incursión en la Experiencia Oaxaquena.* Mexico City: Miguel Ángel Porrúa Publishers.

Jiménez Pacheco, Juan José, director of *usos y costumbres* section of Oaxaca Electoral Institute, interview in Oaxaca, Oaxaca, November 24, 1998.

Juan Martínez, Victor Leonel, interview in Oaxaca City, Oaxaca, November 10, 2010.

López, Clemente de Jesús, interview in Oaxaca City, Oaxaca, November 10, 2010.

López López, Eric, advisor to the secretary of government, Oaxaca State Government, interviewed in Oaxaca City, Oaxaca, November 24, 1998.

Martínez Luna, Jaime, anthropologist, interviewed in Gelatao, Oaxaca, May 14, 2005.

Méndez, Sara, human rights activist at Centro Derechos Humanos Tierra del Sol in Tlaxiaco, interviewed in Oaxaca City, Oaxaca, May 15, 2005.

Moreno Alcantara, Carlos, PAN Representative to the Oaxaca Electoral Institute, interview in Oaxaca, Oaxaca, November 24, 1998.

Molina Maldonado, Orlando, interview with regent for health of San Miguel Tlacotepec and 2007 mayoral candidate, June 24, 2009, in Juxtlahuapa, Oaxaca.

Molina Ramirez, Tania. 2006. "El viento del norte sopla en las comunidades oaxaqueñas: La migración transforma los usos y costumbres," *Masiosare* 421 (January 15).

Morales Canales, Lourdes. 2008. "Conflicto electoral y cambio social: el caso de San Miguel Quetzaltepec, Mixes," in Hernández-Díaz, Jorge, ed. *Ciudadanías diferenciadas en un estado multicultural: los usos y costumbres en Oaxaca.* Mexico City: Siglo XXI Editorial, 151–174.

Oaxaca Electoral Institute. 2009. *Compendio de Legislación Electoral.* Oaxaca: Instituto Estatal Electoral de Oaxaca.

Oaxaca State Legislature. 1993. Registry of Legislative Decrees 13, 1992–1995. Typescript.

Otero, Gerardo. 2007. "Review Article: Class or Identity Politics? A False Dichotomy," *International Journal of Comparative Sociology* 48.1: 73–80.

Pitkin, Hanna Fenichel. 1972. *The Concept of Representation.* Berkeley: University of California Press.

Recondo, David. 2001. "Usos y costumbres, procesos electorales y autonomía indígena en Oaxaca," in Pasquel, Lourdes de León, ed. *Costumbres, leyes y movimiento indio en Oaxaca y Chiapas*. Mexico City: Centro de Investigaciones y Estudios Superiores en Antropología Social and Miguel Ángel Porrúa, 91–113.

Recondo, David. 2006. "Las costumbres de la democracias: multiculturalismo y democratización en Oaxaca," paper presented at the 2006 Meeting of the Latin American Studies Association, March 15–18 (San Juan).

Regino Montes, Adelfo. 1996. "Foro Indígena Nacional – La Autonomía: Una Forma Concreta de Ejercicio del Derecho a la Libre Determinación y sus Alcances," typescript. San Cristóbal de las Casas, Mexico: Servicios del Pueblo Mixe (group based in Oaxaca, Mexico).

Regino Montes, Adelfo. "Taller 2: Libre Determinación de los Pueblos Indígenas," typescript.

Ríos, Viridiana. 2006. "Conflictividad postelectoral en los Usos y Costumbres de Oaxaca." Undergraduate thesis in political science, Instituto Tecnológico Autónomo de México (ITAM).

Rus, Jan. 1994. "The 'Comunidad Revolucionaria Institucional': The Subversion of Native Government in Highland Chiapas, 1936–1968," in Joseph and Nugent, eds. *Everyday Forms of State Formation: Revolution and the Negotiation of Rule in Modern Mexico*. Durham, NC: Duke University Press.

Services for an Alternative Education. 2002. *Informe de Observación Electoral en Municipios de Usos y Costumbres, Oaxaca 2001*. Oaxaca City: Servicios para una Educación Alternativa, A.C. and Comisión Diocesana de Pastoral Social, 77–81.

Services for an Alternative Education. 2005. *Informe: Observación Electoral en Municipios Indígenas que Rigen por Sistemas Normativos Internos*. Proceso Electoral 2004. Oaxaca City: Servicios para una Educación Alternativa, A.C., 77–81.

Storing, Herbert J. 1981. *The Compete Anti-Federalist—Volume I: What the Anti-Federalists Were For*. Chicago: University of Chicago Press.

Tapia, Alma Alejandra. 2010. "Prevalece marginación de mujeres en materia electoral: Alanís Figueroa," *La Jornada-Zacatecas* (March 10), 1. http://www.trife.gob.mx/comunicacionsocial/resumen/resumen/pdf/2010/140310.pdf (accessed September 16, 2010).

Velásquez Cepeda, María Cristina. 2000. *El nombramiento—Las elecciones por usos y costumbres en Oaxaca*. Oaxaca: Instituto Estatal Electoral de Oaxaca.

Yashar, Deborah J. 2005. *Contesting Citizenship: The Rise of Indigenous Movements*. New York: Cambridge University Press.

Zafra, Gloria. 2009. "Por la ley o la costumbre: obstáculos en la participación política de las mujeres en el surest mexicano," in Victor Leonel Juan Martínez and Maria Clara Galvis, eds. *Derecho y Sociedad Indígena en Oaxaca*. Washington, D.C.: Due Process of Law Foundation, 63–73.

CHAPTER 9

Elusive Demodiversity in Bolivia: Between Representation, Participation, and Self-Government

José Luis Exeni Rodríguez

N early 30 years into the uninterrupted process of democratization in Bolivia, marked by successive episodes of political-institutional reform, a new adjective has come into use to describe its form of government: "intercultural democracy." This label captures the three types of democracy—representative, direct-and-participatory, and communitarian—each of which is given equal recognition in the reconfigured regime that has emerged from the recent constituent process. The model of the state that underpins this regime remains unitary, but is evolving toward a set of plurinational institutions with recognition of indigenous autonomy.

The first part of this chapter discusses the actors, institutions, and practices emerging from the recent constituent process. It traces the 30-year transition from a pacted to an intercultural democracy and contrasts the provisions of the 1967 and 2009 constitutions. The next section shows how social mobilization brought about and drove forward the constituent process, resulting in new forms of direct participation that complement liberal-representative democracy. The final sections examine communitarian democracy, which may be designated "postliberal." Its guiding vision is "living well" in harmony with nature (*buen vivir*). The main features of a communitarian democracy—indigenous self-government in local and departmental autonomous territories—are outlined, as well as indigenous participation and representation.

The principal question is to analyze the possibilities and limits of reconciling political representation, citizen participation, and self-government in a context of democratic experimentation. The problem can be posed accordingly: how is this complementarity managed beyond mere coexistence? This chapter examines these issues from the perspective of the current Bolivian experience of extending/transforming democracy in a context of transformational constitutionalism.

(Post) Constituent Consolidation

Bolivian democracy—its institutions, actors, and practices—is no longer what it once was. As the late Octavio Paz might have said, *dijo adiós a lo que fue, se detiene en lo que será* ("it said goodbye to what it was, and hesitates in what it will be.") And it projects, like a hazy horizon under construction, what the norm is yet to be: an *intercultural democracy*. Thus, there is continuity, but also expansion, and of course, substantive change. The path is clear: on the foundations, limits, and lessons of liberal-representative democracy, without giving it up but with some disdain, the institutionalized practice of direct and participatory democracy is also moving forward. The challenge is called demodiversity.[1] The first question is how the expansion and institutional (re)design of Bolivian democracy develops from a "pacted democracy" in principle centered on political parties/elections and then dressed up with mechanisms for direct participation, moving toward what is today a majoritarian democracy in the service of interculturalism. Additionally, the consequences for the general normative framework and, especially, for extra/institutional politics need to be considered. In other words, what is the channel for the new direct participation mechanisms, decision-making, consultation, autonomy, and deliberation in the struggles for constructing democracy in Bolivia?

An initial observation is that the Plurinational Legislative Assembly's development legislation for the principles established in the new (2009) constitution[2] reflects trends of both continuity and distancing. This is fundamental to understanding the set of organic laws approved by constitutional mandate in 2010: the law establishing the Plurinational Electoral Body, the electoral law, the law governing the judiciary, the Plurinational Constitutional Tribunal Law, and the Framework Autonomous Areas and Decentralization Law.[3]

However, this difficult effort at experimenting with change led by President Evo Morales and the Movement Toward Socialism (Movimiento al Socialismo—MAS) is marked by tensions between the normative agenda of Bolivian democracy with respect to complementarity (no cooptation, not merely coexistence) and the really existing everyday practices of the relevant actors. At the same time, the complex legislative agenda and the statutes for the autonomous territories (especially at the departmental level) are for now significantly behind schedule.

Apart from these issues, it is indisputable that the debate around building democracy in Bolivia must be understood as a nodal and complex process that is still in its infancy: the refounding of the state. We are facing nothing less than a new "model of the state" adopted as the constitutional foundation. What is its reach? Article 1 answers this precisely. It is a state with no fewer than 11 attributes: unitary, social welfare, rule of law, plurinational, communitarian, free, independent, sovereign, democratic, intercultural and decentralized, and with autonomy for internal territories.

This is no minor challenge. Moreover, this new model of the state, this structure with unresolved tensions from its long history,[4] poses serious challenges in terms of the (re)definition of rules, imaginaries, and practices. The scaffolding of democracy is part of this. How can democratic institutionality be reconciled with plurinationalism? And with communitarianism? What does the existence of autonomous areas (plural)[5] mean for the form of government? And how can the centrality of the indigenous nations and indigenous rural communities be articulated from an intercultural perspective?

Table 9.1 compares the previous and the newly adopted constitutions in terms of continuities and transformations in the model of the state.

As the comparison shows, seven of the 11 "fundamental bases" of the current Bolivian state were included/recognized in the previous constitution.

Table 9.1   Bolivia: Model of the state in the constitutions of 1967 and 2009

Constitution of 1967 (Partially reformed in 1994 and 2004)	Constitution of 2009 (Approved in National Constituent Referendum)	Comparison
Bolivia: (Article 1)	Bolivia is constituted as a state: (Article 1)	Adjective—Attribute:
Unitary	Unitary	
Social welfare	Social welfare	
Rule of law	Rule of law	
Free	Free	Maintained
Independent	Independent	
Sovereign	Sovereign	
Democratic	Democratic	
	Communitarian	Added
	Decentralized and with autonomous regions	
Multiethnic	Plurinational	Transformed
Pluricultural	Intercultural	

Source: Prepared by author.

Thus, there is significant continuity. For example, there is continuity in the three qualities of a modern state: *free state*, no subordination to any other state or decision-making restrictions imposed by international conventions; *sovereign state*, meaning it reserves for itself the power to define and resolve domestic issues without interference from other states or multilateral institutions; and *independent state*, in that there are no colonial relationships or protectorates enforced by other states or powers. Could there have been a change in this?

The new model of the Bolivian state conserves another three attributes from the previous constitution that are inherent in modern constitutionality: *social welfare state*, which must be concerned with the welfare of the citizenry based on the guarantee of social rights; *rule of law*, which requires all state bodies to be subject to law, and thus avoid arbitrary acts; and *democratic state*, which adopts democracy as the form of government and as the principle for legitimacy of its authorities and representatives.

What else is retained from the previous constitution? One characteristic, the seventh, *unitary state*, is the territorial organization that occupied the center of the old political order, albeit with polarization and confrontation, as well as the constituent debate and its regional disputes. This is not a minor point, since in 2007 the elites of the so-called *Media Luna* (east and south of Bolivia), responding to the progress of the constituent process and in conflict with the Departments of Chuquisaca and La Paz (the Andean highlands) resuscitated the idea of federalism (which in the early nineteenth century had led to the Federal War).

So, what is new about the constitution's model of the state? There are at least two basic qualitative leaps. First, the explicit declaration that the Bolivian state is *communitarian*, in that it recognizes the existence of not just individuals but also communities, with all that implies for the affirmation of collective rights. Second is the territorial structure and organization of the state, which is *decentralized*, and especially, with *autonomous areas*.

And what is transformed? Here the fundamental change is in the plurinational-popular aspect of Bolivia, since it represents cross-cutting changes throughout the state structure. The new constitution declares the Bolivian state *intercultural* as well as *plurinational*. Thus, unlike the prior constitution, Bolivia is defined not only as "pluricultural," it is also an *intercultural state*. This involves not only the recognition-coexistence of different cultures but also the greater challenge of constructing a common sphere, the society of *vivir bien* ("living well").[6] Naturally, this directly influences the form of government, since it requires embracing an intercultural democracy.

The other substantive change in the state model is the transformation of the "multiethnic" state into the *plurinational state*. This is indeed a substantive change. The Bolivian constitution recognizes that there are not only different "ethnicities" in the country but also a complex of nations and indigenous rural communities that make up a foundational and necessary part of the Bolivian nation.[7] This plurinational character is reflected throughout the state framework, beginning with public agencies, and entails—as de Santos (2010) would say—the notion of self-government and self-determination.[8]

Thus, the controversy around constructing democracy in Bolivia in a postcolonial and postliberal reality is closely related to the state-in-society model and the reconfiguration of public authorities, which have a profound effect on democracies (plural) and the exercise of political representation and direct participation. We are witnessing a complex experimental challenge of (re)construction of institutions.

But if Bolivian democracy is not what it was and is projecting what it will be, what should be the design of the "system of government"? Given the constitutional mandate, how should the path to the expansion and transformation of democracy be expressed? Table 9.2 offers a synthesis.

Table 9.2 Bolivia: Principled expansion of democracy

Constitution of 1967		*Constitution of 2009*
National Congress / 1994–1995 Reform	National Congress/ 2004–2005 Reform	Constituent Assembly / Approved by Referendum
Bolivia adopts the form of democracy for its government		
Representative	Representative	Representative
Suffrage is the basis for the democratic regime. Based on voting that is universal, direct and equal, individual and secret, free and obligatory. The people *do not deliberate or govern* except through their representatives and the authorities created by law	*Suffrage* is the basis for the democratic regime. Based on voting that is universal, direct and equal, individual and secret, free and obligatory	Via the election of representatives by universal, direct, and secret vote
	Participatory The people deliberate and govern through their representatives and through the *Constituent Assembly, citizens' legislative initiative,* and *referendum*	Direct and Participatory Through *referendum,* citizens' *legislative initiative, recall elections, assembly, town council,* and *prior consultation*
		Communitarian Through election, designation, or nomination of authorities through *the norms and procedures* of the indigenous nations and indigenous rural communities

Source: Prepared by author.

The process of expansion is clear. At first there was the individual ballot. And then there were elections. Subsequently, mechanisms for participation, deliberation, and collective decision-making were adopted. And now the challenge of self-government for indigenous nations and peoples is established. The following section examines this trajectory.

Broadening of Democracy: Representation and Participation

Over three difficult decades, many Latin American countries transitioned from bureaucratic-authoritarian regimes (mostly military dictatorships) to electoral democracies. In Bolivia this transition happened in the early 1980s: on October 8, 1982, the government of the Unidad Democrática Popular (Popular Democratic Unity) came to power. Since then, the process of democratization has moved toward significant expansion in successive political-institutional reforms that fine-tuned the democratic framework while overcoming situations of instability and crisis. At the center of these developments, in addition to the strong adhesion to neoliberal policies of structural adjustment and state reform (following the letter and spirit of the Washington Consensus), there was an obsession around governability and an interesting preference for multiparty coalitions as a condition for stability.

In this period a series of reforms were made, mostly as a result of political pacts and constitutional reforms in response to citizen demands for better quality political representation and greater participation in defining public issues. First, "not just voting, electing," reform in the 1990s included the election of uninominal representatives and popular participation at the local-municipal level; second, with the "not just electing, deciding," reform in the early part of this century, direct forms of consultation involving the referendum emerged. Thus, expansion of democratic representation advanced (election of local and departmental authorities as well as constituent representatives) along with participatory democracy (referenda on gas, autonomous regions, recall votes, and the constitution).

However, without a doubt, the system of government is one of the most relevant normative developments expressed in the new constitution because of its structural character (article 11).[9] The basic principle is that there is no single-hegemonic model of democracy (read liberal-representative) at which to arrive; rather, there are diverse concepts and practices of democracy in permanent interaction and conflict.[10] This is a break with the teleological framework that predicts that after the transition there will be more or less linear processes of democratic consolidation, and later on, inexorable deepening and persistence of democracy that brings us close to *ideal democracy*. Included in this tradition, with some important variations, is the reflection on *citizenship democracy* (UNDP—OAS, 2009 and 2010) as a "new phase on the democratic road" in the consolidation of electoral democracy in the region.[11]

There were several milestones in Bolivia's democratic expansion. A prolonged period of hegemonic party (MNR) rule following the 1952 revolution brought with it the right to universal vote; and after the military dictatorships of the 1970s, electoral democracy in Bolivia—and its institutionality—dealt with an intense process of transition-learning. Three successive general elections (1978, 1979, and 1980), punctuated by coups and interim governments, led to a pacted transition that formed a government in October 1982 (presidency of Hernán Siles Zuazo) and whose tonic was the sum of hyperinflation, institutional deadlock, and excess of social demands-expectations with the well-known result of crisis-trauma of governability.

Then came the multiparty pact. After 1985, with the Pact for Democracy involving the Revolutionary Nationalist Movement (MNR) and the Nationalist Democratic Action (ADN) party, there was a period of systemic governability through minority governments, dispersed vote, and parliamentary and government multiparty coalitions. This phase, which lasted two decades, was characterized by periodic general elections with alternation in power of the triad MNR-ADN-MIR (Revolutionary Left Movement) and, at the end of the 1980s, the inclusion of "neopopulist" forces, CONDEPA (Conscience of the Fatherland) and UCS (Civic Solidarity Union), as well as the eventual competition for the "national left" from the MBL (Free Bolivia Movement). This was the party system that led the political-institutional reform process in the country, especially the second generation reforms of the 1990s. In October 2003 this *pacted democracy* succumbed to an overdose of party patronage and terminal crisis of the hegemonic consensus rooted in the marriage between representative democracy and economic neoliberalism. During this period, elections and electoral institutions functioned in the service of a political system—the "partyarchy"—that was self-reflective.

Thus, for more than two decades Bolivia had what the UNDP's *Report on Democracy in Latin America* (2004) defines as an electoral democracy along with what it criticizes as the so-called Latin American triangle: the coexistence of democracy of voting with high levels of inequality and poverty. And it has a deficit, which is also an unresolved issue, of the absence of "comprehensive citizenship," that is, that citizens have the totality of their rights guaranteed, not just civil and political rights, but also economic, social, and cultural rights.[12] The final phase of this period has been well defined in Bolivia as one of "crisis, inflection and change" (UNDP-IHD, 2002): crisis of the political model of pacted democracy and its party system, crisis of the narrowly based neoliberal export model for the economy, and crisis of the model for social integration associated with mere recognition, generally declarative, of the "pluri-multi" nature of Bolivian society. The literature concurs that the April 2000 Water War in Cochabamba marks the point of inflection.

As for the expansion of democracy, during the period of pacted democracy there were important changes. The agreements among political party leaders in 1991 and 1992 advanced the 1994 constitutional reform with fundamental reforms in the judiciary, the inclusion of uninominal representatives, and other public policy actions, such as popular participation in local-municipal democracy and affirmative action for women's political participation. The electoral democracy of the new millennium enjoyed relevant progress in the limited democracy of transition. In fact, these were advances in terms of representative democracy, with guarantees for the exercise of suffrage and the inclusion of new powers whose source of legitimacy came from voting, but they were insufficient in terms of participation in decision-making.

After several social mobilizations—the "politics of the streets," extrainstitutional and at times antisystemic—and the failed governing coalition of the MNR-MIR-NFR, which ended abruptly in October 2003 with the Gas War in the city of El Alto, conditions were ripe for a new expansion of democracy, again through constitutional reform. The challenge was to advance toward the adoption of mechanisms for direct and participatory democracy. Thus, the 2004 reform included in the constitutional order, and therefore in political and democratic practice, the *referendum,* as a mechanism for collective decision-making through voting; the *citizens legislative initiative,* for developing legislation outside of parliament, the recognition of group citizenship and indigenous peoples—which eliminated the monopoly of the parties on political representation—and the *Constituent Assembly*, as a mechanism for the "total reform" of the constitution.

These reforms, which complemented liberal-representative democracy with mechanisms for direct and participatory democracy, presented the subsequent years of Bolivian democracy with unprecedented and complex challenges for electoral institutionality and practice. To start off, in July of 2004, the same year as the reform, the first national referendum took place, on oil policy. Two years later, a popular initiative sponsored a referendum on autonomy. And then there were two difficult processes of citizen consultation in the midst of unresolved unrest and polarization that tested the referendum mechanism, and even tested the institutionality of democracy itself. The processes were the popular referendum recalling the president, vice-president, and departmental prefects in August 2008; and the Dirimidor referendum (on the limits of land ownership) and the National Constituent referendum (on the new constitutional text emerging from the Constituent Assembly) in January 2009. Before that, in December of 2005, as part of democratic expansion, departmental authorities (prefects) were for the first time directly elected through voting. And in July 2006, 255 assembly members were elected with the mandate to draft a new constitution.

The third substantive moment in democratic expansion in Bolivia arrived with the approval of the new constitution. In addition to reaffirming the bases of representative democracy in the election of authorities and representatives through universal suffrage, direct and participatory democracy was extended with the inclusion of four mechanisms for deliberation and decision-making: recall of elected officials, assembly, town councils, and prior consultation. It also established the centrality of public participation in defining public policies and social control of accountability. But perhaps the most important change was the adoption of communitarian democracy, which is discussed further in the next section of this chapter.

Communitarian Democracy

In addition to complementarity between political representation and direct and participatory democracy, one of the most important innovations to come out of the Bolivian process in terms of expanding democracies (plural), is the inclusion in the constitution of *communitarian democracy*.[13] For the first time the state is recognizing self-government of indigenous nations and indigenous rural communities.

What is the significance of the institutional recognition of communitarian democracy? First, it means that in the plurinational state of Bolivia there are 36 nations and indigenous rural peoples with different types of political organization. Second, that their self-determination is guaranteed within the unitary state.[14] Third, that Bolivia's democratic government is direct and participatory, representative and communitarian. And fourth, that indigenous nations and indigenous rural communities, in accordance with the constitution and the law, can elect, designate, or nominate their authorities and representatives through self-determined norms and procedures.

In this context, communitarian democracy has implications for demodiversity. What are its "constituent elements"? According to Zegada (2011: 164–193), communitarian democracy is characterized by its collective nature, directly embedded in the community; the predominance of the assembly as the space-mechanism for deliberation and decision ("the assembly rules"), which limits the scale; consensus in collective decision-making; a system of authority based on rotation and the obligation to serve, as well as an understanding of authority as service; and mechanisms for recalling officeholders, social control, and accountability of public administration to the community. These communitarian forms of self-government have complex relationships with syndicalist, and of course, party forms of self-government. Communitarian democracy's diversity of practices clearly show that it is not limited to mere recognition of collective rights within an expanded liberal democratic framework.

This recognition poses a set of challenges for the Bolivian democratic regime and its new institutionality. It also presents challenges for communitarian democracy itself, which must contend with its projection "beyond the community." Preliminary developments illustrate this.

In 2009, the popular election of seven indigenous deputies, even though they are only 6 percent of the 130 national legislators, was an important step toward plurinational presence in the legislature. Although obviously highland indigenous peoples (Aymara and Quechua) do not need special districting to be elected to the assembly (where they have a strong presence), the law guarantees minimum representation for lowland indigenous peoples who are minorities in their departments. This was also the case for the April 2010 direct elections, which were not exempt from disputes,[15] of 23 indigenous representatives according to their own norms and procedures to the departmental assemblies. The result, summarized in Table 9.3, is the direct inclusion of indigenous people from many nations and groups in the legislative bodies at the central as well as the departmental level.

But intercultural democracy also has a territorial dimension inherent in the existence of autonomous areas within the newly forming state. This is expressed in the "Andrés Ibáñez" Framework Law for Autonomous Areas and Decentralization, which recognizes and essentially regulates the four levels of autonomous areas: departmental, regional, municipal, and indigenous rural communities. A precursor to this last level of autonomous governance was created in December 2009 with the vote to convert 11 municipalities into autonomous indigenous rural communities (the proposition was rejected in only one municipality. See Table 9.4).[16]

Thus, intercultural democracy in Bolivia is no longer just a constitutional mandate or a normative ideal; it is an experimental scheme under construction. It has in its favor important steps and experiences of complementarity that without doubt can serve as the basis for an intercultural agenda. But it also harbors unresolved issues, limits, and challenges, as well as instrumental and even hegemonic tendencies.

For example, there are difficulties implementing an equal hierarchy among different forms of democracy; to date, communitarian democracy has had to pass through the filter, if not the frank supremacy, of representative democracy. Indeed, there are deputies from special districts, but they are elected by

Table 9.3 Bolivia: Assembly members belonging to indigenous groups of rural origin

Department	Special Districting Indigenous Rural Community		
	Plurinational Legislative Assembly	*Departmental Assemblies*	*Indigenous Rural Communities (minorities in their department)*
La Paz	1	5	Afroboliviano, Mosetén, Leco, Kallawaya, Tacana, and Araona
Santa Cruz	1	5	Chiquitano, Guaraní, Guarayo, Ayoreo, and Yuracaré-Mojeño
Cochabamba	1	2	Yuki and Yuracaré
Potosí	0	0	
Chuquisaca	0	2	Guaraní
Oruro	1	1	Chipaya and Murato
Tarija	1	3	Guaraní, Weenhayek, and Tapiete
Beni	1	4	Tacana, Pacahuara, Itonama, Joaquiniano, Maropa, Guarasug'we,Moxeño, Sirionó, Baure, Tsimane, Movima, Cayubaba, Moré, Cavineño, Chácobo, Canichana, Mosetén, and Yuracaré
Pando	1	1	Yaminagua, Pacahuara, Esse Ejja, Machinerí, and Tacana
TOTAL	7	23	

Source: Prepared by author.

individual vote and under a political party acronym; municipalities are moving toward converting into autonomous indigenous communities, but first referenda are required, after which statutes for autonomy can be approved. Paradoxically, these advances depend on the individual vote. The next section of the chapter reviews some implications of building this so-called intercultural democracy.

The Intercultural Agenda

The Bolivian constituent process began more than two decades ago as a demand from lowland indigenous groups in the legendary March for Dignity and Land (1990). It then followed a prolonged and complex path, not without obstacles, until first it became an electoral offering (2002), after which it was adopted as a promised agenda (October 2003) and subsequently a government program (2005), until it was expressed in a new constitution with 411 articles and 10 transitional provisions that came out of the hard work of the elected Constituent Assembly (2006–2007) and a sensitive process

Table 9.4 Bolivia: Referenda for autonomous indigenous communities

Department	Province	Municipality	YES	NO	Participation
La Paz	Bautista Saavedra	Charazani	3,035 (86.62%)	469 (13.38%)	96.67%
	Ingavi	Jesús de Machaca	2,787 (56.09%)	2,182 (43.91%)	98.24%
Santa Cruz	Cordillera	Charagua	3,817 (55.66%)	3,041 (44.34%)	94.48%
Potosí	Rafael Bustillo	Chayanta	3,151 (59.9%)	2,109 (40.1%)	96.68%
Chuquisaca	Luis Calvo	Huacaya	337 (53.66%)	291 (46.34%)	92.94%
	Yamparáez	Tarabuco	6,408 (90.8%)	649 (9.2%)	96.54%
	Zudáñez	Villa Mojocoya	2,462 (88.31%)	326 (11.69%)	96.8%
Oruro	Sabaya	Chipaya	397 (91.69%)	36 (8.31%)	65.01%
	San Pedro de Totora	San Pedro de Totora	1,467 (74.5%)	502 (25.5%)	97.29%
	Ladislao Cabrera	Pampa Aullagas	825 (83.67%)	161 (16.33%)	97.85%
	Ladislao Cabrera	Salinas de Garci Mendoza	2,047 (75.09%)	679 (24.91%)	95.57%
	Sajama	Curahuara de Carangas	925 (45.08%)	1,127 (54.92%)	94.78%

Source: Prepared by author with data from the CNE.

of regional and especially parliamentary compromise (2008), to be finally approved by majority vote of the citizenry for the first time in our history, in a National Constituent Referendum (2009).[17]

Although the Bolivian constituent process leading to the new constitution may have been difficult and conflictive, it currently faces the truly enormous task of normative adaptation and institutional (re)design, as well as adapting the practice of citizenship and political culture in order to implement the principles and aspirations contained in the constitution. One of those fundamental challenges is creating the conditions to advance the complementarity of direct and participatory, representative, and communitarian democracies.

This agenda had its first normative moment, which was mostly a trace of a foundation, but was also symbolic, in the laws governing the Electoral

Regime and the Plurinational Electoral Body promulgated by President Morales as part of the five fundamental laws. These laws establish the ideal of intercultural democracy.[18] The antecedent of this substantive electoral reform, as an illustration that "institutions matter" and that they generate conflict at the time of their adoption, was the tense and uncertain way, but finally achieved through compromise, that Law No. 4021 of the Transitional Electoral Regime (2009) was passed. That law facilitated the General Elections of December 2009, the first under the new constitution.

The laws for the Electoral Regime and the Plurinational Electoral Body were passed without significant conflict by the ruling majority with limited public deliberation and generally no contest or contribution from the opposition. In any case, the relevance of these laws for our purposes is that this inaugural legislation not only establishes the principles of a body with public authority in the plurinational state (in this case the newly formed Electoral Body); it also establishes rules and procedures for the practice of demodiversity in the sphere of Bolivian intercultural democracy.[19]

In this context, clearly even more than the institutional design and its innovations, and beyond the process of constructing a new hegemony in Bolivia, the fundamental democratic challenge rests in the practice itself of the complementarity—its institutional, territorial, and symbolic dimensions—among the three forms of democracy recognized in the constitution and regulated in the Electoral Regime Law. There are fertile avenues in these structures, but of course there are unresolved issues, occasional reverses, and plenty of blockages.

The *advances* on this journey, built on the foundational bases of the constitution, are the norms established to guarantee the expanded practice of the three forms of democracy.

In the case of *representative democracy*, in addition to carefully regulating the already existing national elections for president/vice-president, senators, and deputies, the dimension of territorial autonomy is consolidated through the election of authorities and representatives at the departmental, regional, and municipal levels.[20] Moreover, interesting innovations have been introduced, such as direct election of the highest authorities in their respective jurisdictions (magistrates of the Supreme Court and the Plurinational Constitutional Tribunal),[21] supervision of elections of authorities in administration and oversight of public service cooperatives, and the administration, on demand, of elections in universities and civil society organizations. Direct election of representatives to supranational organizations, such as the Andean Parliament, is also included. In all of these areas the principles of parity and rotation are rigorously observed to guarantee the "equivalency" of conditions for women and men.

As for *direct and participatory democracy*, the referendum is regulated with respect to its scope and limits, especially the requirements for popular initiatives, such as subject matter, technical validation of the questions and constitutional review. Additionally, referenda to establish autonomous areas, constitutional referenda, and international treaties are differentiated. Moreover, progress is being made in defining rules for recall referenda to establish their conditions and effects. And general guidelines, rather than regulations, are established for the Supreme Electoral Tribunal's "monitoring," to create a record, and provide information and encouragement, of nonbinding public deliberation in assemblies and town councils. Finally, a supervisory procedure has been established for prior consultations to assure that they are mandatory, preliminary to actions, and informed, especially those involving natural resources and environment.

Finally, *communitarian democracy* incorporates two levels of normative definition. The first, monitoring, is mostly symbolic, in that the Supreme Electoral Tribunal has a mandate to "supervise," when appropriate, election, designation, and nomination processes for authorities and representatives of indigenous nations and indigenous rural communities following their own norms and procedures, whether those procedures are written or based on oral tradition or other forms of recordation. The second level of normative definition relates to more specific questions coming from other forms of democracy. Following the transitional electoral regime, the law establishes the creation of (only) seven special districts for indigenous rural communities for the Plurinational Legislative Assembly. It also establishes the direct election of at least 23 departmental assembly members. And it requires future municipal charters to include direct indigenous representation on municipal councils. Applying the constitutional mandate, the law also includes indigenous membership in the Plurinational Electoral Body and the Plurinational Constitutional Tribunal. And it references the aforementioned prior consultations with indigenous nations and peoples as subjects.

However, this democratic experimentation also has *limitations* and even reverses (which can be understood as "deconstitutionalization"), in that some of the intended changes can be displaced, or at least postponed, because of the distribution of power.

In this respect there are two very powerful tensions in that they remain as unresolved issues or issues partially resolved in favor of central hegemonic power. One tension is *autonomy*, in which the law impedes full exercise of this territorial dimension of democracy. This is reflected, for example, in the regulations included in the Electoral Regime Law that should actually be defined in the departmental development legislation, such as the method for electing the governor or denying the governor the authority to call referenda.

It is also evident in the prolonged effort at distributing jurisdictional authority between the central level and the autonomous territorial entities. And
in the critical definition—in the Framework Law for Autonomous Areas
and Decentralization—of the mechanism for suspending elected authorities
that has led to the removal of two governors and ten mayors, mostly from
the opposition. Democracy "without a center," then, including legislative
development in departmental assemblies, whether because of strength at the
central level or weakness at the subnational levels, continues to be a matter
that is "in limbo."

The other tension in the law, in Bolivia's long history, is the exercise of communitarian democracy and the full inclusion of the *indigenous
nations and indigenous rural communities* through self-governance and self-
representation. A clear unresolved issue is the decision to keep the number
of special districts to seven, when a reasonable compromise existed to
increase them to 14, or at least 11.[22] Because of this, plurinationality is
underrepresented in the Plurinational Legislative Assembly. Also pending
implementation is the Law for Prior Consultations, which recently, in early
2012, has been put on the agenda by the government because of the pressure from the dispute around a highway that would cross through a national
reserve, the Territorio Indígena Parque Nacional Isiboro-Sécure (TIPNIS).
And there are still several blockages/resistances to autonomy for indigenous
rural communities.[23] For example, although the new constitution recognizes indigenous jurisdiction as a substantive part of legal pluralism, the
legal framework undermines this advance, since the law governing jurisdiction (Law No 073, December 2010) limits the subject matter, personal and
geographic jurisdiction of indigenous rural communities.

Finally, there are legislative gaps in implementing the constitution's establishment of "intercultural democracy." At least two fundamental laws have
yet to be drafted: Political Organizations Law to substitute for the current
outdated ones, the Political Parties Law and the Citizens and Indigenous
Groups Law; and the constitutionally mandated Law for Participation and
Social Control over all levels of public administration. On balance, the agenda
for intercultural democracy is still pending.[24]

Epilogue with Uncertain Outcome

Bolivia offers a vision of a postliberal democracy in which plurinational
voices are incorporated into the constitutional order through direct forms of
participation and self-government. Many of the participatory innovations we
observe throughout the region have been enshrined in Bolivia's constitution.
It represents, perhaps, a more ambitious process than anywhere else in the

region. The tensions between representation and participation are present; and the complexities of reconciling diverse mechanisms for institutionalizing plurinational and multicultural voices in a democratic regime should not be underestimated; but there is no question that much can be learned from this case of deep democratic experimentation.

One of the fundamental lessons of Bolivian political culture is that the most creative democratic moments occur through extrainstitutional mobilization. Important adjustments and expansions in institutions cannot be explained without this "politics in the streets." This organizational density with an ample repertory of collective action—and confrontation—is at the center of construction of the state and the demand for building democracy in Bolivia.

It is important to explore whether the new participatory and self-government mechanisms limit or distort the principle of political representation, displacing electoral mechanisms based on individual suffrage. In fact, another important lesson has been that representation and direct action are not necessarily mutually exclusive. To the contrary, at times of tension, conflict, and moments of crisis, these two systems interacted to give rise to current Bolivian democracy: extrainstitutional when the formal system closes up on itself, institutional when collective action becomes antisystemic.

What is the current "road map," if one even exists, for demodiversity in Bolivia? This question seeks to examine what democracies (plural) pass through and how they transform within the new model of the state as plurinational; in other words, how does democratic experimentation project the path of complementarity between political representation, citizen participation, and self-government? The following are notes on this future.

Clearly, recognition, and especially, adoption of demodiversity as a constitutional and normative guide is an important step toward *inclusion* of sectors, such as indigenous peoples, women, and peasants, that have traditionally been marginalized and discriminated against by state structures and in the corridors of democracy. It is also invigorating for *representation*, since democracy has been expanded beyond elections/voting to incorporate forms of direct participation and collective decision-making into the principle of political representation. However, effective mechanisms for *transparency* and *accountability* have yet to be implemented, since the constitutional mandate for social control of public administration is still awaiting legislation. And intercultural democracy is defenseless against persistent *clientelist* practices of a corporatist nature as well as authoritarian tendencies in various spheres and levels of politics in Bolivian political culture.

Rather than move from electoral to citizenship democracy[25] based on the expansion of "necessary democracy," democratic experimentation requires negotiating the complementarity of democracies with political and institutional pluralism, guaranteeing the "republican dimension" of democracy and the always complex challenge of educating citizens to live in democracy. There are a surfeit of temptations and concerns.

This impulse toward democratization, in the political conjuncture of "democratic and cultural revolution" (i.e., not just reformist), is (re)presented in a scenario of anticapitalist and anticolonialist struggles. As described above, there is a long history of unresolved tensions (especially ethnic-cultural and regional tensions) that are inscribed within these struggles; it is a time horizon that transcends political transitions and their political-institutional reform processes. It is no coincidence that the social expression of this democratic project wears the poorly explained and little-debated clothing of "communitarian socialism" to differentiate itself from (or perhaps to resemble, with nuance) the vaunted "socialism for the 21st century."

Should we think in terms of representation versus participation? Citizen participation, direct action, politics in the streets—are these threats to political representation (especially during times of crisis)? Are they like a necessary good as long as they do not weaken, and are functional to, structures for representation?[26] Or are they perhaps complementary and therefore indivisible? This question contains two analytic consequences that knock at the door of the debate agenda: first, the supposed *tension* between the two forms of democracy; and second, the tendency to restrict participation to the local-municipal level. Political representation and direct participation are *complementary*; they do not merely coexist, nor do they merely divide functions as a matter of scale.

As for political actors, it is important to consider what happened with the once robust party system of moderate pluralism that made the pact possible. Where are these actors hiding? In what corner of the *ancien régime*? Where are the political parties that should have modernized and democratized internally (in their leadership, their candidates), as well as made themselves more "transparent" (in their use of public financing), to perpetuate their monopoly of representation in democracy? What happened to those electoral machines that, littering the landscape with promises, would contend for citizens' preferences at the ballot box?

Without doubt another aspect of the current conflict around the construction of democracy in Bolivia is that representation and especially participation occur beyond, and at times outside of, (traditional) political parties. This reality requires acceptance of the centrality of *other subjects* in the public-political space: social movements, indigenous nations and rural communities, civic committees, neighborhood associations, unions, professional associations, women's movements, and so on. This is the exercise of popular sovereignty without limiting it only to delegation.

However, complementarity in democratic practice is also related to communitarian democracy, which has existed since precolonial times but has only recently gained recognition in the constitutional framework and its legislative development. The mere presence of indigenous nations and indigenous rural communities shakes, like an earthquake, many of the mono-cultural layers and fantasies of the old nation-state in Bolivia. In this area we have identified not only important advances but also barriers, limits, and even regrets. Be that as it may, democracy's interculturalism cannot be imagined today without its communitarianism.

Also on the normative and practical agendas is the infrastructure required to guarantee the expansive rights recognized in the constitution: not just individual rights but also collective rights; not just civil and political but also economic, social, and cultural rights; not just of persons but also of the *Madre Tierra* ("Mother Earth," which has sacred connotations among Andean indigenous peoples).[27] This is interwoven with the other great refoundational and democratic challenge of practicing a plural economy within the constitutional framework of *buen vivir* (*Suma Qamaña*). These are most certainly fundamental questions, but to date, they have been posed exclusively in a declaratory mode.[28] In order to address the so-called Latin American triangle of *electoral democracy, inequality,* and *poverty*, these issues, in addition to the persistent neocolonial structures of marginality, discrimination, racism, and exclusion, cannot be deferred.

Moreover, although the tone tends to be one of condemnation ("authoritarianism," "concentration of power," "hegemony"), a fundamental question on the democratic horizon is presidentialism and the predominance of the executive with respect to other branches of government (two-thirds of the legislature is from the ruling party, and the judiciary is subordinate). It appears we are moving from a failed tendency toward coalition presidency based on multiparty pacts to a "monochrome" majoritarian presidency resting on a new hegemony. This raises questions about the requirements of a "democratic form of governance" (Munck 2010), and I would propose, as an exploration, some minimum criteria: the effects of concentration in the executive (Cameron 2010), the incentives-risks of (both horizontally and vertically) divided government, mechanisms for social control and accountability of public administration, "republican organization of government," among others.

Additionally, in a model of the state that seeks to grant internal autonomy, it is critical to situate the conflict over democracy building in the framework of *the territorial organization of power* and its tensions. This is especially the case when the regionalization of politics and electoral behavior are inescapable facts. What is the proper institutional design of a democracy in a setting with uneven and multiple geographies (including autonomous indigenous rural communities)? This challenge necessitates adopting the agenda of intercultural democracy, the ideal of redistribution of power in a plural and diverse society. "Democracy without a center" would be the goal.

Finally, what direction will the current process of political and institutional reconfiguration take given the heightened level of conflict that might be defined as "creative tensions" in the change process, according to Vice-President García Linera, or as "degenerative tensions," as might be indicated by some premature signs of deconstitutionalization, remains to be seen. The challenge is to guarantee political pluralism, with equivalent conditions between men and women, in a framework of interculturality and institutional heterogeneity. It is necessary to cement a "plurinational-popular block" as the basis for an intercultural democracy with equality. These are some of the problems emerging from the current experimentations in the building of Bolivian democracies; they will require continued analysis and debate.

Notes

1. The concept of "demodiversity" (*demodiversidad*) comes from the Portuguese scholar Boaventura de Sousa Santos (2004). It is based on two fundamental principles: (a) there is no single concept of democracy; rather there are several, and (b) the hegemonic model of democracy (elitist, liberal, representative) does not guarantee more than a "low intensity democracy."
2. As a result of a prolonged and complex constituent process begun in 1990 with the March for Territory and Dignity by lowland indigenous peoples, and after the difficult development of the Constituent Assembly (2006–2007), in January 2009 for the first time in Bolivian history a new constitution was approved in a national constituent referendum.
3. In its Second Transitional Disposition, the constitution establishes a maximum period of 180 days following its formation (January 22, 2010) for the Plurinational Legislative Assembly to approve these five organic laws. Despite the complexity of the task, and without sufficient public deliberation, in addition to limited agreements with the opposition, the laws were passed on time.
4. For an extensive and consistent analysis of the state and its imaginaries see the National Human Development Report 2010: *The State of the State in Bolivia*, which proposes the idea that the Bolivian state is a "State with holes." UNDP-IHD, La Paz.
5. The new territorial organization of the Bolivian state recognizes four levels of autonomy: departmental, regional, municipal, and indigenous rural

communities. Although the regional level does not, the other three have legislative capacity.

6. *vivir bien (Suma Qamaña)*, a perspective that goes beyond the idea of development or of mere social welfare, has been adopted as one of the fundamental principles of the Bolivian state. It also predicates the plural economy.

7. The new constitution officially recognizes 36 nations and indigenous rural communities and their languages, guaranteeing self-determination (Article 2). Additionally, it recognizes intercultural Afro-Bolivian communities as part of the "Bolivian nation" (Article 3).

8. Santos (2010) argues that "recognizing plurinationality entails a radical challenge to the concept of the modern state that is rooted in the idea of the civic nation, and the idea that in every state there is only one nation conceived as belonging to a common ethnicity, culture or religion."

9. In its first paragraph, Article 11 of the new constitution establishes that Bolivia's form of government shall be "democratic, participatory, representative and communitarian, with equality of conditions between men and women." According to de Santos (2010), "it is one of the most advanced constitutional formulations of democracy in the world."

10. As Cameron, Hershberg, and Sharpe argue in Chapter 1 of this book, the competing models of democracy in Latin America that express tensions between democratic principles are not necessarily inevitable, despite the proliferation of descriptors.

11. The posttransition proposal/challenge of advancing toward citizenship democracy in Latin America involves "expanding the horizon of necessary democracy" and its sustainability on the basis of the full guarantee by the state of a *comprehensive citizenship*. See UNDP and UNDP—OAS, 2009 and 2010.

12. See the UNDP/OAS discussion in the working document, "*La democracia de ciudadanía. Una agenda para la construcción de ciudadanía en América Latina*", November, 2009.

13. This self-government has been called different things, such as ethnic democracy, communal democracy, and *ayllu* (traditional Andean political and social units) democracy.

14. This recognition, in accordance with Article 2 of the constitution, provides for the right of nations and indigenous rural communities to autonomy, self-government, culture, recognition of their institutions, and consolidation of their territorial entities. All the languages of the indigenous nations and indigenous rural communities are recognized as official languages, and their ethical-moral principles are also recognized.

15. The first direct election required supervision from the Departmental Electoral Tribunals because of disputes between the ruling party and the opposition, especially in the "Media Luna" Departments. In Santa Cruz, for example, with the majority in opposition to the MAS government, it became necessary to seek judicial intervention so that the Departmental Assembly would recognize and seat the legitimate representatives of two indigenous groups.

16. As mandated by the Framework Law for Autonomous Areas, these municipalities are currently in the process of drafting their own statutes; their legislation must pass constitutional review and a referendum in order for the autonomous indigenous rural communities to be legally established. One of the most advanced, which has already been completed, is the statute for Jesús de Machaca. Other communities that have not approved the conversion to indigenous municipalities are also moving forward in drafting these statutes, such as Raqaypampa in Cochabamba, which approved its statute in assembly in May 2011.

17. The new political constitution of the state was approved on January 25, 2009, with 61.43 percent of the valid votes; an unprecedented percentage of the electorate, 90.24 percent, participated in the vote. It went into effect on February 7, 2009.

18. The constitution does not mention intercultural democracy. This notion is the result of normative construction—and its conceptual basis—defined in development legislation, and is essentially the recognition of different forms of understanding and practicing democracy in Bolivia, especially from the perspective of the diversity of nations and indigenous rural communities.

19. *Intercultural democracy* according to Santos (2010) is thus understood: (a) the coexistence of different forms of democratic deliberation; (b) different criteria for democratic representation; (c) recognition of collective rights of peoples as a condition for the effective exercise of individual rights; (d) recognition of the new fundamental rights; and e) education oriented toward forms of relating and subjectivity based on cultural reciprocity.

20. Bolivia directly elects departmental governors and legislatures (including assembly members by population and assembly members by intradepartmental territory), as well as mayors and municipal councils.

21. Elections for members of the Supreme Court, Agro-Environmental Court, Judicial Council, and the Plurinational Constitutional Tribunal are a democratic innovation adopted by the constitution and legislated through the Electoral Regime Law. The first ballot took place on October 8, 2011, with a high percentage of blank votes. An unprecedented and complex process, there were significant risks in the preselection of candidates by the Plurinational Legislative Assembly, the dissemination of candidates' qualifications by the Supreme Electoral Tribunal (because of the explicit prohibition against campaigning), the design of the ballot (77 candidates on five pages), public information (with debatable limits on the media), and the voting and counting processes themselves (every voter had to mark five votes on the ballot).

22. The redistribution of seats in the Plurinational Legislative Assembly was left undetermined by the law until a new population census (planned for 2011) is carried out. With the new data the seats should be reallocated by department, the number of uninominal and plurinominal districts per department should be adjusted, and the number of seats for indigenous rural communities should be increased. This is a complex issue that bodes conflict.

23. The demand to increase the number of special districts to elect assembly representatives from indigenous rural communities was expressed in a hunger strike

by some indigenous deputies, and was part of the CIDOB's agenda in its inconclusive July 2010 march around the approval of the Framework Law for Autonomous Areas and Decentralization. This reveals two disturbing fissures (but not breaks): between the government and lowland indigenous groups, and between the former allies in the Pact for Unity—indigenous communities and smallholder colonizers.

24. Mayorga (2011: 218), on the paradox of the contradictions in the new model of democracy, observes that "democracy has expanded but political power is concentrated."
25. See UNDP and OAS, 2009 and 2010.
26. In the words of UNDP-OAS: "more participation *for* better representation" (italics mine).
27. Unlike in the Ecuador constitution, the Bolivian constitution does not explicitly mention the "rights of Nature." However, these rights were already incorporated in the Law of the Madre Tierra (Law No 071, December 2010), which recognizes the rights of Mother Earth as well as the obligations and duties of the plurinational state and society to guarantee them.
28. An essential issue that cannot be deferred in Bolivia's democratic debate is the definition of the "development model." There is currently a tension between the dominant current that privileges an extractive industry route, challenged as a reconstruction of the old nationalism; and another recurrent vision that defends the rights of Nature, for which it has been dubbed *pachamamismo*.

Bibliography

Altman, David (2010): "Plebiscitos, referendos e iniciativas populares en América Latina: ¿mecanismos de control político o políticamente controlados?", in *Perfiles Latinoamericanos* (No 35, January-June). FLACSO-México.

Cameron, Maxwell A. (2010): "The state of democracy in the Andes", in *Revista de Ciencia Política* (Volume 20, N° 1), pp. 5–20. Santiago: Universidad Católica de Chile.

Cameron, Maxwell, Sharpe, Ken and Hershberg, Eric (2012): "Voice and Consequence: Direct Participation and Democracy in Latin America," in Cameron, Hershberg and Sharpe, (eds.), *New Institutions for Participatory Democracy in Latin America: Voice and Consequences.* New York: Palgrave-Macmillan.

Exeni Rodríguez, José Luis (2011): "Andamios de la demodiversidad en Bolivia", in *Cuadernos de Futuro.* La Paz, IDH-PNUD, N° 26, March 2011.

—— (2010a): "Bolivia: hacia una democracia intercultural con igualdad", in *Revista Cuarto Intermedio.* Cochabamba, N° 95, September 2010.

—— (2010b): "Un órgano electoral para la demodiversidad", in IDEA Internacional y Vicepresidencia del Estado Plurinacional de Bolivia, *Miradas a la Constitución Política del Estado.* La Paz.

Mayorga, Fernando (2011): *Dilemas. Ensayos sobre democracia intercultural y Estado Plurinacional.* La Paz, CESU-UMSS y Plural.

Munck, Gerardo L. (2010): "Repensando la cuestión democrática: la región andina en el nuevo siglo", in *Revista de Ciencia Política* (Volume 20, N° 1), pp. 149–161. Santiago, Universidad Católica de Chile.

UNDP-OAS (2010): *Nuestra democracia*. México D.F., Fondo de Cultura Económica.

—— (2009): *La democracia de ciudadanía. Una agenda para la construcción de ciudadanía en América Latina*. New York: OAS.

PNUD (2008): *Una brújula para la democracia. Aportes para una agenda de gobernabilidad democrática*. Buenos Aires, PNUD and Siglo XXI.

—— (2004): *La democracia en América Latina*. Buenos Aires: PNUD.

PNUD Bolivia (2010): *Los cambios detrás del cambio. Informe Nacional sobre Desarrollo Humano 2010*. La Paz, IDH-PNUD.

—— (2007): *El estado del Estado en Bolivia. Informe Nacional sobre Desarrollo Humano 2007*. La Paz, IDH-PNUD.

—— (2002): *Informe Nacional sobre Desarrollo Humano 2002*. La Paz, IDH-PNUD.

Santos, Boaventura de Sousa (2010): *Refundación del Estado en América Latina. Perspectivas desde una epistemología del Sur*. La Paz: Plural and CESU-UMSS.

—— (2004): *Democracia de alta intensidad*. Cuadernos de Diálogo y Deliberación. La Paz: Corte Nacional Electoral Court.

Santos, Boaventura de Sousa and Avritzer, Leonardo (2004): "Para ampliar el canon democrático", in Santos (coordinator): *Democratizar la democracia. Los caminos de la democracia participativa*. México D.F., Fondo de Cultura Económica.

Zegada, María Teresa et al. (2011): *La democracia desde los márgenes: transformaciones en el campo político boliviano*. La Paz, CLACSO and Muela del Diablo.

Legislation

Constitución Política del Estado [Political Constitution of the State], 1967 (partially reformed in 1994 and 2004).

Constitución Política del Estado [Political Constitution of the State], 2009 (approved in the National Constituent Referendum).

Ley de Régimen Electoral Transitorio [Law of the Transitory Electoral Regime] (Ley N° 4021, April 14, 2009).

Ley del Órgano Electoral Plurinacional [Law of the Plurinational Electoral Organ] (Ley N° 018 June 6, 2010).

Ley del Régimen Electoral [Law of the Electoral Regime] (Ley N° 026 June 30, 2010).

Ley Marco de Autonomías y Descentralización [Framework Law of Autonomy and Decentralization] "Andrés Ibáñez" (Ley N° 031 July 19, 2010).

Ley de la Madre Tierra [Law of Mother Earth] (Ley N° 071 December 21, 2010).

Ley del Deslinde Jurisdiccional [Law of Jurisdictional Demarcation] (Ley N° 073 December 29, 2010).

CHAPTER 10

Institutionalized Voice in Latin American Democracies

Maxwell A. Cameron and Kenneth E. Sharpe

Introduction

Latin America has made progress toward more open and democratic political systems over the last three decades, but the quality and performance of democratic institutions remain uneven (O'Donnell et al., 2003; Dagnino et al., 2006; Organización de Estados Americanos, Programa de Naciones Unidas para el Desarrollo, 2010). In one respect, however, Latin America is emerging as a pioneer: there has been an explosion in democratic participation. Citizens have begun to demand more say in the decisions that affect them directly. One consequence has been a wide range of participatory innovations designed to reinforce the option of "voice" (as opposed to "loyalty" or "exit," in Hirschman's [1970] argot).

The contributors to this book have documented some of the new forms of institutionalized voice in Latin America. In this chapter we step back and ask: How can their research help us to better understand Latin America's diverse democratic regimes? We argue that greater attention to mechanisms of direct institutionalized voice can help us understand both the diversity and quality of democracies in the region. When we think about democracies in Latin America we should include local initiatives like participatory budgeting and community councils as well as elections, parties, and legislatures.[1] Democratic regimes have many dimensions, and diverse forms of participation are essential to all of them. Put differently, democracy is unthinkable without institutionalized voice.

Building on the work of the Andean Democracy Research Network (see Cameron and Luna 2010), we distinguish between three dimensions of democracy: (1) elections-representation, (2) constitutions, and (3) citizenship. The first dimension of democracy involves the election of representatives. The second dimension implies liberal protections for minority and individual rights, and republican arrangements for self-government under the law. Democracy is not only about how officials are elected but also about *how* they govern. The third dimension of democracy entails the protection of the civil, political and social, economic and cultural rights necessary for full membership in the political community.

Participation plays a critical role in each of these dimensions. In electoral-representative democracy, participation means voting or running for office. Citizens select representatives to speak on their behalf. This, of course, implies that there is competition among parties, with winners and losers (Przeworski, 1991). Elected representatives are accountable to those who have selected them and can be removed if they fail to deliver on their promises. Guillermo O'Donnell called this vertical accountability (O'Donnell, 2003). Democratic theorists from Joseph A. Schumpeter (1942) to Adam Przeworski (1991) emphasized the centrality of this form of accountability by suggesting that elections enable voters to "throw the bums out."

But elections are not enough. As O'Donnell (1999, 1994) argued, democracy requires more than the vertical accountability of elections; it also demands horizontal accountability to ensure rulers are held to account between elections. Horizontal accountability means that agencies of government have the legal power and the capacity to ensure that other agencies are fulfilling their legal and constitutional duties. Agents of government are empowered to act on behalf of citizens to hold each other accountable. The separation of powers means that no one branch of government speaks univocally for "we the people" (Ackerman, 1988: 170). Each is, indirectly, a voice of the demos.

None of these institutions will work well unless citizens vigilantly and actively promote and defend their own rights. Both the horizontal accountability of liberal constitutionalism and the vertical accountability of elections rest on the foundation of citizenship (O'Donnell, Iazzetta and Vargas Cullell, 2003). Unless citizens have the ability and opportunity to speak and act in defense of their rights and interests, other mechanisms of accountability may become mere formalities. The collapse of party systems and the lack of legislative initiative coupled with the fragility of judicial institutions not only weaken the rule of law but also create what has been called "low intensity citizenship" (O'Donnell, 2004). What the UNDP calls a citizens' democracy, by contrast, rests on the social control and accountability made possible by active and vigilant citizenship (Organización de Estados Americanos, Programa de Naciones Unidas para Desarrollo, 2010). Sometimes these expressions of voice take the form of protests in the streets or the expression of opinion through the media, but in this book we are interested in direct participation through institutional channels.

There is, of course, no one model of democracy that fits all regimes. We use the metaphor of ecologies to suggest the complex interactions between the three dimensions of democracy.[2] Other scholars narrow their focus to the procedural minimum required for a regime to be classified as democratic. The Schumpeterian (1942) school of thought (what C.B. Macpherson [1977] called the "equilibrium model of democracy") reduces democracy to competitive elections. This approach often implicitly (or sometimes explicitly) assumes the existence of other dimensions of democracy because, quite simply, elections do not tend to work well as mechanism of social choice in the absence of a framework of constitutional rules and citizenship rights (see O'Donnell, 2007; Macpherson, 1977).

In the research on Latin American democratization, the normative baseline is more typically some variant of constitutional democracy: that is, electoral-representative democracy plus constitutional protections for basic rights and freedoms of individuals and minorities. This approach highlights the weakness of many Latin American democracies that often fall short when assessed in terms of constitutionalism. But this approach often neglects certain sources of strength in these regimes. O'Donnell made this point when he delivered a powerful broadside (1996a, 1996b) against what he called the teleological assumptions implicit in theories of democratic consolidation.

In his view, theorists of democratic "consolidation" all too often took established Western European and North American democracies as their normative baseline. This led them to emphasize the features that new democracies lacked, and would have to acquire in order to become consolidated. And yet, as O'Donnell noted, many of the so-called unconsolidated democratic regimes in Latin America have proven remarkably robust. They are consolidated because they rest on informal institutions that social scientists have not sufficiently appreciated.[3] Although Latin American democratic regimes have tended to weakly institutionalize liberal and republican features, they are not altogether undemocratic. They are more majoritarian than their Western Europe or North American counterparts; this makes them less liberal, but not necessarily less democratic.

Another perspective that starts with liberal democracy as its normative baseline is the literature on competitive authoritarianism (Levitsky and Way, 2002, 2010). This viewpoint rightly underscores the fact that elections can be held in nondemocratic regimes where basic rights and freedoms are not respected. In recent years we have witnessed the emergence of hybrid regimes that combine democratic and authoritarian features. The case of Fujimori's

Peru is an exemplar of a civil-military regime with elections that degenerated from a kind of "delegative democracy" (or electoral democracy without horizontal accountability; see O'Donnell 1994) into a competitive authoritarian regime in which elections served as a mechanism to legitimate a plebiscitary leader (see Carrión, 2006).

Yet important democratic innovations may be missed by researchers who classify regimes as nondemocratic simply because they do not uphold important liberal rights and freedoms. Not all delegative democracies become competitive authoritarian regimes. Some may experiment with innovations in participation that reinforce majoritarian features of democracy while undermining liberalism. Several of the regimes that we analyze in this book (Bolivia under Morales and Venezuela under Chávez, for example) have encouraged active participation at the same time that basic liberal rights and freedoms have been undermined. High levels of participation do not make a regime democratic, but neither can the participatory dimension of democracy be reduced to participation in elections. Indeed, frustration with representative institutions increases the demand for more direct forms of participation.

This brings us to a literature that suggests that failures of representation can undermine the maintenance or quality of democracy: "The widespread dissatisfaction with democratic representation is a core ingredient in the crisis of democracy in the Andes and throughout much of Latin America," claim Scott Mainwaring, Ana María Bejarano, and Eduardo Pizarro Leongomez (2006: 1). Failures in mechanisms of representation, particularly the collapse of party systems, have undermined democracy by contributing to the rise of political outsiders who have attacked or dismantled democratic institutions (Mainwaring, Bejarano, and Pizarro Leongomez, 2006: 4). This crisis in representation may indeed invite in demagogues, but in identifying this danger we also want to be alert to the opportunities created for participation. The pessimism implied by the crisis of representation may be juxtaposed against the optimism of theorists of participatory democracy (Houtzager and Gurza Lavalle, 2010: 5). Indeed, more participatory approaches to democracy may blossom in the context of a crisis of representation, as we see in the cases of Bolivia and Venezuela. A full assessment of the quality of democracy must look at the impact of new forms of institutionalized voice on the functions previously reserved exclusively for parties and legislatures in emerging hybrid regimes.

Can the spread of direct participation close the gap between citizens and their democratic regimes, as suggested by Selee and Peruzzotti (2009: 1–16)? New participatory practices have the potential to improve the performance and legitimacy of democracy, increase accountability and responsiveness, and foster more active and engaged citizenship. They may develop because of a crisis in representative institutions, but such institutionalized voice is also a valuable feature of democracy even where representative institutions are robust. Indeed representative bodies often depend on institutionalized voice for their vitality. Robust representative institutions may atrophy without the energy generated by more direct forms of citizen participation. Indeed, direct participation, by taking citizenship beyond the passive act of voting, may contribute to what Benjamin Arditi (2008) calls "post-liberalism." Post-liberalism implies a participatory politics that exceeds liberal citizenship, but does so "in the best tradition of liberal democracy" (Macpherson, 1977: 115).

Institutionalized Voice and Post-liberal Democracy

Voice matters for a wide range of democratic goods: representation, inclusion, responsiveness, accountability, disruption of clientelism, and encouragement of citizenship. Voice may strengthen the formal institutions of representative democracy by *including* underrepresented citizens, teaching citizens how to represent themselves, and making elected representatives more *accountable* and *responsive*—to use some of the categories outlined in the introduction. But the effects of voice depend on how it is institutionalized—and, above all, whether it is expressed directly or indirectly.[4] Representative democracy is based on indirect voice, in which people have the right to choose decision-makers. Participatory democracy implies that the people govern themselves—they participate in making decisions that affect them directly. But this can mean a number of different things.

One form direct participation can take is "direct democracy" (a term often used to denote plebiscitary democracy). Critics like Max Weber (1978) have rightly worried that direct democracy may circumvent or circumscribe the power of elected representatives in the legislature and the executive. But not all forms of direct, institutionalized voice have such illiberal effects. Here we will argue that there are forms of institutionalized voice that are consistent with the liberal ideal of political equality, that reinforce representative institutions, and that may even enhance the best traditions of liberal or representative democracy.

Participatory democracy works best in small-scale, face-to-face communities because meaningful public deliberation is impossible when the size of the political community is too large. Ancient Greek democracy, in which citizens numbered in the thousands not millions, approximated the conditions necessary for direct participation, although it also included features of indirect democracy (Hansen 1999: 59–60). Representative government, which was initially thought to be opposed to democracy, and a more palatable alternative, has been successfully grafted on to this traditional concept of democracy. In large-scale mass societies, meaningful deliberation is not possible among all the members of the political community, and this makes it necessary to replicate the kind of deliberation possible in a face-to-face community by creating representative institutions in which elected officials engage in public deliberation on behalf of the members of the polity.

This leaves citizens without an active role in their own self-government. Participation is limited to the passive role of choosing those who decide. Participatory democracy seeks to recapture the experience of active self-government. One way of doing this is through the use of referenda or plebiscites so that citizens can make decisions collectively without the mediation of representatives while retaining the formal equality of the suffrage.

Plebiscitary democracy involves referenda initiated by the executive, and there are many examples of democracies around the world that use plebiscites. Referenda convened by legislators or voters are comparatively more infrequent (except in Uruguay and Switzerland—see David Altman, 2010). As Alicia Lissidini shows in Chapter 7, the use of plebiscites in Venezuela has reinforced the power of the presidency at the expense of other elected officials. In Uruguay, by contrast, most referenda are proposed by the legislature and they have served to place a check on the president. Citizen initiatives, perhaps the most infrequent type of public consultation, begin with petitions from the citizenry. They require voters to overcome powerful collective action problems; their effects on democracy, social justice, and the efficiency of government are hotly debated, as supporters of successful citizen's initiatives in California (hamstringing the taxing power of the legislature, decriminalizing the medical use of marijuana) will readily admit.

Plebiscitary democracy may short-circuit the entire process of representation. Representatives are elected to make laws but not to decide their application or interpretation in particular cases, which is the task of the courts. In a small, face-to-face community it is not always necessary to make the distinction between deliberation aimed at reaching general rules that cover all equally and the judgment necessary to interpret and apply these rules in particular cases. But such a distinction is crucial to the idea of representative democracy. The danger of plebiscites is that it invites rulers to bypass legislatures and courts, and appeal to the public to make decisions that may well undermine the work of the legislature—and thus hinder the rule of law. That is why direct democracy is so often seen as illiberal.

Yet such plebiscites may not be the cause of illiberalism, but the consequence. Representative institutions are often weak in Latin America because many of the states in the region lack the capacity to enforce the law. This is another way of saying that liberalism is weak in many Latin American democracies: there are elections, and for the most part they are free and fair, but officials do not govern democratically. If citizens' lives are not regulated by the law, and they experience impunity and injustice every day, then mechanisms of direct institutionalized voice—like the use of recall to remove unresponsive authorities or to provide a mandate for sweeping political reforms—are likely to be embraced with considerable enthusiasm. What motivates this is not illiberalism so much as popular liberalism (Postero, 2007).

Plebiscites are not the only forms of direct institutionalized voice. And many of the authors in this book have looked at new forms that do not depend on a national up-and-down vote. These include small-scale deliberation and collective action at the local level, like community councils, participatory budgeting, or indigenous self-government. Such participation is likely to be experienced as a more real and more effective exercise of democracy than participation in elections if all that they accomplish is the alternation of elites, especially when these elites seem to be either unable or unwilling to address the conditions that give rise to the experience of injustice and neglect.

Through such direct participatory experiences citizens can be involved in agenda setting, policymaking, or holding officials accountable, and this may (or may not) be accomplished without producing the same ill effects of the plebiscitary tendencies inherent in electoral democracy. We are particularly interested in such direct institutionalized voice because of the potential it has to encourage citizens to acquire the habits and dispositions necessary to deliberate and act collectively—not as a mass responding to the appeals of demagogues, but as citizens acting in concert.

In these forms of participation, distinctions between legislation, adjudication, and administration are less crucial. The give and take of face-to-face communication facilitates consensus building in small communities where everyone knows everyone else. In participatory democracies citizens normally deliberate not over whether impersonal rules affect all citizens—although this may be the case in, for example, Brazil's policy conferences in Brazil—but rather whether to take decisions in particular contexts that will affect them directly and immediately in their own communities.

Perhaps the most minimal form of such direct institutionalized voice is consultative mechanisms that aim to provide information, ideas, feedback, and public sentiment to government officials, bureaucrats, or lawmakers. These consultative mechanisms may legitimate or empower civil society organizations, nongovernmental experts, or influential individuals. Or they may simply be window-dressing. Often the biggest risk they entail is simply wasting peoples' time. But participants tend to value such experiences and, when well designed, they can improve public policy outcomes.

Felipe Hevia and Ernesto Insunza Vera (Chapter 4 in this book) found over 400 instances of consultative mechanisms in the Mexican federal government. Although they are given different terms as *committees, councils, commissions, juntas, or arbitral organs,* they are especially important in the areas of social policy, economic development, renewable resources, education, and culture. Hevia and Insunza conclude that although these mechanisms are institutionalized and often attract highly qualified participants, they have, as yet, only occasionally had a real policy impact. This is partly because they serve to provide feedback either before or after decisions have been taken but they are not involved in the policymaking itself or its implementation.

In contrast, Thamy Pogrebinschi's (Chapter 3) analysis of policy conferences in Brazil suggests an example of a kind of consultative mechanism that government officials or legislators take seriously. She describes them as arenas for public deliberation and participation that are designed to provide policy guidelines at the federal level. They are convened by the executive through its panoply of ministries and secretariats, typically around a particular policy issue area. Individuals from both government and civil society participate on behalf of their respective affiliations, and the process works bottom–up, from rounds of dialogue at the municipal level, to the state level, and finally to the national conferences. Each round of dialogue includes participants from previous rounds, and the outcome is often taken up and submitted as bills in the federal (or state) legislature.

Participatory budgeting represents another kind of institutionalized voice which aims to directly have an effect on policy and policy agendas. As Françoise Montambeault describes it (Chapter 5), the idea is to involve ordinary citizens in the municipal governance process by giving them a voice in the decision-making and the setting of collective policy priorities through face-to-face deliberation. Participatory budgeting has been adopted throughout Brazil and in many places in Latin America and beyond. Enthusiasm for this mechanism is largely based on the expectation that it can produce more effective government policy-making, and that it can deepen democracy by including citizens in the policy process in ways that give them expertise, experience, and influence. Montambeault characterizes participatory budgeting as a school of democracy because it helps *educate citizens* in the kinds of practices they need to be influential.

Yet another goal of nonelectoral institutionalized direct participation is policy implementation. Michael McCarthy (Chapter 6) uses the term "coproduction" to refer to the joint provision of public goods by the state and citizens. Venezuela's community councils are an exemplar of this approach. They are grassroots organizations of between 150 and 400 families in urban areas (a minimum of 20 families in rural areas) that are constituted, under the aegis of a state agency, to address local issues. They are state-sponsored entities composed of community activists, and over 35,000 have been formed in recent years. They are good illustrations of the tensions inherent in such direct participation. State funding under the aegis of a powerful executive like Chávez who is resistant to the traditional system of checks and balances creates the possibility that such councils can be used to consolidate executive or party control. But the mandate given to state agencies to help the projects initiated by local councils may increase the *responsiveness* of the state to formerly excluded citizens and make the very legitimacy of the regime dependent on such responsiveness. And further, the responsibility given to the local community councils to execute the projects themselves encourages, despite the risk of corruption, a margin of local autonomy, participation, and decision-making that did not exist in many of these neighborhoods before.

Another example of direct, institutionalized voice—which may or may not have an electoral component—is indigenous self-government under customary law. As described by Todd Eisenstadt and Jennifer Yelle (Chapter 8), indigenous communities in areas of Mexico like Oaxaca that are governed by traditional customary law (*usos y costumbres*) often elect their own authorities in accordance with the means of their own choice. Such elections may take place through communitywide assemblies or appointed councils of elders, by a show of hands or by marking a ballot. The *inclusion* of indigenous people is more likely to be accomplished by means of institutionalized voice that is congruent with existing practices than it would be through the kind of voting and running for office generally accepted in liberal notions of citizenship.

A final issue that has emerged in many chapters of this book, which was not anticipated by the editors at the outset of the project, is *partisanship* and its impact on institutionalized voice. Elections have the effect of transforming politics into an adversarial struggle between opposed groups of citizens. As Giovanni Sartori (1976) notes, "parties," as suggested by the etymology of the word, are designed to represent parts of society, not the whole. The hostility toward parties, however essential they may be, arises from the sense that they divide rather than unify people. Good deliberation requires searching for compromise and common ground, listening to other perspectives, and seeking solutions that serve the public good. There is a tension in electoral democracy between the partisanship that is necessary at election time and the deliberation and action in the public interest that is the key function of a legislature.

Institutionalized voice offers opportunities for people to work together on common projects, to deliberate in smaller groups, and to act in concert toward shared objectives. People are often attracted to this kind of politics because it is both more rewarding than electoral competition and an alternative to the negativity of partisanship. But partisanship can also interfere with participation, turning the search for common ground into another arena of battle between leaders. Participatory innovations often require a firewall against partisanship. In the absence of some means of diminishing partisan contestation, participatory experiences can fail. Partisan disputes over participatory budgeting weakened the process in Recife. In postconflict El Salvador, partisanship undermined the institutionalization and effectiveness of participatory experiments in municipal governments (Gregori, 2012). But in other cases, successful institutionalized voice coexisted with and sometimes was made possible by strong parties and their representatives, and even complemented elected governments. The policy conferences in Brazil were convened by the executive and nested in the legislature, and their recommendations shaped legislation. Participatory budgeting in places like Porto Alegre would not have been possible without the initiative of elected representatives like the mayors whose training and orientation had been within a party that had an ideological commitment to participation and were willing to give away some budgetary authority to the process.

Parties and partisanship often seem like the enemy of participatory democracy. That is why some advocates of participatory democracy reject partisanship wholesale. But parties often serve key democratic functions—aggregating interests, holding officials accountable, creating the unity to bargain over legislation, and getting the votes needed to pass legislation. The key is to find the right ways to institutionalize citizens' voices—as the participatory budgeting in Porto Alegre demonstrates, and as the policy conferences in Brazil also show—to carve out a space where this nonpartisan deliberation can coexist and work with elected party officials in municipal governments. Institutionalized voice can be corroded by extreme partisanship, but can coexist quite comfortably with parties that do not seek to politicize everything.

Institutional Ecologies: Participation, Representation, and Democratic Politics

The issue of partisanship brings us to a larger point. The various dimensions of democracy form ecologies of institutions, in the sense that they interact to reinforce or undermine each other, so that changes at one level influence the others. It is possible that innovations in one area of democratic governance may damage the performance of democracy in another, but it is also possible that innovation in one area will reinforce the performance of democratic institutions in another. For example, direct participation may complement representation (Selee and Peruzzotti, 2009: 3–6), but it can also be used to bypass representative institutions. Similarly, representation can demobilize participation, but it can also create opportunities for participatory practices.

In assessing the quality of democracy it seems both appropriate and normatively desirable to identify areas in which participation and representation reinforce rather than undermine each other. This requires eschewing the presumption that there is a necessary trade-off between participation and representation. Radical advocates of participation who are critical of representation often emphasize such trade-offs, as do more conservative advocates of representation who are skeptical of direct participation, but emphasizing trade-offs may lead to polarization and oversimplification. For example, we may take an illustrative set of countries from Latin America and array them on a continuum from most participatory to most representative, where the extreme ends of the continuum are occupied by countries that score high on one variable and low on the other (in other words, we are looking at the coefficient between representation and participation). The ranking would place Venezuela and Nicaragua on one end of the spectrum, and Mexico and Chile on the other.

Venezuela and Nicaragua are among the cases most often mentioned as examples of regimes that encourage direct participation at the expense of representative institutions. Venezuela's community councils, and other participatory mechanisms, have been used to bypass existing representative institutions (opposition-held municipalities and state governments). When Chávez came to power in 1998, he used plebiscitary means and the creation of a constituent assembly to overhaul Venezuela's entire political system, and in the process he accumulated extensive instruments of executive power. Chávez has captured and politicized state institutions and used public resources in ways that undermine the fairness of electoral processes. He has used supermajorities in the legislature during much of his tenure in office to turn the National Assembly into an instrument of executive rule (most notably with enabling laws).

Venezuela is one of the world's most presidentialist systems, with no term limits for the president and few meaningful checks on his power. Chávez has attempted to keep the opposition off balance by undermining them whenever they gain office. He has blacklisted opponents and undermined democratically elected opponents (especially governors and mayors). There are, therefore, good reasons to be worried about representative democracy in Venezuela. At the same time, Chávez has actively promoted direct participation through a variety of mechanisms and organizations, and he has attempted to legitimate his rule through repeated plebiscites. He has also continuously updated the rules governing community councils and other similar mechanisms in an effort to filter *who* benefits, and to use this as a carrot for partisan advantage.

Nicaragua is similar to Venezuela in crucial respects. Daniel Ortega's Sandinista Front (FSLN) has encouraged councils of citizens' power at the local level, but has ensured their subordination to the government party. These councils are similar to Venezuela's community councils, in that they are aimed to reinforce "popular power" by organizing direct participation within the framework of development plans under the aegis of the presidency. In practice, these councils are strongly linked to the ruling FSLN.

On the other end of the spectrum, Mexico and Chile are laggards when it comes to participation. Even before it shed the institutional features of 65 years of single-party rule, Mexico had begun to develop a range of consultative bodies. Although Mexico has moved toward competitive party politics, in practice, due to its long history of corporatism and clientelism, these bodies have little influence and remain subordinate to the incumbent party.

Chile has a robust representative democracy with a relatively stable party system but has not experimented with the mechanisms of direct participation. It has neither referenda nor recall, nor does it have citizen initiatives or community councils, and participatory budgeting is rarely practiced. Moreover, it has an authoritarian constitution, adopted under the military dictatorship in 1980. That constitution imposed an exclusionary electoral system (a binomial system, in which the second strongest party is assured representation) that limits choices for the voter and makes the construction of new political options extremely difficult (Altman and Luna, 2010). As a result, there is a high level of apathy and indifference toward the political system, especially among youth.

A highly simplified mapping of the region—with Chile on one end of the spectrum and Venezuela on the other—has become conventional wisdom. Such thinking has dominated debates over the "two lefts" in Latin America, to which various contributors to this book allude (Arditi, 2008). The problem with this sort of dichotomous thinking is that it obscures as much as it reveals, and it is a council of despair. It misses the ways in the Chávez regime tried to respond to the failures of the previous system by including broad sectors of the population in policymaking and implementation; it misses the way in which the community councils, for all their partisanship and executive control, have provided a voice, and granted some measure of power and control to local communities. And it misses the alternative, potentially more positive ways in which direct participation and representation might be balanced, something the Chilean regime has failed to achieve.

A step toward a more nuanced comparative analysis is presented by Gisela Zaremberg in Chapter 2 of this book. She distinguishes between countries in

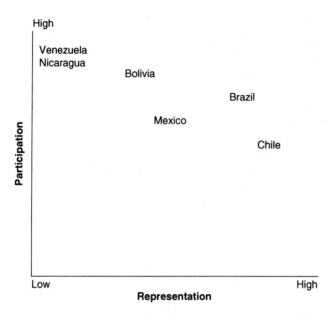

Figure 10.1 Participation and representation in Latin America

which representation *and* participation are encouraged (Brazil and Mexico) and those where participation *versus* representation is fostered (Venezuela and Nicaragua). We can locate each case in a two-dimensional space. Instead of a trade-off, in which more of one dimension implies less of the other, we can look at mixes of both.

The heuristic purpose of Figure 10.1 is to highlight the fact that countries on the extreme end of the spectrum are underperformers rather than models to be emulated. Whereas Chile is one of the most robust representative democracies in Latin America, and Venezuela is one of the most participatory regimes, countries like Bolivia and Brazil appear to be better examples of regimes that combine participation and representation. In the case of Brazil, the combination seems to work smoothly; in Bolivia it is more fraught. The important point is that in any one-dimension ranking they seem unremarkable, but when we consider the mix of participatory and representative institutions together, their significance is brought into relief. Mexico, on the other hand, is an underperformer from the perspective of *both* representation and participation.

Bolivia and Brazil contrast with Venezuela and Nicaragua in the sense that participation is less controlled from above and representative institutions have been better respected. Elected in 2005, and reelected in 2009, President Evo

Morales has presided over the collapse of the Bolivian party system and has confronted significant opposition at the subnational level, but he has also managed to undertake a process of constitutional reform that resulted in the adoption of a new constitution in a referendum in 2010. This new constitution fostered new legislative institutions at the departmental level and has allowed the creation of indigenous autonomous self-government. As José Luis Exeni shows in Chapter 9, the new constitution is a hybrid of representative, participatory, and communitarian (read: self-governing indigenous) conceptions of democracy.

The collapse of political parties in Bolivia is disturbing. The conflict with the "half moon" departments (Santa Cruz, Beni, Pando, and Tarija) placed stress on representative institutions. The manner in which the constitution was reformed raised doubts about the legitimacy of the process. More troubling yet, the judiciary has been used as a political instrument against the opposition. Nevertheless, Bolivia has emerged from a difficult period of conflict without a military coup, civil war, or breakdown in the democratic regime. Moreover, it has deepened long deferred reforms, which began in the 1990s, aimed at creating a more inclusive and pluralistic political system. Bolivia is a laboratory in which almost all the different participatory mechanisms that are discussed in this book have been adopted, but what is most extraordinary is that they have been enshrined in the nation's constitution with the result that the Morales government set for itself the task of reconciling them with one another. This is no easy task.

But Bolivia is not a model for the region any more than Chile is. If Chile is unique in lacking problems that plague other Andean countries, Bolivia is perhaps unique in having them all. A better model for the region's democracies is Brazil. As a Portuguese-speaking country with a very different colonial past and a size that allows it to be insular, Brazil is often overlooked in Latin Americans' search for models. But it has emerged as a leader in the hemisphere in terms of direct democracy, and it has managed to reconcile new forms of institutionalized voice with robust representative institutions. Participatory budgeting is widely used in major cities throughout the country, but it is institutionalized in a way such that elected mayors and other municipal officials are responsive and accountable to this participatory institution. At the national level, policy conferences provide an institutionalized way in which the experts and stakeholders in different policy arenas can participate in policy formulation in ways that can be heard by the elected representatives who write the laws. At the same time, Brazil has reinforced its representative institutions, it has not altered basic constitutional rules around reelection, nor has it undertaken changes in the constitution to reinforce the hegemony of a single party. "Brazil," Archon Fung (2011) recently wrote, "is an epicenter of democratic revitalization and institutional invention" in Latin America and he noted that there "are simply no analogs of similar scale or depth in North America, Europe, Asia, or Africa."

Participation Within Diverse Regimes

There is no single model of participation and representation in Latin America. As Latin America moves toward the construction of diverse democratic regimes, the role of participation will continue to vary. In assessing the role of participation within diverse regimes, it becomes necessary to explore the aims of participation. What "goods," both intrinsic and instrumental, are mechanisms of participation designed to achieve? For example, participation may or may not enhance democracy; some kinds of participation are compatible with authoritarian regimes. Cuba offers an example of a highly participatory political system in which the Communist Party monopolizes power.

Even within a democratic context, participation may be designed not to deepen or even radicalize democracy, but as part of an effort to initiate a process of a transition to Cuban style authoritarian socialism. Popular participation in Venezuela, for example, might be aimed at building the same kind of top–down, state-controlled mass organizations found in Cuba, and therefore not aimed at strengthening democracy.[5] Yet, crucially, Venezuela, unlike Cuba, does retain competitive elections. The state does not simply impose its candidate; further there has not been an election that Chávez has won in which any opposition candidate could credibly claim to have been denied victory by fraud. Chávez and his supporters likely have little interest in reinforcing democratic citizenship when they promote grassroots participation like the community councils; and it may be that they have encouraged these councils not simply or mainly to foster the coproduction of public goods like water or electricity but to foster popular support for the regime. But the direct participation occurs through an ensemble of practices and mechanisms that form part of a constitution very different from that of Cuba. The crucial difference is that in Cuba one party, the Communist Party, monopolizes electoral competition and exercises far greater centralized control over popular organizations.

Can more models of direct participatory democracy be constitutionalized, such that a more radical vision of popular empowerment is reconciled within liberal democracy? As we wrote this book, an issue that vexed us was whether direct institutionalized voice can be "scaled up" to higher levels. The chapter by José Luis Exeni (Chapter 9) contains the answer. The key to making democratic constitutions more participatory is not scaling up direct voice but devolving more power to the local level and entrenching multiple models of participation within a national constitution. This is easier to do in theory than practice, but Bolivia provides an interesting model.

Exeni argues that Bolivia's new constitution is an amalgam of three distinct democratic models: representative democracy, direct participatory democracy, and communitarian democracy. Expanded participation plays a role in each of these models. Indigenous participation is increased in the national legislature, in the electoral supervisory body, and the constitutional tribunal, but it does not stop there; the laws have been changed to create new legislative bodies and self-governing institutions at the local level. Referenda have been used to decide which communities will acquire autonomy. Recall referenda have been adopted and used for both national and subnational authorities. The creation of autonomous self-governing bodies in indigenous communities is the key innovation designed to foster a more communitarian democracy. The cumulative effect of these innovations is to use direct institutionalized voice to transform and democratize the state as a whole—not by scaling up but by devolving more democratic power to small-scale self-governing communities everywhere.

Conclusion

This book project began, in part, with the recognition that efforts to assess the state of democracy in Latin America (particularly, that with which a number of contributors to this book have been associated, the Andean Democracy Research Network) need to grapple with the challenge of how to include citizenship and participation, as well as elections and constitutional institutions, in our efforts to evaluate the strength or weakness, the quality, and the diversity of democracy in Latin America. Recognizing the complexity of the issues, we commissioned a group of scholars involved in primary research on participation and gave them the task of examining the participatory practices and institutions they knew best from the perspective of a number of key issues that seemed to us to be relevant to the state of democracy.

The studies in this book suggest that the assessments of democracy should begin by examining the practices and mechanisms of direct institutionalized participation. We contest the presumption that there is a zero-sum trade-off between participation and representation, and instead seek to understand how these dimensions of democracy may reinforce or undermine each other in diverse "ecologies." Further recognizing that some of the benefits of participation may lie outside the sphere of formal democratic institutions, we also stress the ways in which different forms of participation can contribute to the diversity of democratic regimes as well as their quality. Although we need to examine each mechanism in terms of its own specific features, a more holistic understanding is necessary to capture the ways in which participation contributes to alternative models of democratic regimes.

In moving to the next stage of ongoing research on democratization in Latin America, the challenge will be to integrate the insights discussed in this book into democracy assessment exercises so as to recognize both the pitfalls and potential of participatory innovation to make democracy work better. Efforts to assess democracy need to take seriously the whole gamut of mechanisms of direct institutionalized voice without which a more participatory democracy is unattainable. We trust that the results will be relevant not only to Latin America but also beyond, since the problems of representation, of citizen engagement, and the quality of democracy can be found worldwide, in established as well as new democracies. Not only is Latin America emerging as a pioneer of more participatory models of democracy, its innovations are relevant to the growing doubt and disaffection of citizens in the world's older democracies.[6]

Notes

1. A recent attempt to define and measure democracy seeks to encompass various alternative "models," including participatory and deliberative democracy, by Coppedge and Gerring et al. (2011), but it does not include the kinds of institutions for direct participation analyzed here, such as participatory budgeting or community councils.
2. We are grateful to Mark Warren for suggesting this metaphor.
3. See Helmke and Levitsky (2004).
4. In the spirit of Harold Lasswell's (1936) famous definition of politics—"who gets what, when, and how"—our findings suggest not only that voice matters: *how* it is institutionalized also matters. The role of voice depends on *what* mechanisms are used, *who* is given a voice through these mechanisms, and *when* they are able to exercise their voices.
5. This topic was actively discussed in a workshop on "Participation and Representation in Latin America," Universidad Nacional de San Martín, Buenos Aires, Argentina, December 9–11, 2010. We are particularly grateful to Manuel Antonio Garretón for sharpening our thinking on this point.
6. For a lucid discussion of the multiple crises of democratic legitimacy, see Rosanvallon (2011).

Bibliography

Ackerman, Bruce (1988). "Neo-federalism?" in Elster and Slagstad, eds. *Constitutionalism and Democracy*. Cambridge: Cambridge University Press.

Altman, David. (2010). "Plebiscitos, referendos e iniciativas populares en América Latina: ¿mecanismos de control político o políticamente controlados?" *Perfiles Latinoamericanos* (No. 35, January-June). FLACSO-México.

Altman, David and Juan Pablo Luna (2010). "Chile ¿Institucionalización con pies de barro? In Cameron and Luna, eds. *Democracia en la region andina: Diversidad y desafíos.* Lima: Instituto de Estudios Peruanos.

Avritzer, Leonardo. (2009). *Participatory Institutions in Democratic Brazil.* Johns Hopkins University Press.

Avrtizer, Leonardo. (2002). *Democracy and the Public Space in Latin America.* Princeton: Princeton Univ. Press.

Arditi, Benjamin. (2008). "Arguments About the Left Turns in Latin America: A Post-Liberal Politics?" *Latin American Research Review,* 43 (3): 59–81.

Cameron, Maxwell A. and Juan Pablo Luna, eds. (2010). *Democracia en la region andina: Diversidad y desafíos.* Lima: Instituto de Estudios Peruanos.

Carrión, Julio, F. ed. (2006) *The Fujimori Legacy: The Rise of Electoral Authoritarianism in Peru.* University Park, Pennsylvania: The Penn State University Press.

Coppedge, Michael and John Gerring et al. (2011). "Conceptualizing and Measuring Democracy: A New Approach," *Perspectives on Politics,* 9 (2): 247–267.

Dagnino, Evelina, Alberto J. Olvera, and Aldo Panfichi, eds. (2006). *La disputa por la construcción democrática en América Latina.* Mexico: Fondo de Cultura Económica.

Fung, Archon. (2011). "Reinventing Democracy in Latin America (Review Essay)," Unpublished ms. prepared for *Perspectives in Politics,* July 31, 2011.

Gregori, Karina (2012). "Democratizacion y participacion ciudadana en El Salvador de la pos-guerra," Unpublished paper prepared for the project on "Participation and Representation in Latin America."

Hansen, Mogens Herman (1999). *The Athenian Democracy in the Age of Demosthenes: Structure, Principles, and Ideology.* trans by J.A. Cook. Norman: University of Oklahoma Press.

Helmke, Gretchen and Steven Levitsky (2004). "Informal Institutions and Comparative Politics: A Research Agenda", *Perspectives on Politics,* 2 (4): 725–740.

Hirschman, Albert O. (1970). *Exit, Voice, and Loyalty: Responses to Decline in Firms, Organizations and States.* Cambridge: Harvard University Press.

Houtzager, Peter P. and Adrian Gurza Lavalle (2010). "Civil Society's Claims to Political Representation in Brazil," *Studies in Comparative International Development,* 45: 1–29.

Lasswell, Harold D. (1936). *Politics: Who gets what, when, how.* London: Whittlesey house, McGraw-Hill book Co.

Levitsky, Steven and James Loxton (2012). "Populism and Competitive Authoritarianism in the Andes." Paper prepared for the XXX International Congress of the Latin American Studies Association, 23–25 May, 2012, San Francisco, CA.

Levitsky, Steven and Lucan A. Way (2010). *Competitive Authoritarianism: The Origins and Evolution of Hybrid Regimes in the Post-Cold War Era.* New York: Cambridge University Press.

Levitsky, Steven and Lucan A. Way (2002). "Elections Without Democracy: The Rise of Competitive Authoritarianism," *Journal of Democracy* 13, No. 2 (April): 51–66.

Mainwaring, Scott, Ana María Bejarano and Eduardo Pizarro Leongómez (2006) "The Crisis of Democratic Representation in the Andes: An Overview," in Mainwaring, Bejarano and Pizarro Leongomez, eds. *The Crisis of Democratic Representation in the Andes*. Stanford: Stanford University Press.

Macpherson, C.B. (1977). *The Life and Times of Liberal Democracy*. Oxford: Oxford University Press.

O'Donnell, Guillermo (2007). *Dissonances: Democratic Critiques of Democracy*. Notre Dame: University of Notre Dame.

O'Donnell, Guillermo (2004). "Why the Rule of Law Matters," *Journal of Democracy*, 15 (4): 32–46.

O'Donnell, Guillermo (1999). "Horizontal Accountability in New Democracies," in A. Schedler, L. Diamond, and M. F. Plattner, eds. *The Self-Restraining State: Power and Accountability in New Democracies*. Boulder: Lynne Rienner Publishers.

O'Donnell, Guillermo (1996a). "Illusions About Consolidation," *Journal of Democracy*, 7 (2): 34–51.

O'Donnell, Guillermo (1996b). "Illusions and Conceptual Flaws," *Journal of Democracy*, 7 (4): 160–68.

O'Donnell, Guillermo (1994). "Delegative Democracy," *Journal of Democracy*, 5 (1): 55–69.

O'Donnell, Guillermo, Osvaldo Iazzetta and Jorge Vargas Cullell, eds. (2003). *Democracia, desarrollo humano y ciudadanía: Reflexiones sobre la calidad de la democracia en América Latina*. Rosario, Argentina Homo Sapiens Ediciones.

Organización de Estados Americanos, Programa de Naciones Unidas para Desarrollo (2010). *Nuestra Democracia*. Mexico: Fondo de Cultura Económica.

Pateman, Carole. (2012). "Participatory Democracy Revisited," *Perspectives on Politics*, 10 (1): 7–19.

Pinnington, Elizabeth and Daniel Schugurensky, eds. (2010). *Learning Citizenship by Practicing Democracy: International Initiatives and Perspectives*. Newcastle Upon Tyne: Cambridge Scholars Publishing.

Postero, Nancy Grey (2007). *Now We Are Citizens: Indigenous Politics in Postmulticultural Bolivia*. Stanford: Stanford University Press.

Przeworski, Adam. (1991). *Democracy and the Market. Cambridge*. Cambridge: Cambridge University Press.

Roncagliolo, Rafael, Carlos Meléndez, Jorge Valladares (2010). "Ejercicio de la representación y la participación política," In Cameron and Luna, eds. *Democracia en la region andina: Diversidad y desafíos*. Lima: Instituto de Estudios Peruanos.

Rosanvallon, Pierre (2011). *Democratic Legitimacy: Impartiality, Reflexivity, Proximity*. Princeton: Princeton University Press.

Sartori, Giovanni (1976). *Parties and Party Systems: A Framework for Analysis, Vol. 1*. Cambridge: Cambridge University Press.

Schumpeter, Joseph A. (1942). *Capitalism, Socialism, and Democracy*. New York: Harper & Row.

Selee, Andrew and Enrique Peruzzotti, eds. (2009). *Participatory Innovation and Repre-
sentative Democracy in Latin America.* Washington, D.C. and Baltimore: Woodrow
Wilson Center Press and The Johns Hopkins University Press.
Weber, Max (1978). *Economy and Society, Vol. I and II.* G. Roth and C. Wittich, eds.
Berkeley: University of California Press.

List of Contributors

Maxwell A. Cameron is a professor of political science and the director of the Centre for the Study of Democratic Institutions at the University of British Columbia in Vancouver, Canada.

Todd A. Eisenstadt is a professor of government at American University.

José Luis Exeni Rodríguez is a postdoctoral researcher, ALICE Project, Centre for Social Studies (CES), University of Coimbra, Portugal.

Eric Hershberg is a professor of government and the director of the Center for Latin American and Latino Studies at American University.

Felipe J. Hevia de la Jara is a research professor at CIESAS (Centro de Investigaciones y Estudios Superiores en Antropología Social), Mexico City.

Ernesto Isunza Vera is a research professor at CIESAS (Centro de Investigaciones y Estudios Superiores en Antropología Social), Mexico City.

Alicia Lissidini is a professor of political science at the School of Politics and Government, Universidad Nacional de San Martín in Buenos Aires (UNSaM).

Michael M. McCarthy is a PhD candidate in the Department of Political Science at Johns Hopkins University.

Françoise Montambeault is an assistant professor of political science at the Université de Montréal

Thamy Pogrebinschi is a professor of political science at the Institute of Social and Political Studies of the State University of Rio de Janeiro (IESP-UERJ), where she also coordinates the Laboratory for Studies on

Democracy (LED). She is also Humboldt fellow and a visiting researcher at the Wissenschaftszentrum Berlin für Sozialforschung (WZB).

Kenneth E. Sharpe is the William R. Kenan Jr. professor of political science at Swarthmore College.

Mark E. Warren is Merilees Chair and professor of political science at the University of British Columbia in Vancouver, Canada.

Jennifer Yelle is a PhD candidate in the Department of Government at American University.

Gisela Zaremberg is a professor of political science at FLACSO (Facultad Latinoamericana de Ciencias Sociales), Mexico.

Index

Note: The letter 'n' followed by the locator represents notes in the text.